PENGUIN AFRICAN LIBRARY AP3

Edited by Ronald Segal

Portugal in Africa

JAMES DUFFY

JAMES DUFFY

Portugal in Africa

Penguin Books

Penguin Books Inc
3300 Clipper Mill Road, Baltimore 11, Maryland

This edition first published 1963

Copyright © James Duffy, 1962

Printed in the United States of America

Contents

List of Maps

Editorial Foreword

The London *Daily Telegraph* of 20 December 1961 reported the mourning of Lisbon at the swift fall of Goa to the Indian Army.

> Thousands attended a special Mass for Goa tonight in the fifteenth-century church of the Jeronimos and celebrated at the same portable altar that Vasco da Gama took with him on his voyage of discovery to India.
>
> All day long Portuguese radio programmes confined themselves to solemn music. It sounded like, and it was, the funeral of an empire.
>
> This is the day when the Portuguese have realized for the first time that they are not in any sense an imperial power. The sudden loss of Goa destroys once and for all the myth that for years has sustained the Salazar régime.
>
> It is an assumption that Portugal, though militarily and economically weak, possesses a peculiar spiritual strength to enable her, alone among European nations, to remain in Asia and Africa in the furtherance of a non-racial, Christian civilizing mission.
>
> It is this faith that has enabled the Portuguese to fight in Angola a colonial war that to the rest of the world looks utterly hopeless. One wonders whether they will now have the heart to continue it.

The Portuguese have maintained a faith in their imperial mission for almost 500 years, increasingly substituting fervour for the evidence of accomplishment. Such self-deception is not, of course, unique; in less intense and lasting a form, it has characterized in varying degrees the missions of other colonial empires like the Belgian, the French, and – despite polite cries to the contrary – the British. Portugal has been exceptional only in the success with which it has deceived itself and so much of the outside world, leaving to its subjects all the disenchantments of experience.

From time to time in the past, scandals broke round Portugal's imperial rule, but it was only in 1960 that events within the Afro-Asian world seemed capable of submerging at last so long-established a dominion, and public opinion in the West began seriously to measure the Portuguese mission. That this has been a tribute to the efficient savagery with which Portugal has contained rebellion and stifled protest, rather than a victory for the mission itself, there are two urgent witnesses in the speed with which its rule in Goa collapsed before the invading Indian army, and the hatred revealed by the shape of the Angolan rebellion. A more measurable consequence of Portugal's 'non-racial, Christian civilizing mission' was produced by no less an authority than the Lisbon Instituto Nacional de Estatistica in 1959. Drawing on the figures of the last available census, conducted in 1950, the Institute disclosed that there were 1,478 civilized and 502,457 uncivilized Africans in Portuguese Guinea, 30,089 civilized and 4,006,598 uncivilized in Angola, and 25,149 civilized and 5,646,957 uncivilized in Moçambique. Portugal's almost five centuries of spiritual and intellectual labour in Africa, therefore, had by 1950 produced a harvest of 0·39 per cent in Portuguese Guinea, 0·44 per cent in Moçambique, and 0·74 per cent in Angola. Even those who perpetually protest the sincerity of the Portuguese cannot reasonably excuse so small a return for the investment of so much moral capital. Doubtless the processes of Portuguese civilization require patience. But one may properly wonder whether the civilization is worth sowing at all if it takes so long and demands such sacrifices to cultivate.

Antonio de Figueiredo summarized the record in *Portugal and its Empire* (Gollancz, London, 1961):

Out of ten and a half million people (Angola 4,500,000: Moçambique 6,000,000), over ninety-nine per cent are illiterate. Less than four per cent in Moçambique and less than eight per cent in Angola know how to speak Portuguese at all. Less than five per cent in Moçambique and less than ten per cent in Angola live in or around the white man's towns, the only centres where some development is achieved by the natural process of social contact. If there has been any serious interest in these people, it has been in how better to shape their lives to economic exploitation.

Portuguese and foreign students of African affairs, misled by the talk of 'assimilation', have come to think that the *assimilado* system has been devised to give Africans the rights of citizenship. At first sight, by contrast with other colonial policies, the idea that Africans, after meeting with some qualifications, could earn the 'generous concession' of citizen rights looks stimulating. But assimilation, 'partnership' and their friendly opposite, 'apartheid', are all features of colonialist mythology. The white man cannot ignore the realities of African demography, and out of moral and political necessity he finds elaborate theories which he applies more or less to suit himself.

For a few years at the outset of its colonial career, Portugal propagated a genuine policy of assimilation. When her explorers reached the Congo River in 1483 they found a kingdom of complex administration, whose inhabitants worked iron, copper, and other metals, wove mats and clothing from raffia or palm-cloth, and raised pigs, sheep, chickens, and cattle. The King or Manicongo, Nzinga-a-Cuum, showed a readiness to accept the ways of Western civilization, and his successor, Mbemba-a-Nzinga, who reigned from 1506 to 1543 as Dom Afonso I, not only adopted Christianity himself but did his utmost to spread the new faith amongst his subjects.

The early Portuguese embassies and missions contained priests, artisans, and even two German printers, who emigrated to the Congo in 1492, while several Portuguese women were sent to teach the domestic skills of Western civilization. A number of young Congolese nobles travelled to Lisbon for their education, and Dom Afonso himself soon began modelling his court on that of Lisbon, even borrowing the intricate Portuguese etiquette and costuming. But the German printers died, the priests surrendered to secular distractions, of which the slave-trade was soon found to be the most profitable, and the artisans assimilated themselves to or collapsed under the climate. To repeated complaints and cries for help, King Manuel I of Portugal issued a *regimento* in 1512 comprising advice to the Manicongo and royal instructions for the Portuguese community at his court, but the

regulations were carefully ignored, while the necessary investment of men and materials never arrived. Portugal increasingly
occupied herself in promoting the slave-trade – from headquarters on the island of São Tomé – to feed her colonial
experiments in South America and the East. By the end of the
eighteenth century, reduced by periodic Jaga invasions and the
Portuguese slave-raids, the Congo kingdom had shrunk to a few
scattered remnants around the village of São Salvador, once the
haughty capital of Mbanza Congo. Establishing herself in those
vast stretches of Africa now known as Angola and Moçambique,
Portugal paid no more attention to her civilizing mission than
the predatory appetite of the Brazilian plantations demanded.
In the end, the crown of her accomplishment was to be her
introduction of maize, manioc, citrus fruits, and potatoes into
Africa, new foods from America whose cultivation was to have
dramatic effects on the growth and security of settled populations.

The disorderly Liberal governments of the nineteenth century
made sporadic attempts, under mounting criticism in Europe
and America, to regulate the slave-trade and then the cruelties
of forced labour that followed its superficial suppression. But
their *regimentos* were as ornately futile as the intervention of
Manuel I had been. Portuguese Africa itself remained unruffled,
merely substituting 'contract labour' for slavery when slavery
had, under largely British pressure, at last been outlawed.

It was left to Dr Antonio de Oliveira Salazar, a Professor of
Economics, to brush the dust off the myths of Portugal's spiritual
mission and use them to furnish the Fascism of the *Estado Novo*,
the New State into which Portugal was to be transformed. From
27 April 1928, when he first assumed public office as Minister of
Finance, he set out to mould Portugal into a corporate society,
its economy and culture sustained by industrial discipline and
the labour of 'inferior races' – the phrase is his own – in the
overseas territories. 'Through the designs of Providence by
which the world is ruled,' he said in a speech on 28 April 1934,
'Portugal has no need of wars and conquest.' Indeed, the con-
quests had been achieved in the past, and the present clearly
existed to exploit them.

Using the State Security Police, the Policia Internacional e de Defesa do Estado, or P.I.D.E. for short, he surrounded Portugal and its empire with a screen of silence which secured for a time the assiduous propagation of his fantasies.

Concentrating upon *desenvolvimento de fachada*, the development of the façade, his régime hid squalor and illiteracy, disease and chronic unemployment, behind a programme of decorative public works, which impressed tourists and journalists from Britain and Brazil, and comforted government emissaries from the West in search of stable alliances against Communism.

Article 5 of the Constitution promised 'equality of the citizen before the law, and the free access of all classes to the benefits of civilization', while newspapers were censored or banned, television and radio strictly controlled, and political opponents sent to the safety of Lisbon gaols. In 1960 alone there were over 3,800 convictions in Portugal for crimes against religion and the state; in the colonies, restive Africans were more summarily silenced.

Despite an empire of some 800,000 square miles, from which Portugal takes twelve and a half per cent of her imports and to which she sends twenty-five per cent of her exports in return, the national income *per capita* in Portugal itself has not yet reached £70 a year, remaining less than one-sixth of that in un-imperial Sweden. The infant mortality rate at almost 90 per 1,000 is double that in Czechoslovakia and Japan, while the figure for illiteracy, at just under forty per cent, should embarrass any society with pretensions to a spiritual or intellectual mission.

Far from being embarrassed, however, Dr Salazar has proclaimed himself triumphant. In 1934, he announced:

The prestige of Portugal will shine forever . . . everywhere the pride of being Portuguese will quicken the life-blood of the people and will vouchsafe peace and repose to the ashes of our heroes who are no longer with us. To reach our goal we have experienced a far-reaching revolution in economics, politics, ideas, customs, institutions, and in our collective life.

Twenty-seven years later, faced with mass rebellion in Angola,

13

he was to proclaim, 'I can see no other attitude for us than to continue on our way.' The Portuguese themselves, no less than the Africans in their empire, might be forgiven for wondering whether the way of the Salazar régime has, after all, been a very profitable one to follow.

In his *Mission to Portugal* (Editorial Civilização Brasileira SA, 1960) the former Brazilian Ambassador to Portugal, Alvaro Lins, wrote of:

... the mark of dictatorship and police terror on the faces of the Portuguese. Their tormented expressions reflect demoralization, revolt, often despair and always intranquillity, insecurity, and fear. Fear of unemployment, fear of prison ... The same phenomenon is visible in the country, in areas where collective life is not on the show-window pattern of Lisbon and Oporto. The tourist ... is often heard to exclaim: 'Magnificent roads! Well-cultivated fields! How these workers produce and how well-organized they are!' ... But a Brazilian who knows the reality knows what is behind and beyond this façade. He knows that none of these things belongs to the Portuguese people; he knows that these things belong on the contrary to a handful of rich bankers and feudal landlords, to a small group of men who control the reins of political power. This group is formed by prosperous businessmen who hold monopolies and who are engaged in the pursuit of official prestige and the amassing of quick fortunes; who receive the sanction of the State in their dubious transactions. ...

The fantasy within Portugal itself merely reflects the fantasy of the whole Portuguese empire. Behind the myth that Portugal's colonial possessions are 'Overseas Provinces' – the myth officially proclaimed on 11 June 1951 and ever since then frenziedly waved in the face of international criticism – the Salazar régime bleeds the empire for the benefit of that same small 'handful of rich bankers and feudal landlords' who are busy bleeding Portugal itself. Despite Portugal's economic backwardness and political terror, Salazar passionately proclaims the civilizing mission of Portugal in history. Despite the degradation and squalor, ignorance and want of Portuguese Africa, Salazar maintains that those who talk of emancipation

come too late, for the job had already been done. ... Many of those who ... demand the emancipation of Portuguese territories ... will come to think that we did a great service to mankind ... having spared them new forms of slavery (30 November 1960).

Chikomuami Mahala described Portugal's 'great service to mankind' in 'The Horror of Moçambique' (*Africa South*, October–December, 1960):

Approximately ninety per cent of the Africans live off the soil, for Moçambique, like all African countries, is essentially agricultural. Since traditional methods of agriculture are today of very little commercial value, the land is largley divided up into huge 'concessions' and 'plantations', which belong solely to Europeans and produce the main export crops. The 'concessions' are vast regions of small-holdings in which the peasants are compelled to produce a predetermined quota, assessed and imposed by the administration. ... The planters put their demands to the administrative authorities and these are responsible for forcibly recruiting enough labour in the village to satisfy the demand. ...

To this picture of forced and underpaid labour, must be added the unpaid compulsory labour imposed 'in the public interest'. The law actually allows that prison sentences may be replaced by compulsory labour. As any excuse is enough to arrest an African, the state is assured of a considerable supply of workers without spending the smallest sum.

In January 1947, one of the senior officials within the Portuguese colonial administration attempted to show Portugal the reality of its rule. Henrique Galvão, then a member of Salazar's União Nacional, reported to the Portuguese National Assembly on conditions in the African empire.

Entire frontier regions are being depopulated, and only old people, sick people, women and children are now to be found there. ... The most accurate description of this impoverishment is given us by the catastrophic fall in the birthrate, the incredible level of infant mortality, the growing number of sick and infirm, as well as the mortality figures due to various causes, the most important being the conditions of work and the recruitment of labourers.

On 9 December 1952 Henrique Galvão was charged with plotting a *coup d'état* and sentenced to a preliminary three years in prison. Kept in gaol on a series of different charges until 1959, he finally escaped from prison hospital to the Argentinian Embassy and was granted political asylum there. The Salazar régime does not encourage scrutiny.

It is not enough that Portugal should retain her empire because she needs it economically; her government must claim that its rule is a service to mankind. This fantasy – that forced labour and political repression, illiteracy and starvation, are signposts of civilization – is one which it must be difficult for the governing families of Portugal themselves to believe. That they should expect Africans to believe it as well is grotesque.

A study of Portugal in Africa, such as Professor Duffy has here undertaken, is, therefore, an urgent task not only as a measure of Portugal's historic mission in Africa, its achievements and its devastations, but also as an examination of delusion itself, significant for its application to the whole contemporary world and, in particular, the present-day relationships between Africa and the West.

Writing on the Belgian Congo in *Africa South* (July–September 1960) Colin Legum claimed:

The self-deception of Europeans in multi-racial societies is undoubtedly the major political problem still facing Africa. European supremacy is firmly maintained on an elaborate structure of propaganda both intentionally and unintentionally designed to reassure the white rulers of the justice of their cause, and to prevent the outside world from understanding what is really happening.

The Belgians excelled at this practice. They genuinely deceived themselves about the success of their own paternalist policies; they laid a massive smoke-screen that prevented a proper assesssment of the wide gaps between the claims of their policies and their actual achievements. Nobody achieved greater success in providing a rationale for their paternalism; moral fervour and intellectual argument were harnessed to their cause. *Inforcongo* – the Belgian Department of Information in the Congo – was one of the finest propaganda machines in the world; the only pity of it is that it was not put to any better use.

But the efficiency of Belgian propaganda was a double-edged weapon. For the awakening came with such shattering swiftness and force that it left the Belgians bewildered and aghast at their own self-deception.

For Belgium the moment of awakening came with the furious

race rioting in Leopoldville on 4 January 1959. For Portugal it came with the sudden rebellion in the North of Angola on 15 March 1961. The delusions of centuries were among the first victims of the ferocity with which Portuguese rule was assailed by Portugal's African subjects. The Portuguese, in Lisbon and Luanda alike, had been stunned by their own superstitions. Now, suddenly deprived of their fantasies, they are placing their faith in force. That they will be driven from Angola – and Moçambique and Guinea – as they were driven under different circumstances from Goa, there can be no doubt. Only the number of the months left to them allows speculation, and the thoroughness of the break. The longer that force is employed, the more the chances will dwindle of any Portuguese association with Africa on those essential terms of creative equality which five centuries have flouted.

RONALD SEGAL

Introduction

Portugal in Africa is a brief history of Portuguese policies and traditions in Africa, principally in the two large colonies of Angola and Moçambique. In the preparation of this work I have relied to a large extent on my book *Portuguese Africa* (1959). I have tried to isolate and describe the persistent problems and characteristics of the Portuguese presence in Africa and to show how they lead inevitably into the troubled and uncertain present. There is an extraordinary continuity of Portuguese behaviour and policy in Africa which helps to explain the crises of today and the developments of tomorrow. I have brought the story to a close with the Portuguese government's announcement in late summer 1961 of drastic administrative reforms. To go beyond that point would have been to attempt to write tomorrow's newspaper headlines. I am fully aware that the onrush of present events in Angola and, almost certainly, future events in Moçambique will make this termination point less than satisfactory.

I have dedicated the major part of the work to a study of Angola and Moçambique. These two colonies have long been the most important areas of Portuguese interest in Africa and are today the principal reasons why Portugal is determined to remain in Africa. My reasons for neglecting Portuguese Guinea and the Cape Verde Islands are three: their relative lack of importance in Portugal's colonial schemes; my own uncertain knowledge of the areas; and the difficulties of presenting the story of these minor territories, whose historical orientations are often at variance with those of Angola and Moçambique, within the limited space and fairly complex organization of the present work. For information on the course of history in Portugal itself, I would refer the reader to H. V. Livermore's excellent *History of Portugal* (Cambridge, 1947) or, for a briefer survey, to Mr Livermore's essay in *Portugal and Brazil* (Oxford, 1953).

In general I have used the Portuguese version of African proper names, although these may occasionally be different from the English usage. I believe they will be easily recognizable most of the time. Conventional orthography and accentuation, which may have led to a few inconsistencies, have been used throughout in the (historically very inconsistent) Portuguese – but I hope this will not distract the reader unduly. All translations in the work are my own.

My debt to many individuals, who have helped so generously in so many ways, is enormous. I can only acknowledge this debt collectively by saying that I am very grateful for their kind assistance. Much of the additional research that has gone into the work was made possible with the support of a grant from the Penrose Fund of the American Philosophical Society.

November 1961   JAMES DUFFY

Part I: The Past

1. Political map of Africa, showing the situation in 1961

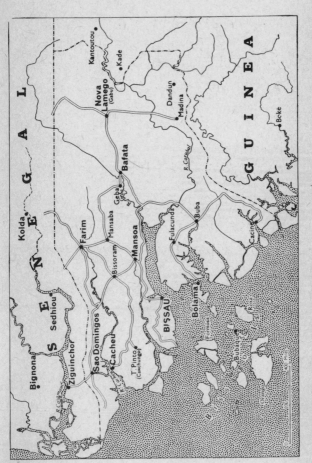

2. Portuguese Guinea, 1961

23

1 Portugal, West Africa, and the Congo

The Portuguese African territories of Angola, Moçambique, Guinea, the Cape Verde Islands, and the islands of São Tomé and Principe make up an area about twenty-three times the size of Portugal itself. Only Angola and Moçambique are of primary significance; but the other fragments of what the Portuguese liked to call until very recently their African empire are still of romantic importance – as are other scattered outposts of the Portuguese world in South-East Asia and China. They give an exotic dimension to Portugal's concept of herself as a small nation in Europe, but a great nation in the world. This sense of pride in the size and scatter of overseas Portugal has for a long time been part of Portuguese colonial sentiment and a real if amorphous factor in the formation of colonial policy.

Portugal has been in Africa more than 500 years, and her territories there are the oldest European colonies in the world today. Set against the fleeting history of other colonial powers in Africa, this is a remarkable record of endurance, if of nothing else, and the Portuguese confession that they have the vice of history – by vice, they imply virtue – is perhaps a legitimate affirmation of a venerable colonial tradition. The Portuguese maintain that their presence in many parts of the world has been a creatively unique experience characterized by heroism and idealism. Racial tolerance, Christian endeavour, human fortitude in distant lands – such are the values which the Portuguese declare have been visible from the beginning in Africa, in America, and in the East. Such are the values which, it is said, have determined colonial policies in Africa from the fifteenth century to the mid twentieth century; they provide an explanation of the past, a defence for the present, and the hope for the future. They are the substance for the rhetorical elaboration which goes into the making of the myth of Portuguese Africa.

A sense of space, then, and a sense of historical tradition have for centuries moulded the Portuguese imperial consciousness. The words of the Portuguese ambassador at the United Nations, in defence of his country's policies in Angola, sound like words from the past precisely because they are words from the past. The colonial mystique of the Salazar régime is not a new creation; it is only a careful refinement of earlier Portuguese attitudes now given authority and distribution by a reasonably efficient propaganda machine. From the beginning Portugal's adventure in Africa has been chronicled and glorified by historians and poets – by Prince Henry's chronicler Zurara, by the great Renaissance historians Barros, Couto, and Faria e Sousa, by the gifted epic poet Camões, and by a succession of lesser poets and historians through the centuries. It is vital to realize that the psychic reality which the Portuguese call their overseas consciousness has been a deep and pervasive force in national thought and in African policy – just as it is equally vital to know that the facts of the Portuguese presence in Africa are somewhat different from those the myth suggests.

A few remarks here on Portuguese difficulties at home in the nineteenth and early twentieth centuries may help toward an understanding of the recurring colonial problems which lead down to the present. In 1807 the Portuguese royal family removed to Brazil in order to escape the French armies, which invaded the country in that year. One of the results of the Peninsular War was the spread of a Liberal revolution in Portugal, and when João VI finally returned to his country in 1821 he was confronted with a constitution, an elected Cortes, and, most important, a land deeply divided into constitutionalist and absolutist camps. The secession of Brazil and questions of succession to the Portuguese throne following the death of João in 1826 added to the complexities of the political scene.

Portugal was a constitutional monarchy from 1821 to 1910. During the first third of this period, the country was rent by dissension and occasional civil wars. The triumph of the Liberal cause did not, save for several brief periods, such as the enlightened régime of Sá da Bandeira in the 1830s, bring a truly liberal rule to Portugal. More often than not, the country was governed either erratically or autocratically. In these troubled years, the Portuguese government was in no position to do more than promulgate elaborate colonial legislation and attempt to deal with the pressing issue of slavery.

If governments in the second half of the century were more orderly, they were hardly more effective. By agreement the conservative and liberal parties rotated in government, but none was able to solve the continuing financial crises that beset Portugal. The country was in no position to assert itself during the years of the scramble for Africa. The British ultimatum to Portugal in 1890 at the height of the controversy in Moçambique had the effect of precipitating a Republican uprising in Oporto. It was only through tenacity and delaying tactics that various otherwise unstable governments had managed to hold on to the African possessions by the end of the century.

The creation of a Portuguese Republic in 1910, following twenty years of agitation and the assassination of King Carlos with his eldest son in 1908, brought neither harmony nor economic progress to Portugal. The Republicans were united only in their contempt for the monarchy and the Church. The radical and moderate elements soon fell out with one another. The country sank deeper into bankruptcy and, in the absence of either consistency or stability in the government, much of the régime's reforms, including those for the African colonies, could not be implemented. In the early years of the 1920s, the political scene in Portugal was marked by violence, assassination, frequent changes of government, and complete confusion.

In 1926 a military uprising led by General Gomes da Costa brought down the government of President Machado. Gomes da Costa was replaced within a month by General Oscar de Fragoso Carmona as head of the military junta. Carmona held

27

together the new government, but he could not solve the country's pressing economic problems. In 1928, a professor of law and economics at the University of Coimbra, Dr António de Oliveira Salazar, agreed to become Finance Minister if granted absolute control over national expenditure. Within two years Portugal had a budgetary surplus; within four, Salazar was Prime Minister and virtual dictator of the country. With the new constitution of 1933, the *Estado Novo* or New State had come to Portugal.

The Exploration of the Coast

In the middle of the year 1415 Portugal stood poised on the edge of an extraordinary colonial career. Three centuries of political, religious, and economic development had their culmination in the decision of João I, of the newly established dynasty of Aviz, to invade the North African stronghold of Ceuta. A new generation of men had come to power with João, merchants and captains who were ready to forsake the traditional routes of commerce that had already made Lisbon and Oporto cosmopolitan centres. The country was strong, unified, and reasonably prosperous, independent from covetous Spain, and completely free for almost a century from Moorish domination. On 21 August, Ceuta fell after one day of heavy assault, and Portugal, as Bailey Diffie has written in *Prelude to Empire*, 'was now launched on the imperial road from which there was no point of voluntary return . . . The hope for profit, the conquest of souls, the cutting off of Castile, were now identified with Portugal's national spirit.'

The fifteenth century is the period of African coastal exploration. After the fall of Ceuta, Henry, the third son of João, directed the maritime thrust of Portugal which was to culminate at the end of the century in Vasco da Gama's first voyage to India. Devout, humourless, austere, Henry the Navigator possessed the capacity for patient, hopeful planning. His practical and idealistic motives, trade and evangelization, are still voiced in the twentieth century to justify Portuguese colonialism in

Africa. At the height of the diplomatic attack on Portugal in 1960, the Salazar government organized vast and elaborate ceremonies to celebrate the five-hundredth anniversary of Henry's death. In Africa, Brazil, and Portugal, Henry's contribution to science and humanity was extolled in thousands of speeches and pamphlets. The purpose of the celebrations was to extract from the life and works of the prince a philosophy of overseas conduct and to give it reality in the present crisis. At the formal opening of the commemorative sessions Premier Salazar's administrative assistant, Dr Pedro Theotónio Pereira, spoke in these familiar phrases:

> We live in an age of renascence which links us with the past and which we will try to project into the future . . . the unity and solidarity which hold together the pieces of Portuguese territory have never been stronger, and the sentiment of all the peoples has never been more unanimous.

(Six months later, in March 1961, the Angolan rebellion began.)

Early expeditions along the African coast were slow and painstaking; only the settlement of the Canary Islands in 1424 was a clear-cut indication of Portuguese progress. During this period coasting was an uncertain enterprise; lack of geographic knowledge and the fears of the mariners were serious handicaps. But in 1434 Gil Eanes rounded Cape Bojador, and for the next thirty years Portuguese voyagers continued pushing beyond that point: in 1436, the Rio de Oro; in 1441, Cape Blanco; in 1446, the Senegal and Cape Verde. By 1460, when Henry died, Portuguese caravels had reached the coast of Sierra Leone. In 1475 the ships of Fernão Gomes, who held a five-year monopoly on the trade of the Guinea coast, crossed the equator. In 1483 Captain Diogo Cão, one of the greatest of Portuguese navigators, came to the mouth of the Congo River. Four years later, Bartolomeu Dias rounded the Cape of Good Hope. In 1498 Vasco da Gama, following in the wake of Dias, sailed up the East African coast to Malindi and thence across the Indian Ocean to Calicut. Islam had been outflanked, and the sea-road to the East, the ultimate goal of Henry's patient planning, lay open to Portuguese navigation.[1]

The hundred years after Ceuta compose the grandiose century of Portuguese exploration and expansion. They encompass an age which, beginning with Prince Henry and ending with Afonso de Albuquerque, includes captains and warriors like Cão, Dias, Cabral, da Gama, and d'Almeida. They furnish a seemingly endless source of inspiration to chroniclers, poets, scientists, in Portugal and abroad, who so define, elaborate, and redefine past glories that these years have become an age of supermen whose inspiration is still a living presence in Portuguese colonial thought. While the study of Portuguese Africa is only in passing concerned with their heroics, many of the prevailing attitudes in every part of the Lusitanian world have their nationalistic foundation in the *século maravilhoso*.

The Key-Points of Power

Until about 1550 much of Portugal's interest in Africa was centred on the lands of first exploration, the coast from Cape Blanco to the Cameroons. By 1480 Portuguese navigators had sailed to Cape St Catherine and had probably established contact with the volcanic island of São Tomé. João II in the 1480s claimed *exclusive* jurisdiction over the 2,000 miles of coast which the Portuguese called the land of Guinea. Then, as now – and during all the years between – Portuguese policy in Africa admitted, whenever possible, no foreign intrusion or influence into those areas which Portugal chose to consider hers by virtue of priority.

Portuguese enterprise in West Africa in the fifteenth and sixteenth centuries did not and could not follow the same patterns of exploitation and development which were to be followed in Angola and Moçambique. The extent of coast was too vast,

1. Although Portugal may claim the greater part of the credit for the early exploration of the Guinea coast, the myth of absolute Portuguese priority in West Africa is false. During the fifteenth century, particularly in its third quarter, Andalusian sailors and merchants made frequent sailings to West Africa and in several areas fiercely contested Portuguese dominance. Not until the discovery of America and the division of the new worlds into Spanish and Portuguese spheres of influence did Spanish competition in Africa diminish, and even in the sixteenth century Castilian interlopers continued their West African voyages.

the work of continuing exploration in other parts of the world too distracting, and the difficulties of maintaining garrisons in a feverish, often hostile country too great, for a small nation of limited demographic and financial resources. Much is known about the Portuguese exploration of the West African coast, but not a great deal about its exploitation. (European historians have long regarded Portuguese history in Africa with a curious ambivalence. The maritime exploits are viewed with awe; the operations on land with disdain.) In recent years the history of Portugal in West Africa has begun to come into better focus, and Portuguese activity along the Guinea Coast and inland is seen to have been more extensive than had been assumed, although there is still little evidence to indicate that this activity had any lasting cultural influence on the African inhabitants of the area. Compared with the success of other European performances in the same regions before 1800, the history of Portuguese activities there is not inconsequential.

But, from the beginning, Portuguese policy in West Africa was modest. Since the object of the policy was trade, not territorial domination, and since the Crown never had a consuming interest in the Guinea coast, the presence of Portugal was usually limited to the factories and forts set up at key coastal points. Where possible the Portuguese tried to extend their authority into the countryside beyond the forts: they made diplomatic and trade alliances with African princes and attempted to evangelize the native population. Their efforts were adapted to the situation, to the particular strengths and weaknesses of the Portuguese garrison, and to those of the African peoples in their vicinity. Several attempts were made to settle small white communities along the coast, but these were largely unsuccessful. To supply and defend white towns implied an effort which Portugal could not sustain, and she was content to maintain a profitable commercial monopoly which cost relatively little. By 1500 Portugal had established a West African trade complex which brought Portuguese cloth, glass, and metal to be exchanged for gold, slaves, gum arabic, and ivory.

The major key-points of Portuguese power in West Africa

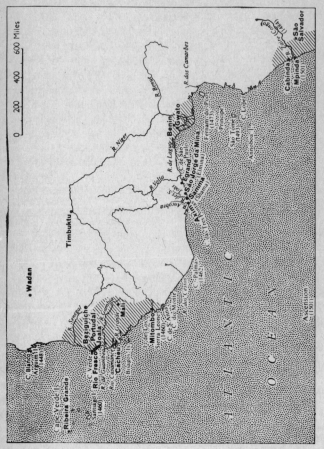

3. West Africa as far as the Congo River, showing the limits of Portuguese influence c. 1500

were Arguim, Santiago, São Jorge da Mina, and São Tomé. Arguim was the least important. An island beneath the hook of Cape Blanco, Arguim flourished for about seventy-five years after a fortress and factory had been established there in the mid fifteenth century. From Arguim the Portuguese successfully intruded into the commerce of the western Sudan. Originally Portugal intended to penetrate the interior, and seek out the mysterious Timbuktu, centre of the gold trade, but this ended in failure and Arguim became an *entrepôt* for traffic in another kind of gold. Arguim lived on a slave-trade which dispatched 1,000 slaves or more each year to Portugal or to São Jorge da Mina. With the rise of the transatlantic trade, Arguim, always difficult to supply, languished into insignificance.

Another centre of Portuguese activity in West Africa was the Cape Verde Islands and the mainland opposite, roughly the coastal area between Senegal and Sierra Leone. The Islands and a portion of the coast, now known as Portuguese Guinea, were to be the only West African territories to survive in Portuguese hands. On Santiago Island the Portuguese government carried out an early attempt at colonization. Portuguese, Spanish, and Genoese settlers came to the island, and Africans were brought from the mainland to work the island's plantations. Over the succeeding centuries an amalgamation of European colonists and African slaves was formed. The proportions of the amalgam are unknown, but certainly the African contribution was the greater. By the 1950 census, seventy per cent of the Cape Verdian population was mulatto; and from the island's citizenry, the Salazar régime has recently chosen administrators and diplomats to serve as public examples of Portugal's non-discriminatory practices in Africa.

Santiago soon became the centre of trade in Upper Guinea. From the island Portuguese settlers and traders crossed over to the coast, there to trade, to found small posts, and often to reside in native towns. These original settlers were soon followed by a population of freebooters and renegades whose unruly ways disrupted the commerce between Santiago and the mainland. The settlers from Santiago and the adventurers formed a number of white pockets along the coast south from Cape Verde. Several of these stations, such as Cacheu and Bissau, have a continuous history into the present. Occasional missionary sorties from Santiago penetrated the interior, as did Portuguese traders, while emissaries of the Portuguese Crown travelled as far inland as Timbuktu.

Portugal's policy in Upper Guinea during the sixteenth century was to maintain pacific relations with the more important African princes of the interior. In the absence of armed conflict, trade in the interior generally flourished, and Portuguese or half-caste trading agents moved freely in the Senegal and the Gambia, often intermarrying and spending their lives in the hinterland. The lands of Guinea were split into a number of trading regions, and a monopoly of commerce was let out to contractors.[1] Portuguese became the *lingua franca* of Upper Guinea, and it survived in one part of the area or another long after Portugal's commercial hegemony had disappeared.

Portuguese influence in Lower Guinea was not so widespread as in the lands to the north, but in some ways it was more spectacular. On the Mina coast, at the Village of Two Parts, the Portuguese in 1482 constructed the imposing fortress-city of São Jorge da Mina which, with the fortress of São Miguel in Luanda, was one of the two great Portuguese installations along the Atlantic coast. The construction of São Jorge was symptomatic of a different policy Portugal was obliged to pursue in this region of West Africa. On the Gold Coast Portuguese traders could not move with freedom and security through the interior. They were obliged to use whatever force or methods of terror they had at their disposal, and when this failed they relied on intrigue and bribery. The various factories established north and south of São Jorge were fortified, and the passage between

1. John Blake, in his *Europeans in West Africa*, makes these divisions: the trade of the Senegal, the trade of the Gambia and Cantor, the trade of the rivers of Guinea (probably the Casamanca, the Farim, and the Geba), and the trade of Sierra Leone. The contractors usually employed factors who were resident in the area to supervise their transactions.

them was by sea or in armed company. São Jorge was the warehouse and administrative centre for the area. Here lived the governor and his officials, whose duty it was to ensure the safety and legitimacy of commerce.

Although African opposition made Portugal's position in the Gold Coast difficult and often tenuous, Portuguese trade here was the richest in the whole of Guinea. It is estimated that gold to the value of £100,000 a year was sent to Portugal. Slaves from Arguim and ports to the north, from São Tomé, and from Benin were brought to São Jorge, there to be exchanged, along with cloth and hardware, for the precious metal. Seldom, however, were the Portuguese able to tap directly the source of supply. They were cut off from the mines of Ashanti and had to be content with relying on the supply delivered by African traders. In the shadow of São Jorge an African and Portuguese community grew up; but not even here did the Portuguese achieve a discernible cultural influence, although a segment of the African population became nominally Christian.

South of São Jorge da Mina, the luxuriant equatorial island of São Tomé dominated Portuguese activities. A satisfactory account of the curious and often perverse history of this mountainous tropical island has still to be written, and this is a pity, because in its own way São Tomé has been in miniature an example of the successes and failures of Portuguese colonialism in Africa, and it has even been half-seriously suggested that the island be preserved as a sort of living colonial museum. Settled in the late fifteenth century by a strange company of young Jews, exiles, officials, traders, and slaves from the mainland, São Tomé quickly developed into an important *entrepôt* for the slave-trade between Guinea and the Congo and the New World, as well as into an important sugar-producing area.

From São Tomé the Portuguese set up a trading post at Gwato in Benin, first to deal in pepper and then in slaves. From about 1490 to 1520, when the factory at Gwato was abandoned, the Portuguese enjoyed considerable success in diplomatic dealings with the King of Benin. Missionaries were active, and a small segment of the population was baptized and taught to read and write Portuguese.

During the sixteenth century Portugal was dominant in West Africa, although her commercial monopoly was contested and occasionally broken by European interlopers. It was only through the absence of serious competition, however, that Portugal held her position, for the attentions of the Portuguese throne at this period were seldom directed for very long toward West Africa. With the growing needs of American estates for labour, the slave became the chief commercial commodity as the century progressed. The Spanish contracts were granted to Portuguese, who dispatched in the last seventy years of the century between 500,000 and 800,000 Africans to the Spanish plantations and the Portuguese sugar-estates in Brazil.

The demand increased, and early in the seventeenth century Portugal's monopoly began to fragment under growing competition. The Dutch West India Company was the first adversary of consequence; by 1642, the Gold Coast was in Dutch hands. In the 1660s French and English companies engaged the efficient and tenacious Dutch in a triangular struggle for the whole West African trade. Portugal managed to retain São Tomé and isolated sections of the coast; she held on to the Cape Verdes and Portuguese Guinea, successfully resisting pressures from the north, where the French came to dominate the trade in the Senegal, and from the south, where the English came to control the Gambia. By now Angola provided the bulk of the slaves for the Portuguese trade.

But by 1700 Brazil was demanding 10,000 slaves a year, a quota which could not always be met by Angola, already furnishing slaves to other parts of the New World as well. The Portuguese established a successful station in Dahomey, and Portuguese Guinea entered a new period of prosperity. In the middle of the eighteenth century the powerful Grão-Pará and Maranhão Company, in which the Portuguese dictator Pombal held interest, was formed to finance the rebuilding of Bissau into an important slave centre. During part of the period, Guinea actually surpassed Angola in the number of slaves sent to Brazil. By the end of the century, however, Guinea was virtually slaved out, and the last great flurry of the trade was to occur in Angola and Moçambique.

The subsequent history of Guinea and of the Cape Verdes is neither of real importance nor of more than occasional interest within the larger history of Portuguese enterprise in Africa. In the nineteenth and early twentieth centuries, Guinea, save for the administration of Honorário Barreto, a capable and ambitious African governor-general of the colony, was a backwater of Portugal's colonial design. A handful of officials kept a semblance of authority, and, at the turn of the present century, minor campaigns of pacification were carried out against several dissident tribes. The Cape Verdes, some 300 miles from the mainland, have had an insulated, detached existence, somewhat more Portuguese in its orientations than African. Both territories have had in the last 150 years only the most fleeting of contacts with the larger, more important Portuguese African world of Angola and Moçambique.

The Unique Interlude of the Congo

Standing as a bridge between Portugal in West Africa and in Angola were São Tomé and the Congo. São Tomé faced north and south and made profit from both directions. The Congo was an isolated microcosm of Portuguese enterprise, combining in its brief historical moment the best and the worst features of Portuguese African policy in the early centuries. Portugal's formal associations with the Congo followed the West African pattern of alliance and trade, but the informal reality was that ruthless plundering of an African people which was to make of Angola, whose history is largely separate from that of the Congo, a devastated land. The Congo episode is a unique experience in Portuguese African history, and one which has captured the imagination of panegyrist and critic alike.

Official Portuguese policy in the Congo was not military conquest, administrative domination, or even primarily commercial exploitation, goals which at one time or another determined Lusitanian policy elsewhere in the empire. Instead, the Crown sought to establish with an African potentate a relationship founded on alliance, plans for the spread of a Christian European cultural pattern, and simple economic agreements. In practical terms Portugal hoped to use the conversion of a supreme African chief in order to evangelize his people, to guarantee her own favoured economic position in the region, and to make contact with the Ethiopian kingdom of the supposedly Christian Prester John.

That the Portuguese accepted the paramount chiefs of the Congo as equals and that their penetration into the area was generally marked by pacific relations with the Africans have come to have special and, possibly, distorted significance in the twentieth century, when the whole endeavour is viewed against the subsequent background of European exploitation in Africa. One is faced, on the one hand, by fanciful interpretations of what was, and, on the other, by bitter conjectures of what might have been. For the defenders of Portuguese imperialism, the Congo experiment – in a sense, experiment it was – represents the founding of colonial traditions which continue to the present day. Here they find abundant historical examples for avowed sentiments of racial equality, for sincere attempts to educate and Christianize the African – with the African's consent – and for a programme of relatively disinterested economic and military assistance. The Congo interlude is still invoked by Portuguese spokesmen as an example of the altruism of their country's conduct in Africa. But critics of the Portuguese see a cause that was lost. When the Congo experiment failed – as it was doomed to do because of the Portuguese commitments in the East, which drained the mother country of men and resources – and the slave-trade became the dominant interest in the Congo and Angola, the failure is viewed as a betrayal of the Africans. 'Seldom', writes Basil Davidson, 'was there a more obvious example of people asking for bread and being given a stone.' Ultimately, however, what the Portuguese did or did not accomplish in the Congo is neither a triumph nor a betrayal. It is a small segment of European history in Africa which at an early date offers insight into the problems of African colonialism.

Diogo Cão came to the mouth of the Congo in the middle

months of the year 1483. On the left bank of the majestic brown river, Cão and his men put into shore; on a spot of land they erected a stone *padrão*, bearing the arms of Portugal and the bare facts of their visit. Having briefly established friendly relations with the leaders of an African community, Cão left four Portuguese companions to be conducted with gifts and messages to the paramount chief dwelling in the interior and pursued his coastal voyage. On his return from the arid shores to the south, Cão put in again at the village. Discovering that the four Portuguese had been retained at the Manicongo's court, Cão seized four Africans. Though the men were taken as hostages for the safety of the Portuguese ambassadors – if they were still alive – Cão attempted to make it clear to the local prince, a relative of the supreme chief, that his subjects would be returned in fifteen months. Cão's action was to be turned into a masterstroke of diplomacy by the Portuguese king and his advisers.

An alliance with the Manicongo seemed to the advisers of João II to offer an opportunity to penetrate the interior of Africa and so reach the kingdom of Prester John. Accordingly every effort was made to impress the hostages with the wealth and spiritual values of Portugal, and from victims of a kidnapping the unsophisticated visitors were transformed into messengers of goodwill, who were able to explain to their chief better than any Portuguese the benefits to be gained from friendship with Europeans.

The return trip of Diogo Cão to the Congo in 1484 or 1485 was thus more of a triumphal embassy than another voyage of exploration. He carried rich presents for King Nzinga-a-Cuum (or Nzinga Nkuwu) and the traditional messages of hope that the Manicongo would embrace the Christian faith.[1] The king proved

---

1. The king of the Congo, in the late fifteenth and sixteenth centuries, was paramount chief of a loose confederation of tribal organizations roughly contained in the area bounded in the north by the Congo River, by the Dande in the south, the Cuango River in the east, and the Atlantic Ocean in the west. The kingdom was split into six provinces, over which the Manicongo's authority was usually supreme. It is apparent that João II believed that he was dealing with a king of more sophistication and political power than was actually the case, for there is little evidence that the Manicongo's people enjoyed a civilization more advanced than they do today. Certainly the civilization of the Congo was not comparable to that of certain other West African states of an earlier or even contemporaneous period.

receptive to Portuguese persuasion, prepared a small group of his people to be sent to Portugal in order to be trained in European ways, and asked that João I I send his missionaries, builders, and traders to instruct his people. João's response was a fleet of three ships dispatched to the Congo in 1490 carrying priests, skilled workers, tools, and religious objects. The purpose of the expedition was peaceful; the company was to evangelize and in a sense to nationalize, to seek alliance not conquest. The first results were auspicious. The Manicongo, his eldest son Afonso, and various notables of his court were baptized, and the Portuguese priests and technicians who remained in the capital Mbanza set about their tasks of instruction.

From 1492 until 1506, when the young Christian Afonso succeeded to his father's ivory seat, little is known of events in the Congo. It is apparent, however, that Portugal did not regularly send men and supplies to Mbanza. In the absence of royal authority, the residents of the newly populated São Tomé began to trade for slaves in the area; in the absence of European example, the old king lapsed into his traditional habits and turned against the few remaining priests. Thus, when Afonso became king, he was confronted with a factious nobility and a cancerous slave-trade.

The long reign of Mbemba-a-Nzinga, or Afonso I, Christian king of a pagan land, represents the golden age, from one point of view, of the Congo. Ten years of clerical instruction had made the prince more than a superficial imitator of European ways. Afonso's contact with his own traditions was broken. One of the earliest examples of Portuguese success at assimilation, Afonso was versed in the Portuguese language and familiar with Portuguese history and customs. But his opportunity to change the customs and destiny of his people was destroyed by one of the side-effects – the slave-trade – of the civilization that he had accepted. His reign was marked by a steadfast though frustrated dedication to bring the benefits of European culture to the Congo. His greatest flaw was a naïve refusal to believe that some Portuguese were able to betray the virtuous principles he had been taught to hold.

From the beginning of his reign, Afonso was bedevilled by the intrigues of the lords proprietor of São Tomé, who made the Congo a commercial and often political dependency of the island. The slave-trade became the dominant interest in his kingdom. A company of missionaries sent to the Congo in 1508 did little to counteract the evil. Succumbing to the moral climate of the capital, they participated in the commerce until they died of fever or succeeded in returning to Portugal. In his letters to the Portuguese king, Manuel I, Afonso complained bitterly of their immorality and of the depredations wrought by freebooters from São Tomé.

Only in 1512 did Manuel move to salvage the situation in the Congo. He had composed an unusual document, which has been widely interpreted as one of the theoretical cornerstones of Portuguese colonial policy. This *regimento*, or set of detailed mandates, consisted of four areas of instruction. The first concerned the help and advice that the bearer of the *regimento*, one Simão da Silva, was to give Afonso in the organization of his kingdom. These instructions were designed in effect to help Afonso create a Portuguese court in Mbanza. The second group of instructions was meant to assure the mission's success and to counteract the harm that had been done in the previous decade. Simão da Silva was required to bring order into the Portuguese house in the Congo. The last two sections of the *regimento* dealt with economic and geographic matters. A royal factor was sent to the Congo with the Silva expedition.

Viewed superficially, the document seems to offer no more than the trappings of a European court. It is difficult to envisage the completed transformation of Congo society; but it is consistent with the terms of the *regimento* and the character of Afonso himself to imagine the establishment of a Portuguese protectorate which, with thoughtful assistance and guidance, could have fulfilled the aspirations of both monarchs for the gradual assimilation of part of Congo society. Such assistance, however, implied a disinterested investment of men and authority far greater than Portugal was prepared to give. And so what might have been – the creation of a Europeanized community within the framework of an African national state – became instead the frustrated strivings of an African chief, against the opposition of Portuguese adventurers and against a strongly dissident element among his own people, for the attainments of European culture.

Simão da Silva died shortly after reaching the mouth of the Congo, and his successor was compromised within a year by the São Tomé faction in Mbanza. At this period São Tomé became the most important slave port in West Africa: in 1522 its administration was taken over by the Crown; in 1534 the town of São Tomé was made a city and the seat of a bishopric. Afonso was isolated from Portugal. His letters and messengers to Lisbon were frequently turned aside at São Tomé. In vain Afonso pleaded for more teachers, more priests, for protection against the unruly traders from the island. At the close of one letter he wrote: 'And we beg Your Highness not to leave us unprotected or allow the Christian work done in our kingdom to be lost, for we alone can do no more.'

By the middle 1520s twenty-five years of slave-trading had left their mark on the Congo. The interior of the country was in turmoil, certain areas were nearly depopulated, and the authority of Afonso undercut in almost every direction. One of Afonso's sons, Henrique, returned to Mbanza in 1521 after thirteen years in Europe. He had been made, through Manuel's perseverance, Bishop of Utica *in partibus infidelium* and Vicar Apostolic of the Congo. Henrique was the first – and last – Negro bishop of the Congo. But his role in the evangelization of his people was insignificant. Constrained by his father from leaving the capital, he was witness to the laxity and selfishness of the white clergy, whose scorn he suffered. Henrique died in the 1530s, a useless product of Afonso's vanity and two nations' aborted hopes.

Manuel's Portuguese resident officers – this much of the 1512 *regimento* had been retained – joined with Afonso in appealing to Manuel and later to João III. They swore that the troubles with the African population were rooted in the egotism and greed of the Portuguese, and they advised their king to replace every civil and religious officer in the Congo kingdom. They urged that the slave-trade be brought under royal control in fact, not merely in name. But the complaints went unheard, and the last decade of Afonso's reign (the 1530s) drew to a close amid disorder and corruption. Afonso, now old, forgotten by Europe, and isolated from his people, became tired and discouraged. The Portuguese, with their celebrated adaptability to any culture or climate, lingered in that backwater of imperial design, quarrelling, meddling, scheming for favour and power. How many Portuguese resided in the Congo in the 1530s, for example, can only be estimated. Probably there were never more than 200 white men there, enjoying an influence out of all proportion to their numbers. Their mulatto children became functionaries, agents of the slave-trade, lesser members of the clergy. Children of two worlds, they paid allegiance to neither and were as responsible as their fathers for the constant turmoil which beset the Congo.

In the early 1540s Afonso died, and with him the last hope for the success of the Congo experiment. An accumulation of ill-assorted resentments burst forth in a bloody revolt for the succession, which saw Afonso's nephew Diogo triumphant over the king's son Pedro. The decline of the Congo toward chaos continued. The slave-trade went unchecked. The arrival of the first Jesuit mission, three priests and a lay teacher, in 1548 brought a brief respite of order. With their usual energy, they set about the task of house-cleaning: 2,100 baptisms in four months; three new churches, one of which, dedicated to the Saviour, was to give Mbanza its permanent name of São Salvador; 600 children in several schools. But the Jesuits were not for long successful. They made the mistake of intriguing against Diogo; they began to collect slaves; they created antagonisms. In 1552 the first Jesuit mission departed in failure. A second Jesuit mission in 1553 fared as badly as the first.

The death of Diogo in 1561 produced a bloodbath greater than the one which brought him to power. A civil war ensued in which black and white citizens perished with surprising lack of discrimination. During the conflict the Congo was closed to ships from São Tomé, and the slave-trade began to pass to the Angola coast. Its violence finally spent, the Congo entered into a peaceful period in the 1560s, which was no more than a lull before the final storm. In 1568 the cannibalistic Jagas, in company with the equally feared Anzicos, descended upon the Congo kingdom. The African court and the Portuguese community fled to the safety of an island in the middle of the river, whence they sent a request for assistance to the young King Sebastião of Portugal. In 1570 a contingent of 600 Portuguese soldiers arrived, and the combined Portuguese–African forces drove the invaders from the land. In gratitude for the restoration of his kingdom the Manicongo Alvaro formally acknowledged vassalage to the King of Portugal, promising to send yearly tribute to Lisbon. Even through Sebastião answered graciously, advising Alvaro only to be a good Christian, the first and most significant period of Portuguese Congo history came to a close in this symbolic act of deference. The Portuguese Congo was not to be the scene of such activity again until 1961.

Except for furnishing slaves and providing a field for periodic missionary endeavours, the Congo was gradually eclipsed by the rise of Angola in the last quarter of the sixteenth century. In 1596 São Salvador was hopefully raised to the rank of city and made the seat of the bishopric of the new diocese of the Congo and Angola, but even this recognition did not halt the decline of the little Portuguese–African world. The Congo chiefs became more and more despotic, and the unity of the kingdom crumbled. By 1615 most traces of Portuguese life had disappeared; the population had died, fled, or been absorbed. Bishop of the Congo Manuel Baptista, writing in 1612, complained of the profitless sacrifices made by European fathers in an unhealthy climate amidst a people so variable in their faith. In the abandonment of São Salvador, the bishops and their aides participated. More often than not the actual seat of the bishopric was Luanda, and after 1676 no bishop sat at São Salvador. A Jesuit college at São Salvador operated spasmodically in the second quarter of the century, but its influence was slight.

The last important missionary effort in the Congo came in the second half of the century, when the field was taken over by Capuchin friars, most of them Italian, Spanish, or Flemish. The first mission of Capuchins arrived there from Rome in 1645, despite Portuguese protest, and baptized an estimated 15,000 Africans a year. Encouraged by such statistics, the Propaganda Fide arranged for a second group of Capuchins to go to the Congo in 1648. When Luanda was regained from the Dutch in the same year, the Portuguese asserted their rights of sovereignty over the area and demanded a measure of control over Capuchin activities in Portuguese territory. For another ten years Capuchin efforts in the Congo blossomed, but by 1660 the inevitable reaction had begun. Plans for a seminary were discarded, and the projected formation of a sizable African clergy came to little. For the rest of the century Capuchin fortunes ebbed and flowed, and in the eighteenth century the work in the Congo was often entrusted to only one or two priests. Although the total of their baptisms was fantastic (100,000 by one priest from 1645 to 1666; 1,750 by another in forty days; 340,000 baptisms and 50,000 marriages by the Capuchins together from 1677 to 1700), not much remained of the Capuchins' work by 1800 except statistics. By 1700 São Salvador itself was a deserted city, its twelve churches in ruins. Stanley, who explored the area in the late 1870s, professed he could find no trace of Christian civilization, no mark of Portuguese sovereignty.

In such a manner one of the unique European experiments petered out. Although in the sixteenth century a policy of colonization meant not much more than the evangelization of a heathen people, the story of the Congo, even in its failure, stands for more. It stands for the pacific good intentions, seldom realized, of the Portuguese Crown, and it stands for the faith of an African prince in his alliance with a European power. For eighty years the Manicongo was political ruler of his kingdom, with authority which frequently extended over the Portuguese residing there. Portuguese intervention was officially limited to commerce and religion. There is no suggestion of official Portuguese tyranny or occupation during these years. The original desire of Portugal to create a civilized African state contiguous with the illusory Ethiopia of Prester John went by the board, but the Portuguese profess that more lasting values were created in the Congo. As a result of the entry of white traders and settlers into the Congo, there emerged in the sixteenth century a biracial community. The practice of easy assimilation with the African, which was to continue in other parts of the continent for 400 years, is one reason, the Portuguese have argued, why there has long been a lack of racial tension in their African colonies.

In conflict with the practices of miscegenation and the willingness of the Portuguese king to accept his African counterpart as a brother, was the Congo slave-trade. 'At the side of the missionary who carried salvation', the great nineteenth-century missionary António Barroso lamented, 'was the buyer of men, who destroyed the ties linking father to son and mother to daughter.' The degradations and frictions arising from the slave-trade and the demands of the empire in the East, which distracted Lisbon's interest from the Congo in the crucial years of the Portuguese–African alliance, were responsible for the failure of the project. Without encouragement and moral authority, it succumbed to the purely material exploitations which have so often characterized the presence of Europe in Africa.

2 Angola

Although the history of Angola in its early years may be considered a part of Portuguese activity in the Congo kingdom, the association is marginal, for the area held interest only in terms of exploration and the projection of the Congo slave-trade. Not until the foundation of Luanda in 1576 and the expeditions of that most celebrated campaigner in Portuguese Africa during the sixteenth century, Paulo Dias de Novais, did the lands to the south become a primary concern to the Lisbon court. For several decades thereafter a declining Congo and a rising Angola shared equally Portugal's modest interest in this part of the world, but by 1600 the territory known as Angola had emerged as the more important. In contrast with her pacific policies of alliance and cultural assimilation in the Congo, here Portugal was often disposed to implant her authority over the African *sobas*, or chiefs, by force and to govern directly. This shift in policy was probably determined by the absence in Angola of any supreme chief of the stature of the Manicongo and by the need for military action to protect the burgeoning slave-trade. The first three centuries of Angola's history are a chronology of small wars, expeditions into the interior, and of a dedicated commerce in black humanity. Angola still retains today some of the harsh frontier aggressiveness that has characterized the past and left its stamp upon the present; it is a quality which sets the province immediately apart from the more leisurely, perhaps more cosmopolitan, Moçambique. One of the most sparsely populated territories of Africa, Angola has not yet recovered from the terrible depredations of conflict and a slave-trade which, by conservative estimate, carried more than three million Negroes to the plantations of the two Americas.

Diogo Cão on his second voyage sailed the entire length of the Angola coast. In the early sixteenth century traders from São Tomé made occasional visits to the island of Luanda. In 1519 the paramount chief of the lands behind Luanda, jealous perhaps of

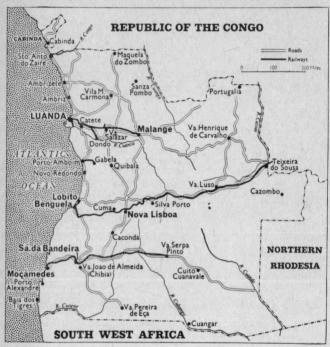

4. Angola, 1961

the attentions received by the Manicongo, asked Afonso to intercede on his behalf for an embassy of Portuguese merchants and priests. Since the request was transmitted to Lisbon along with a sample of silver, Manuel decided to send a small mission to search for souls and silver. The mission was not a success, none of the provisions of the *regimento* was carried out, and for the next forty years official interest in the lands of Angola was negligible. In the same period, however, the slaving trade, with its attendant turmoil, spilled over from the Congo into Angola and was the cause of a small war fought in 1556 between a Congo army, with its European adherents, and an Angolan force also equipped with its Portuguese partisans.

The boundaries to the original lands of Angola are not definitely known. A fair estimate of the area subservient to the Ngola (the dynastic title enjoyed by the chief of the Kimbundu people inhabiting the region) would be the country lying between the Dande River in the north and the Cuanza in the south and extending from the coast back into the Dongo as far as the modern city of Malange, although some scholars project the eastern boundaries all the way to the Cuango River. This was to be the area of Portuguese penetration in the early centuries. The ports of Luanda and Benguela, a few settlements along the Cuanza, and less than a dozen scattered forts in the interior – such was the Portuguese occupation of Angola until the middle of the nineteenth century. The picture is, however, somewhat deceptive, for the Portuguese, because of their promotion of the slave-trade, had an influence over the area more extensive than the modest facts of occupation indicate.

The Africans living in the area during the sixteenth and seventeenth centuries were southern Bantu people who had themselves moved recently into the region and formed into several tribal divisions. Neither of the two contemporary authorities on African affairs in Angola, Andrew Battell of Leigh and António de Oliveira de Cadornega, gives a clear division of peoples and politics. But it is apparent that over the petty chiefs of the Dongo country, nominally under the thrall of the Manicongo, an invader from the lands of Matamba (lying to the west of the southern reaches of the Cuango River) had gained dominance. This Ngola and several of his successors continued to owe informal allegiance to the Manicongo; but the Portuguese in the sixteenth century seemed to regard him as master of his own lands and, as in the Congo, applied his name to the country he governed.

An expedition in 1560, made up of two Jesuit priests and two lay brothers, to the Ngola's court also ended in failure. The scout for the expedition, Paulo Dias de Novais – a grandson of Bartolomeu Dias – was held at the African *embala* for five years before being returned to Lisbon with a supply of slaves, copper, and ivory. In Lisbon, Dias de Novais, with the powerful support of the Jesuits, persuaded the court to name him *donatário* (proprietary landlord) of Angola. Dias apparently sought the appointment for personal aggrandizement. The Society supported, or manoeuvred, the *donatário* because it foresaw an extension of its authority in Africa comparable to the position which it enjoyed in Brazil as protector of the indigenous people. The court hoped to bring about the conquest, colonization, and evangelization of Angola at an inconsequential cost.

The title conferred upon Paulo Dias read impressively: 'Governor and Captain-General of the Kingdom of Sebaste in the Conquest of Ethiopia.' In return for hereditary rights to vast tracts of land – all, in fact, which he could conquer – Dias was to garrison his captaincy with 400 men, bring into Angola 100 families, to whom he was to give seeds and tools, and to build three fortresses between the Dande and the Cuanza. The only significant deeds accomplished by Dias, between his arrival in 1575 and his death in 1589, were the foundation of the city of Luanda and of several forts along the Cuanza. Three years after his arrival, perhaps at the instigation of the Jesuits who wanted to expand their evangelical work into the interior, Dias became involved in a costly campaign with the Ngola's warriors. In this decade of disorder, Dias did manage to push about seventy miles up the river in his search for souls and the alleged silver mines of Cambambe, but about 2,000 Portuguese were lost to fevers or enemy weapons during the same period. The Jesuits profited little from these initial difficulties. But the slave-trade prospered. With the arrival of Dias and the fixing of a permanent settlement at Luanda, Angola became the Black Mother. From Luanda alone, about 2,500 slaves a year were exported from 1575 to 1587; in the next four years, the yearly average tripled. Nor do these figures include the covert commerce from informal ports of embarkation.

In 1592, with the appointment of Governor-General Francisco d'Almeida, a colonial government was created in Angola, and the general pattern of Angola's administrative régime was fixed for the next three and a half centuries. The establishment of a colonial rule in Angola was one of the recommendations made a year earlier in an official report by the lawyer Domingos de Abreu e Brito – perhaps the first modern colonialist in African history. Abreu e Brito urged, among other things in his report, the methodical occupation of Angola by force, the establishment of twelve fortresses, an overland connexion between Angola and Moçambique, a tightening of controls over the export of slaves, freedom of mineral exploitation, a Crown monopoly on salt, and the setting up of a factory at Benguela. Almost every report for the next 300 years on the development of Angola would share, at least in part, the recommendations made in the 1590s by Abreu e Brito.

Development and Exploration in the Seventeenth Century

Until very recently Angola has always refused to be developed, except on its own terms. While there was no systematic policy forthcoming from Lisbon, there was need for none. By 1600 Angola was already firmly set on a profitable if ultimately ruinous course, from which it would not deviate until the twentieth century. By 1600 the old colonists and the Jesuits were entrenched in local power, quarrelling among themselves but uniting against any governor-general who seriously threatened to interfere with their spiritual and economic prerogatives. In the interior the African tribes had already been set one against another. Another fort was established at Muxima up the Cuanza, which had become the main route for penetration of the interior. In 1604 acting governor Manuel Cerveira Pereira reached Cambambe, to discover that there were no productive mines. The silver bubble burst, and everyone settled down to the serious business of dealing in slaves, who were to provide more than eighty per cent of Angola's commerce before 1832.

There was more activity in the seventeenth century, however, than in either the eighteenth or the early nineteenth. To widen the source of supply for slaves, governor Manuel Forjaz sent Baltasar Rebelo de Aragão in 1607 on an expedition eastward. Rebelo de Aragão travelled about 400 miles inland before returning, and in his account of the journey wrote that he believed he could have completed the transcontinental crossing to Moçambique.

In the same period the Dutch set up a factory at the mouth of the Congo, from which Dutch ships occasionally ventured south to attack Portuguese shipping. To the south São Filipe de Benguela was founded in 1617 by Cerveira Pereira. Although a separate conquest, Benguela gradually came under the domination of Luanda, since in its early years Benguela was improvident both in metals and slaves and could not stand alone. But the community at Benguela – renegades from the Congo, exiles and convicts from Portugal, criminals from Brazil – were perhaps the first genuine colonizers in Angola. Frustrated in their search for mineral wealth and unable to compete at first with the slave marts of the north, the handful of settlers was driven to gain an existence from the soil and the sea, and Benguela was almost from the first a self-sufficient little community of traders, fishermen, and farmers. Benguela was no showplace of Lusitanian colonization, but in its own way it exemplified the Portuguese way of life better than other more flamboyant centres of expansion in Africa and the East.

In Luanda the colonial administration of Angola proceeded into the second and third decades of the seventeenth century with scarcely any deviation from the pattern. The limits of territorial occupation were reached with the erection of a blockhouse at Ambaca (on the Lucala River) in 1616, although Portuguese, half-caste, and African traders made their way throughout the area east of the Cuango River. Lisbon's reluctance to finance the costs of the Angola government made the correction of abuses impossible. From the governor down, the administrative officials and soldiers received trifling compensations, and the slave-trade represented the logical and only means of supplementing their income. Attendant irregularities were the steady increases in the head tax (which could be paid in slaves) demanded of the African chiefs and the provoking of local wars to stimulate the flow of captives into Luanda. More than one seventeenth-century Portuguese critic, men like Canon Manuel Severim de Faria, denounced the course of action in Angola, arguing that the colony would never be inherently prosperous as long as the so-called campaign of conquest and pseudo conversion was pursued. But these advocates of settlement and organized trade did not have a receptive audience, and the few Portuguese who attempted to settle in the interior or to carry on business at the scattered fairs were chronically harassed and found themselves caught up in the periodic turmoil that swept the country.

Amid such conditions it is not surprising that occasional royal edicts ordering Portuguese officials in Angola to use a greater clemency in dealing with the native population were usually ignored. The Portuguese there could rightly claim that inter-tribal warfare existed among the 'heathen' before the arrival of Europeans and that they were obliged to confront local necessities. They argued further that the African responded only to brute force, that 'they feared nothing save corporal punishment and the whip ... and it is only by force and fear that we can maintain our position over these indomitable heathen', in the words of Cadornega. Only those Africans who became part of the Portuguese community and the half-caste population sired by Portuguese men were worthy of consideration. So it was that in seventeenth-century Angola a particular Portuguese attitude was already shaped: a contemptuous exploitation of the African mass, coupled with a paternalistic acceptance of the African or mulatto minority who came to share Portuguese cultural values. This attitude can still be said to predominate in Portuguese Africa, although in the last thirty years Dr Salazar's colonial spokesmen have attempted to demonstrate that what has long been true of the minority has also come to be true of Portuguese policy toward the majority.

In these years the Jesuits, occasionally joined by missionaries from other orders, carried on intermittent work in the bush; but it was Luanda which offered excellent opportunities for the unique talents of the Society, and from 1600 they concentrated their activities there, dominating, in the eyes of their contemporaries, life in the capital. As teachers they were responsible for whatever education there was in Angola. They trained both a native clergy and the half-caste administrative class which formed most of Luanda's lesser bureaucracy, to the annoyance of the white residents who held them responsible for most of the colony's problems. The Jesuits also became the centre of controversy. They tried to create for themselves the role they played so successfully in parts of South America, that of protector of the indigenous people. Since the economy was based on the slave-trade – in which the Jesuits fully participated – their pretension brought them into conflict with both governors and local residents, who considered the Jesuits as meddlers and hypocritical trouble-makers. Recriminations to Lisbon against their arrogance were frequent. Enemies of the Society argued that it was more interested in commerce than in catechizing Africans, and that although they received a substantial royal subsidy, the Jesuits were getting rich from real-estate transactions, from the lands under their protection, and from the slave-trade. The Jesuits *were* active in the traffic; most of them subscribed to the prevalent belief that the best way to convert the Negro was to sell him, so that he might be introduced to Christianity through the dignity of labour on American plantations. Ships belonging to the Society were engaged in the Angola–Brazil trade.

The Dutch occupation of Luanda brought a halt to Portuguese missionary efforts. In August 1641 an armada of twenty-one ships appeared off Luanda and captured the city after a slight struggle. In December a smaller fleet entered the fortress at Benguela. The Dutch occupation of the two strategic ports of Angola was one of the repercussions of the struggle in Europe, but the Dutch also needed African labour on the Pernambuco estates of north-east Brazil which they had taken. Control of Luanda and São Tomé was necessary to guarantee the flow of slaves.

The Portuguese community withdrew up the Cuanza to Massangano, where for seven years the garrison withstood separate and joint assaults from the Dutch and from Jaga tribesmen. The Massangano episode is the finest hour of the Portuguese in Angola. As Charles Boxer observes:

> The men who held out so stubbornly at Massangano despite an almost unbroken series of crushing reverses ... were inspired by something more than the expectations of securing slaves. The crusading spirit in its good and bad aspects was still far from dead in Portugal, and war against the Moslem, the heathen, and the heretic was still regarded as a sacred duty. Despite the violence, greed, and cruelty with which the history of Angola is stained, the fact remains that they sincerely believed that they were fighting God's battles and saving Negro souls from the fatal infection of heresy.

Portugal, involved in a military struggle with Spain to ensure the independence declared in 1640, was not able to aid her oppressed African colony directly and called upon another colony, Brazil, to retrieve Angola. A wealthy Brazilian landowner, governor, and general, Salvador Correia de Sá e Benavides, was made governor of Angola in 1647 and given the task of retaking the territory. Twice before armadas from Brazil had failed, but such was the prestige of Salvador de Sá – and such was the need for slaves on the sugar plantations – that he raised fifteen ships and 1,500 men. In August 1648 Luanda capitulated to the Brazilian force. Shortly thereafter Benguela and São Tomé were relinquished by the Dutch.

Two governors-general tower above all others in the history of Angola, Salvador de Sá and the eighteenth-century administrator Francisco de Sousa Coutinho. No sooner had the Dutch departed in their ships than Salvador de Sá set about the reconstruction of Portuguese authority. African chiefs who had collaborated with the invaders were punished for their lack of allegiance. The governor attempted to curtail the activities of the Capuchins in the Congo, who had also taken advantage of Portugal's plight to enter what the Portuguese considered a closed missionary field. The slave supply lines to Buenos Aires and the Brazilian ports were again in operation by 1650. (To compensate the governor and his cohorts for expenses incurred in liberating Angola, an additional tax was placed on each adult slave leaving the colony.) Coastal defences were improved, and, to the creaking administrative organization of Angola, Salvador de Sá brought a new order and efficiency.

When in 1652 Salvador de Sá embarked for Brazil, he left behind an accumulated momentum which was to carry Angola through the rest of the century. Angola now entered its golden age, the most prosperous period of the territory's history excluding the years 1945–60. It is true that native wars were endemic, and that differences between the governors, the old-time residents, and the ubiquitous Jesuits flared up again and again; but such disturbances were accepted as part of Angola's pattern of life and even contributed to its flourishing. Portuguese authority was entrenched at Luanda, where the splendid fortress of São Miguel was finished in 1689, and in the south at Benguela. In the back country, smaller forts at Massangano, Muxima, Pungo Andongo, Cambambe, and Ambaca kept open three slave-routes criss-crossing the colony and provided centres of military strength to keep troublesome *sobas* from seriously interfering with that all-important commerce. By the end of the century Portugal held nominal control over, according to Ravenstein's estimate, 50,000 square miles of Angola and the Congo. European population decreased proportionately with the distance from the coast, but traders and soldiers could move with relative freedom throughout the whole vast area.

The prosperity of Angola was inseparably attached to the development of Brazil, a fact recognized by the Crown itself, which was content to collect its tax on slaves and let affairs run their eventually disastrous course. Angola's debt to Brazil was unquestionably great. Her salvation had come from the American colony, not the metropolis, and it was fitting that in the years following 1650 (until 1668 when Francisco de Távora was sent directly from Lisbon), the governors and functionaries responsible for the territory should also have come from Brazil. It was equally fitting that these administrators should have held the interests of Brazil paramount. Portugal was still involved in a tiresome struggle with Spain which consumed her leaders and finances, and it was a useful and inexpensive device to reward the heroes of Brazil's war against the Dutch by giving them the prized and profitable governorship of Angola. Unlike Salvador de Sá, these men contributed little to the welfare of the colony. They and their lesser officials received but a pittance for their services; their military and administrative budget was inconsequential. Their remuneration came from participation in the slave-trade, either through association with resident slave merchants or by personal initiative.

The military and civil administration of Angola was entrusted to the governor-general, whose local authority, if he chose or was able to use it, was substantial. He named his own staff and had a voice in naming the captains of the fortresses, although the latter, once in the back country, were not always ready to pay any heed to his instructions. The police and the treasury were also in the governor's charge. On matters concerning the defence of the colony, or those of general interest, he acted after consultation with his council, composed partly of colonial officers and partly of local inhabitants. The *ouvidor*, or chief justice, was the second most powerful official in the colony. Appointed in Lisbon, he was responsible for juridical authority. How effectively the governor and his staff ran the affairs of Angola depended on the forcefulness of the governor's own personality and his skill in dealing with the permanent Portuguese inhabitants. Most governors were content to leave the situation in Luanda as they found it, using their energies against the dissident tribes of the interior – a more recognizable foe.

The colonists of Angola usually looked with some suspicion on the temporary administrators, particularly when they spoke of policies which threatened the residents' power over the lesser African tribes. These veterans of a score of military and political campaigns formed a feudal caste resisting change and authority. As captains of fortresses, landholders, members of the city councils, they constantly asserted their entrenched independence. Many of them led lives of splendour, constructing palatial homes in Luanda, marrying or taking as mistresses African or mulatto women, with whom they created generations of children equally resentful of the prerogatives of the governor's court. The population of Angola was augmented by exiles, ambitious second sons from Portugal, and freebooters, who, if they survived the first devastating bout of fever, enlivened the colony with their many genial talents. These first and second citizens of the land had occasional allies in the Jesuits, still powerful though their dreams of an African theocracy had vanished, who brooked no interference with their traditional masterful jurisdiction over the well-being of the Portuguese and African population. It was a courageous governor who came to grips with the formidable citizenry of Angola.

The three large African tribes, all too powerful to have been brought to permanent submission, were those of Matamba, where the ancient virago and one-time Christian Queen Jinga still reigned, of the Dongo, where the Ngola held sway, and of the Congo. The paramount chief of each region was theoretically a vassal of the King of Portugal, but actual Portuguese relations with the three peoples normally consisted of a state of truce, which permitted the trader and the stray missionary relative freedom of movement in the back country. But the truce was often broken by sporadic incidents, resulting usually from the intemperance of the slave-traders. From 1665 to 1685, however, the interior was torn by a series of wars. It was no longer a practical policy in Angola to try to maintain peaceful relations with the native population. Treaties with England and Holland in effect allowed these two nations to participate in the Portuguese slave-trade by opening the ports of Brazil to their ships. And the depleted Portuguese treasury brought new demands on the empire. These two factors had a profound effect on the Angola slave-trade. From an estimated 7,000 slaves exported each year, the number began to rise sharply with violent and devastating effects upon the colony. A number of incidents, real and imagined, led the Portuguese to invade the Congo kingdom which, with the death of the Manicongo António I, lost the remnants of its former power. In 1670-1 the Congo was over-run by a force under the twenty-three-year-old Governor Francisco de Távora, and in the late 1680s the area of Matamba was brought more or less effectively under Portuguese influence. From Benguela also the Portuguese pushed into the interior, to Caconda and beyond, and by the end of the century they had scattered the Jaga and set up an outpost 150 miles from the coast, to help swell the supply of slaves from the highlands. The best intentions of the missionary orders could not withstand the turbulent state of affairs. In 1694 only thirty-six priests were active in the interior; most of their churches and schools had fallen into ruin.

To coordinate the government of the occupied countryside, the first administrative code, or organic charter, for the colony was drawn up in the 1670s. It defined the responsibilities and obligations of the captains of fortresses, especially in matters of revenue and justice; but, like most colonial legislation of the period, it was an afterthought in African policy, and as such was not taken seriously by those at whom it was directed. A theoretic concern for the welfare of Angola accomplished little in the absence of steady encouragement to colonize and develop the wealth of the soil, as was being done in the Americas. Henrique Galvão and Carlos Selvagem comment on this period of Angola's history:

Angola was becoming a colony that most betrayed the adventurous nature of Portugal's expansion, diverting its people from their ancestral ways which tied them to the soil and inciting them to covetousness, to an uneasy trivial existence, more disposed to risk all for easy immediate gain, instead of to a slow and legitimate profit from their sober hard work.

The Slave-Trade

But there could not be in Angola during the seventeenth century, or for several centuries afterwards, any such orderly reality. It was not the age, and Africa was not the place, for sober industrious pursuits. Luanda was the greatest slave port in Africa, and Angola and the Congo together were the largest concentrated area of slave supply in the continent. From 1580 to 1836, when the traffic was at last abolished by the Portuguese government, about four million Africans were exported, over three million from Angola alone. Generally, over fifty per cent of the total went to Brazil, about thirty per cent to the Caribbean, and about ten to fifteen per cent to the River Plate area; though these proportions varied, of course, from one decade to another.

In Angola the slave was the only real article of commerce. The principal dealer was usually the governor, whose interest in the trade was not necessarily his own capital, but the power and facilities of his office plus whatever privileges were contained in his *regimento*. Then there was the contractor, working for himself or, more frequently, for a corporation of investors, who had purchased the licences permitting them to export an appointed number of Negroes in a certain period of time. Through the offices of the governor or of his staff the terms of the contract were often discreetly changed during the actual operation in order to allow more slaves, on whom no taxes were paid, to be exported. Working for the contractor or for themselves were local merchants living in Luanda, or sometimes in the interior, whose *pombeiros* (native traders) scoured the country, bringing in captives from the most remote sections of the colony. On the margin of this legal activity, adventurous residents promoted the clandestine trade.

Slaves were acquired in various ways. They were obtained at fortresses in the interior, where they were brought by African chiefs or their agents as barter for manufactured goods. In Angola this method was less successful than on the more commercially advanced Guinea coast. A surer way was for the merchant to send his *pombeiros* into the interior. Accompanied by a number of domestic slaves bearing the goods to be traded (cloth, wine, metal implements), the *pombeiros* ranged through the countryside for more than a year, bartering with local chiefs. The slaves so acquired were then marched to Luanda. It was not uncommon for the *pombeiros*, or for free-lancing Portuguese traders, to stir up a local war in order to be able to buy prisoners. In the many so-called wars of conquest that the colonial administration waged against the great chiefs or petty *sobas* of the interior, a substantial number of captives was taken, many of whom were sold to slave contractors for dispatch to America. Such procedures were not above criticism by the humanitarians of the age who regarded conquest of the heathen as a Christian mission.

Still another source lay in the well-populated lands granted by the governor or the Crown to deserving soldiers and clerics. The taxes demanded of the chief could be conveniently paid in slaves; many of these *sobadas* were in effect slave farms. It was not unknown for missionary orders to run their programme on the proceeds from the sale of slaves from their estates. The Jesuits in particular every now and then drew heavy fire for this practice from their critics in Luanda and in Lisbon.

In Luanda the slaves were held in barracoons, large warehouses, or sometimes open corrals. Since many slaves came from the deep interior, they arrived on the coast emaciated and exhausted. So that they could withstand the incredible rigours of the transatlantic voyage, the slaves were sometimes restored to a semblance of health. Their services were used, should the embarkation be delayed, on municipal and agricultural tasks. Before or while they were led aboard ship they were baptized wholesale. The story has been perpetuated that on the wharves at Luanda stood a great marble chair, the Bishop's Chair, where the Angolan prelate officiated at baptismal ceremonies. The scene is evocative, but only partly true. It is even possible that captives leaving lesser ports and neglected estuaries along the coast were not bothered at all by last-minute ceremonies.

No single step in the slaving process, not even the dreadful Arab slave-gang marches through East Africa in the nineteenth century, was more terrible than the voyage to the New World. The sickening conditions under which the Negro was transported, and the brutal unconcern of the slaver's officers and crew, were the most dramatic examples of slaving horrors cited by European anti-slaving factions in the eighteenth and nineteenth centuries. Portuguese historians have made much of remarks by several Dutch observers of the seventeenth century that the Portuguese were more efficient and humane transporters of live cargo than other nations. Contemporary Portuguese accounts, however, reveal no such distinction. The Portuguese ships were generally smaller than the Dutch ones and carried proportionately more slaves on the narrow lower decks. To Brazil, the Middle Passage was comparatively swift, from five to eight weeks. But much of the cargo never got to Brazil, or died shortly after being unloaded. Through disease, suicide, or suffocation, twenty to thirty per cent of the slaves embarked in Angola perished. Whether, as critics of the traffic argued, conditions got worse from the seventeenth to the nineteenth century, or popular reaction became more imaginative and vehement, is a needlessly tortured point. At no time did the voyages of the *tumbeiros* have anything to recommend them.

The callous violence which attended every step of the procedure evoked a continuing modest protest from a small minority of humanitarians. Isolated Portuguese clerics spoke out, in vain, against the sophistry of defending the Amerindian and closing one's eyes to African slavery. Several Angolan slave merchants realistically criticized the abuses of the trade. Royal *regimentos* repeatedly stressed to no avail the necessity of treating the Negro with Christian kindness. In the eighteenth century a small number of Portuguese anti-slavery tracts took their place in the growing European literature of protest. Governor Sousa Coutinho sought to mitigate the atrocities committed against the Africans. In a series of decrees he condemned and, in some cases, temporarily corrected the traders' extreme conduct. He threatened dire punishment to anyone who robbed the chiefs of their people or enslaved free Africans. Although he did not condemn the trade, he set his face against the wholesale exploitation of the African population.

In Angola local slavery was always subordinate to the export trade. There was insufficient economic life in the colony to support domestic slavery on any large scale. The African was more profitable sold than kept. Slaves, however, were retained. They were labourers on manioc plantations; they were used by the traders themselves as bearers and soldiers. The slaves also formed part of an African craftsman class, since few Portuguese in the colony engaged in such tasks. Africans trained by the Jesuits in carpentry, masonry, or at the forge, were in constant demand. Slavery in Angola was perhaps more indolent than in Brazil, closer to African tribal slavery than to the servitude of American plantation life.

The Eighteenth Century and the Missionary Effort

Very little disturbed the monotonous course of Angolan history in the eighteenth century. In addition to keeping the *sobas* in submission, the governors were at times presented with the cares of coastal defences against would-be European intruders, but these concerns did little more than ripple the surface of the prosperous and negligent country. Local squabbles were more important than international disputes. The conflicts which continued to flare up among the participants in the slave-trade – governors, captains, citizens, clergy – led the Crown in 1720 to prohibit colonial administrators from engaging in any aspect of the commerce, but such distant pronouncements did not burden the conscience of many. The material splendour of Luanda in the early 1700s was the admiration of foreign and Portuguese visitors; the mansions of the established settlers, the ecclesiastical edifices, the palace of the governor made it seem as though a part of Lisbon had been moved to African soil. The gardens at the city's edge were overgrown and rank, however; once again foodstuffs reached Luanda in the holds of empty slavers.

In 1765 the vigorous reforms that the Marquês de Pombal had clamped on the metropolis echoed in Angola, when the extraordinarily determined and far-sighted Francisco de Sousa Coutinho arrived as governor of the colony. It was at once apparent to Sousa Coutinho that a commercial and pseudo-military occupation of Angola resting on slaving held no promise for the future national development of the territory. One hundred years of inertia and expediency, prosperous though Angola was, could not be called a colonial programme. Angola had lost much of its pioneer vitality; an inbred and stagnant society rejected any change in its traditional ways and perquisites. But already voices in Portugal and abroad were being raised against the slave-trade, an institution which could not endure forever.

Sousa Coutinho saw the present and the future. What he envisaged for Angola was a systematic occupation of the country; the settling of colonists in the healthy plateau regions; a curb on the vast number of Africans being exported annually, which now threatened to depopulate the land; and the self-sufficiency of Angolan agriculture. In many respects Sousa Coutinho was the first modern colonial administrator in Africa.

As such he was a man out of his century. The wealth of Brazil was one of the foundations of Portugal's national existence, and Brazil's security continued to rest on Angolan labour. Pombal was no more receptive to ideas which would threaten the economic *status quo* than were the slaving interests in the African colony. The result was that many of Sousa Coutinho's plans for improvement were never realized. Some of the reforms he attempted to inaugurate are still fundamental to the colony's development in the mid twentieth century. He encouraged local industry: sulphur, copper, asphalt could all contribute to Angola's welfare. Under his guidance a shipyard was put in operation. His industrial dream was an iron foundry on the Cuanza, and this was in small-scale operation by the year of his departure.

Another of Sousa Coutinho's visions was a colonization scheme for the plateau country of Biê and Huíla. In 1682, inland from Benguela, the Portuguese had founded a fortress at Caconda near the rising of the Caporolo River. Sousa Coutinho had the fort transferred to the present site of Caconda, with the notion that in a healthier location Caconda would become the nucleus of a settlement and the centre for trade in the region. 'Since the fortress is situated in the best part of the province, we must see that it is populated with industrious and hard-working people. . . .' He went on to suggest that the Africans would be drawn into the community by the good example of the Europeans. But Caconda did not fulfil its high expectations. The Portuguese there intermarried and lived with their slaves and families in their compounds. The fortress remained one of the advance points of Portuguese penetration; it had a population of about 250 men at the beginning of the nineteenth century, with as many as 15,000 Africans residing in the vicinity. By 1840, however, the area was virtually abandoned. Elsewhere on the plateau, Sousa Coutinho urged his government to bring in settlers and small farmers from Portugal and Brazil. He was confident that such colonists would do more for the well-being of the country than the hundreds of wastrels, exiles, and convicts whose only contribution to Angola was a perpetuation of tyranny and scandal. He also threatened to expropriate the large uncultivated tracts in the hinterland of Luanda unless their owners used them to advantage.

To the colonial administration Sousa Coutinho brought temporary order. He demanded propriety and honesty from his subordinates. In Luanda he built large warehouses for food reserves, to be called upon in years of famine or when the ships from Brazil were delayed. He built a technical training-school for young men. Of Sousa Coutinho's work, Lopes de Lima wrote: 'He was the first governor to civilize this semi-barbarous colony, and during his tenure he did more than all his predecessors had ever thought of.'

But the example of Sousa Coutinho was hardly infectious. By the end of the century, the surface splendour of Luanda had begun to tarnish; the fine buildings were falling into disrepair; the streets were unattended. The slave-trade went on, but it was clear that Angola was now playing out the final hands of the game. The population of Luanda had subtly though perceptibly changed. The constant infusion of social castaways had brought a meanness and disregard into the once cosmopolitan capital. Not much more could be said for life in the interior, where Portuguese authority had begun to diminish. Many sections of the interior were denuded of inhabitants; others were in arms.

The condition of Angola and Moçambique at this period could usually be judged by the state of the missionary effort. By 1800 there were nine or ten fathers and perhaps twenty-five parish priests, more than half of them Angolans, in the colony. The sixteen churches still standing in the interior were irregularly attended. The African clergy was half-educated, although more dedicated than the old-time Portuguese clerics who had

T—c

succumbed to inertia and spiritual sloth. Missionary functions were by now a formality, the continuation of a habit started long ago and now kept alive through a passive sense of responsibility. The Africans, if they paid any attention to the vague gestures toward their conversion, were progressively less influenced by the Church, even when it was represented by their own people.

This decline had progressed through the century. In 1716 the seat of the bishopric had been officially transferred from São Salvador to Luanda, thus confirming the reality of the previous sixty years. There were then about twenty-five chapels or parish churches scattered through the interior, each with a priest of its own. The Capuchin activity waxed and waned during the century, until it disappeared entirely. Capuchins and Jesuits alike chose to make their spiritual contribution in Luanda, rather than serving in the interior. The colonial government supported the orders through land-grants while the Crown paid a subsidy, but the work of the secular clergy suffered from a chronic lack of funds. When in the middle of the century the Jesuits were expelled by Pombal, their loss was mostly felt in education; their evangelizing was scarcely missed. But it should be said for the Jesuits that they had for 250 years given the colony whatever dim enlightenment it possessed. And they were, on occasions, the conscience of Angola and the only buffer between the African and his oppressor. Even that harsh critic of Catholic practices in Portuguese Africa, David Livingstone, had praise for their accomplishments.

Where lay the failure of the missionary effort in Angola? Why, looking back across the years from 1800, did it seem that the Church had built on sand? Beyond a handful of converts, the African population had remained untouched by the Church's work. There were deeper reasons than those of climate, scanty personnel, inadequate funds, or the doubtful techniques of evangelization. The principal reason was that the missionary offered nothing to the Africans but a disembodied doctrine, many of whose disciplines were distinctly distasteful. Where were the superior advantages of European civilization which went with this faith? They were not found in the slave-trade, in the armed incursions into the interior, or in the example of the Portuguese traders who often led a life more African than European. Nowhere except in Luanda was Portugal able to transplant a European way of life, and only in a few other areas was her military power permanently convincing. Without other cultural encouragements, the convictions of a few good men, haltingly expressed, could never have prevailed against the suspicions or indifference of an African people with its own traditions, whose passing associations with Europeans were largely violent.

Abolition of Slavery Under the Liberals

As a consequence of the Napoleonic wars in the Peninsula, the Portuguese court removed in 1807 to Rio de Janeiro, where indeed many Portuguese in Angola felt that it had always been. Brazil declared its independence in 1822. Portugal herself was involved in a struggle between the constitutionalists and the absolutists which, though it ended in a victory for the Liberal forces, set the stage for a turbulent political century. The metropolitan unrest reached Angola. A popular uprising in Luanda in 1822 and a mutiny among the troops deposed the incumbent governor, who was replaced by a provisional junta headed by the bishop. Brazil, to guard her economic ties with West Africa, proposed federation to Angola and Moçambique, an overture rejected in Luanda but supported in Benguela, which had a briefly successful separatist uprising. Only with the final constitutional triumph in 1834 and the arrival of the Liberal governor, Bernardo Vidal, did relative calm return to Angola.

The Liberals' colonial policy in Africa was idealistic and confused. The Portuguese Constitution of 1822 made no special provision for the colonies, since the constitution was to be applicable to all national territory, whether in Europe or overseas. The Ministry for Navy and Overseas was abolished in 1821, restored in 1823, abolished again in 1834, and re-created in 1835 with diminished authority. Even though the 1838 constitution provided for special laws to govern the overseas territories, the fact that all important colonial legislation came before the Portuguese parliament – where many deputies believed that special legislation was unnecessary, since metropolitan laws would serve as well overseas – precluded the formation of a consistent colonial policy. The free population of overseas Portugal were declared Portuguese citizens, with the same privileges as their countrymen in the metropolis. In 1832, even during an absolutist régime, the territories were given the name of overseas provinces. (The shift from colony to province to colony to province is one of the vexing aspects of Portuguese colonial history, even though the transitions have implied little more than a change in terminology.) To the enemies of the Liberal governments, in the past century and this, the gestures toward an *assimilação uniformizadora* were pure farce, sins for which the Liberals have never been forgiven by conservative colonial philosophers. In point of fact, the actual status of the Africans in Angola and Moçambique was no more discernibly altered by liberal legislation of the 1830s than it is by the Salazarian pronouncements of our own time.

With many of the reforms projected for the overseas provinces, the name of the Marquês de Sá da Bandeira is intimately associated. Working in the midst of confusion, animosity, and an instability that finally brought down his government, Prime Minister Sá da Bandeira from 1836 to 1840 evolved a programme, most of it never implemented, of colonial development. He planned a permanent Civil Service in the Overseas Ministry, to guarantee colonial stability during ministerial upheavals. Portugal should now, he declared, dedicate to Africa the same energy that had made of Brazil a thriving country. The keys to his programme were capital investment and colonization: African ports should be opened to foreign shipping, and all commerce between Portugal and Africa – this to remain a Portuguese monopoly – made duty free. Angola should not be a place of exile for political and criminal undesirables; settlement there by honest industrious citizens ought to be one of the first orders of business for the new régime.

In 1836 Sá da Bandeira pronounced his boldest decision: all traffic in slaves from Portuguese possessions was to cease in

December of that year. The decree, though long expected, met implacable resistance in Angola. So violent was the reaction that not until 1845 was a governor able to cope with the problem. Only the blunt and arrogant intervention of the English government, who refused any longer to respect the Portuguese flag and ordered ships of the Royal Navy to patrol the West African coast and to seize Portuguese slavers, and the effective work of Governor Pedro Alexandre da Cunha in 1845, brought about a final suppression by the middle of the century.

The next move to shock the residents of Angola was the complete abolition of slavery. Lisbon naïvely hoped by this legislation to promote the peaceful occupation of the interior, since the source of friction between the African and the European would be removed and the need for the expansion of legitimate commerce created. The African would cultivate and sell the products of the land instead of his own kind, and Portuguese traders and estate owners would accordingly develop a healthy economy. The abolition of slavery would also exempt Portugal from growing humanitarian criticism of her African native policy, a criticism which could have unpleasant international consequences. In 1858 a compromise decree, promulgated by Sá da Bandeira and his associates, was signed into law. Under its provisions all Africans presently held in slavery would become free men in twenty years, enjoying an interim status after 1869 as *libertos*, a classification not too clearly defined and less clearly observed. During the twenty-year period no African could be enslaved, while children born of slaves would be free. Even such a modest proposal was angrily received in Angola with manifestations of violence. The spirit of slavery died hard in the province, and many colonists refused to accept the decision of the government, resisting it both openly and covertly. At the beginning of the twentieth century, their oppressions were to burst forth in a scandal which shook the metropolis and the province.

Slowly, ever so slowly, the reality of Angola began to change in the first half of the nineteenth century. Even before the Liberal triumph in Portugal, several strong-minded and enlightened governors began to think practically of the reform and progress of the colony. Men like António de Saldanha da Gama and Tovar de Albuquerque, appalled by the decadence of Angola, argued for a dramatic reorientation of colonial life to strengthen the economy and give direction to the administration. On the local level they urged the formation of a class of craftsmen and mechanics, the encouragement of native cotton production, the promotion of fisheries to make use of local salt, and the investment of capital in local industry and agriculture which would free Angola from its almost total reliance on imported foods and manufacture. What was needed most of all, in the eyes of these men, was white immigration. Both the colonial administration and the Overseas Ministry could do little to attract colonists to Angola until 1848, when nativist revolts in the Brazilian city of Pernambuco made recent Portuguese immigrants fearful of their future there. With financial assistance from Portugal, 170 immigrants sailed to southern Angola in 1849; a year later they were joined by 130 of their friends. Initially settled in the area of Moçâmedes, a region explored and charted by an expedition that had been sent out by Governor Moçâmedes at the end of the previous century, the newcomers suffered incredible hardships. Some moved to Luanda, but others migrated to the plateau outpost of Huíla, where they remained. The settlement of southern Angola had begun.

In the same period native policy, or at least Portuguese relations with the African population in Angola, became the subject of discussion. Arguments which by now have become familiar began to take philosophic shape in the nineteenth century under the influence particularly of reformist and would-be-reformist governors. On the one hand, there were those who condemned the exploitation of the African as a commodity or a beast of burden. They decried the practice of setting tribe against tribe and the reign of terror which certain captains of fortresses pursued in the interior. On the other hand, defenders of Portuguese custom in Angola cited the evangelization of a heathen people and praised the readiness of the Portuguese to take African and mulatto women as their wives. Such arguments were in a sense academic, for the African was still viewed as a commodity, and any way of obtaining the commodity was considered legitimate. This had long been the essence of native policy. It is true that the African women, in the absence of Portuguese ones, offered an outlet for sexual impulse. Miscegenation in Portuguese Africa, however, though often admirably free from the sense of shame which sometimes accompanied it elsewhere in Africa, must still be considered as erotic expediency; it has become colonial policy only in retrospect.

It has been the fashion since the last decade of the nineteenth century, when another, more practical generation of Portuguese colonial administrators documented the miserable condition of Portuguese Africa, for the more nationalistic historians and spokesmen to hold the Liberals responsible for all the neglect and frustrations besetting the overseas provinces. Such assaults are manifestly unfair. In the first place, not much was accomplished in Angola, despite the best efforts of the Liberals. Making the African a citizen of Portugal, ludicrous as it may seem to those who have made this piece of legislation their principal target, had no effect whatsoever on the continuing decline of Angola. As for the slave-trade, by 1830 it had run its ruinous course in the colony. Its final suppression was a belated recognition of its failure to do more than enrich a privileged class and keep the colony in a state of chronic backwardness. The abolition of slavery was a humanitarian gesture virtually meaningless in its effects. There are moments in the study of Portugal's colonial policies in Africa when ideals that failed must be given equal consideration with the dismal realities that they were meant to replace. The aspirations of men like Sá da Bandeira sprang from an enlightenment too frequently absent in the European colonization of Africa. That some Liberal ministers and governors were not content merely with phrasing eloquent legislation, but also tried to implement it in the face of hostility in the colonies and near political chaos at home, is a fact that should not be overlooked by Portuguese critics and by critics abroad of the Portuguese presence in Africa.

And something *was* accomplished. The legal abolition of

slavery severed, psychologically at least, the last link with a discredited past, and Angola was obliged reluctantly to turn toward a new and perhaps more difficult era. In 1854 David Livingstone reached Luanda. He found the colony decadent, but there seemed to be hope for the future, and he noted a modest spirit of change and progress. Certainly such was to be needed in the years ahead, for the consequences of Livingstone's journey were to lead indirectly to the Conference of Berlin. The Englishman's historic travels were more responsible than any other single factor for drawing Angola and Moçambique into the complexities of the modern age in Africa. Ill-fitted though Portuguese Africa was to confront the problems of the second half of the century, it is not likely that the colonies would have survived without the changes which the Liberals had introduced and which led in their turn to other, more radical developments.

3 Moçambique

Although events in both Angola and Moçambique generally followed the same pattern of decline from high promise to a protracted neglect and confusion, historical currents in Portugal's African colonies east and west seldom ran parallel until late in the nineteenth century. Angola early in its development became the Black Mother, with an orientation toward Brazil. In Moçambique slaving, although the *bête noire* of David Livingstone, never achieved Angolan proportions. The Portuguese in East Africa were originally concerned with the promotion and protection of trade in the Indian Ocean and with the pursuit of gold and silver in the mines of Manica. The political orientation was toward India – even after the collapse of the eastern empire and the reduction of the great mercantile complex to a handful of factories on the Malabar coast, in South-East Asia, and on the China coast. In East Africa there was as well a 200-year conflict along the Swahili coast between the Portuguese and their assorted enemies. To a lesser extent, also, the emergence of the Zambezi *prazo* system helped to give Moçambique a different character. The first century of occupation saw in East Africa the formation of the traditional mould of Portuguese expansion in the East, the establishing of forts and factories along the coast for the dissemination of trade. When satisfactory alliances could be made with local leaders, Arab or African, the Portuguese eschewed the use of arms; defiance, on the other hand, was met, when feasible, by a show of strength (frequently an armada or an expedition from Goa) and the installation of a more flexible local prince.

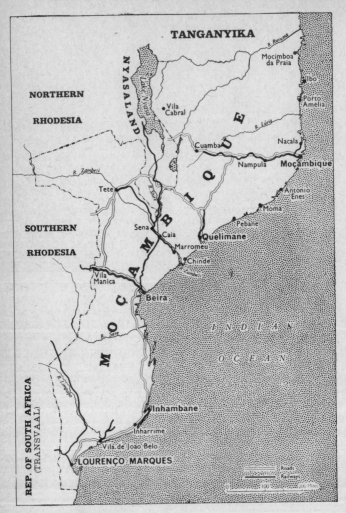

5. Moçambique, 1961

Establishing the Portuguese Mandate ✓

In July 1497 a small fleet of four ships sailed from Lisbon under Vasco da Gama. Early in March 1498 da Gama reached Moçambique harbour.[1] Not the most diplomatic of Portuguese captains, da Gama here and at the next port of call, Mombasa, created perhaps needless difficulties with the local sheiks, and it was only at Malindi, a bitter enemy of Mombasa, that da Gama was generously received and given a pilot to guide him across the Indian Ocean to Calicut. Malindi was to be Portugal's only constant ally among the East African city states. Da Gama visited Malindi again on his homeward voyage and was able to carry to King Manuel protestations of friendship from at least one East African principality.

Only in that area of the interior of Moçambique lying behind the coastline from Sofala to Quelimane did the Portuguese make substantial contact with the black African population during the sixteenth and seventeenth centuries. For the rest, they were dealing primarily with the Swahili (Arab or Islamized African) population of the coast of Zanj, whom the Portuguese generally called 'Moors'. The Moslem sphere of influence extended as far south as Sofala; there were scattered Swahili trading communities in the hinterland. At the time of da Gama's arrival, the main Arab-African city states were Pate, Malindi, Mombasa, and Kilwa, with less important settlements at Zanzibar, Pemba, Kiliji, Moçambique island, and Sofala. Travellers have recorded their prosperity and elegance, and da Gama himself spoke of the fine stone houses and the air of elegance in the local courts and markets. It was a world comparable, if not superior, in material culture to Portugal in 1500. Political unity among these city-states was a transitory burden. Each local prince defended his city's political and commercial independence, and at no time was there an East African nation, although the stronger towns at one time or another dominated their weaker neighbours. In 1500 Kilwa was mistress of the ports and commerce to the south,

1. The island-town of Moçambique is some two-thirds of the way up the coast of the present colony of Moçambique. To avoid confusion, I shall refer to the capital as Moçambique town.

including the vital Sofala gold trade. Portugal was able in part to exploit the differences between the Swahili communities, but she also discovered that in their hostility to her presence there was strong underlying unity.

The civilization of the East African coast reached more than 1,000 years into the past. The inhabitants of the city-states were

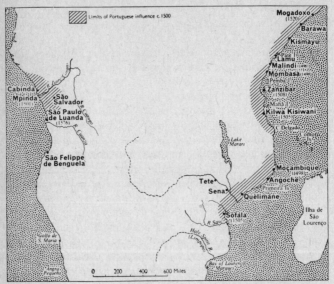

6. Limits of Portuguese influence in East and South West Africa, c. 1600

a mixture of Arab, Bantu, Persian, and Indian elements, in which the Bantu predominated, and the whole community was strongly Africanized, although political administration seems to have remained largely in the hands of an Arab aristocracy. East Africa was part of the Indian Ocean mercantile complex, and the Swahili traders thrived as middlemen who brought the goods of India and the Middle East to Africa. The trade was principally in beads, cotton cloth, and some metal implements, which were exchanged with the Bantu for slaves, ivory, wax, and gold.

The northern frontier of modern Moçambique is Cape Delgado, which has roughly demarcated the extent of Portuguese authority in that direction since about 1700. But even earlier Cape Delgado represented a symbolic point on the East African coast. To the south the Portuguese, having made Moçambique island their centre of power, brought under their domination the Swahili coastal settlements all the way to Sofala. To the north of the cape, the Portuguese were never able, either through steadfast alliance with Malindi or through the construction of the massive Fort Jesus at Mombasa, to impose any lasting commercial or political authority; and by 1700 a resurgence of Islamic power had effectively eliminated Portuguese traders and soldiers from the score of towns in which they had intermittently held sway.

North and south of Cape Delgado, East Africa was a secondary consideration in Portugal's Indian Ocean empire. There was, however, more interest in the area of Moçambique, reputedly rich in gold, and in the harbour of Moçambique island, which quickly became a haven for the ships on the Portugal–India run. Little remains of Portuguese influence north of the cape – only Fort Jesus, the ruins of smaller Portuguese settlements, a few legends in local folklore, and the memories of crooked little Portuguese Street in Zanzibar. Portuguese contact with the pattern of life here was superficial. No real attempts at settlement were made, and the population north of the cape was always smaller than south of it. Hardly more than a hundred men made up the Portuguese population in the city-states during normal times.

In 1505 twenty-three ships under Viceroy Francisco de Almeida sailed for East Africa and India. A fortress-factory was to be built at Sofala, Mombasa and Kilwa were to be subjugated, and a Portuguese commercial monopoly was to be established in the Indian Ocean. Almeida carried out the instructions of his *regimento*. Mombasa and Kilwa were pillaged, and other ports less forcibly persuaded to submit. Mombasa was sacked and burnt again in 1529. But, after such a dramatic arrival, Portuguese attention was drawn away from the Swahili coast, to

Hormuz, to Malabar, and to the Far East. Not until the end of the century did Portugal pay serious attention to this part of Africa. In the meantime, Swahili commerce, which had survived other disasters through the centuries, went on much as before. The Portuguese were unable to guarantee their monopoly or their control over coastal shipping. A contraband commerce sprang up which, though periodically put down by visiting armadas, thrived much as it had before 1500. Without a fortified base and a permanent navy, Portugal could hope to accomplish little.

In 1585–6 a Turkish adventurer, Mir Ali Bey, razed the Swahili coast with a small force of men, collecting rich prizes and receiving submission from all the city-states save Malindi. On his second invasion in 1588–9 the Turk was not so lucky; a Portuguese force from the sea and the cannibalistic Zimba from the land trapped Mir Ali Bey in Mombasa, where he and a few of his men who escaped the Zimba were captured by the Portuguese squadron. In 1591 the Crown authorized the building of Fort Jesus at Mombasa; begun in 1593, the work on the fort was not completed until the late 1630s, although it was in use during most of the period. The captain at Mombasa had under his jurisdiction the Swahili coast north of Cape Delgado; his factors were situated at Kilwa, Pemba, Zanzibar, and other ports. In 1594, a customs house was established at Mombasa through which all coastal trade was supposed to pass, with import duties at about six per cent of valuation. And in 1597 a monastery of Augustinian friars was established in Mombasa, a sign of the first real missionary interest in the region. Neither in 1600 nor later was the work of Christian evangelization among the 'Moors' notably successful.

The good years for Portugal in the Swahili coast were the early part of the seventeenth century. The city-states paid allegiance and even occasional tribute to the King of Portugal. But in 1631 Portuguese fortunes began to decline. The puppet sultan of Mombasa, Malindi, and Pemba, an Augustinian-educated convert, reverted to his childhood faith and murdered the Portuguese captain of Fort Jesus with most of the garrison.

Although he abandoned the fortress a year later, other troubles ensued to beset the meagre Portuguese forces in the area. Other city-states began to grow restless. The strength of Portugal's maritime empire was now being sapped by English and Dutch intrusions, and the assistance of armadas from Goa could not always be counted on. By 1650 the entire coast was in revolt. The city-states found allies in the seafaring Omani Arabs who periodically attacked Portuguese factories and shipping along the coast. The struggle was nearly equal, and, had it taken place fifty years before, Portugal would have prevailed. Now she had neither the ships nor the forthright courageous leaders to cope with the constant pressures and the revolts bursting like fire-crackers at her skirts. In 1698, a thirty-three-month siege by an Omani expedition took Fort Jesus, where about 1,000 Portuguese men, together with some 5,000 Swahili auxiliaries and residents, lost their lives. Within a few years the remnants of Portuguese authority were concentrated on the island of Moçambique. From then on, as if by tacit agreement, Arab rule north of Cape Delgado was accepted as supreme, and the Portuguese mandate to the south was not seriously challenged.

Sofala and Moçambique Island

Although factories were established at both Sofala and Moçambique within seven years of da Gama's first voyage, Sofala, the gateway to gold, retained a more powerful hold on official imagination during the first decades of the century. In 1505 men from the Indies fleet of Francisco de Almeida were left there to construct a fortress. The Portuguese convinced the Swahili sheikh of the advantages to be gained from their friendship and protection, and built a small mud and wattle fort. In the first months of occupation trade flourished, since the Portuguese cut off communication with the Arab markets. The exasperated Moslem traders prevailed upon the sheikh to dislodge the intruders, but he fell during the attack, and a more amenable man was put in his place by the Portuguese.

The outpost consolidated its position in the next several years, and the bulwarks of the fort were reinforced with stone. A fairly steady flow from the mine-workings scattered in the interior, roughly between the Zambezi and Limpopo Rivers, fed the aspirations of the slowly increasing European population, although neither then nor later did the supply of gold measure up to the expectations of the Crown. It seems clear that the Portuguese believed they were in contact with the mines of Solomon and so had an exaggerated notion of their capacity. During the years 1506–10 the receipts from Sofala scarcely sufficed to maintain the fortress and its small garrison. In cutting out the Swahili traders as middlemen, with whom the Bantu were long accustomed to trading, the Portuguese diminished the supply. And these traders set up other lines of communication with the interior which by-passed Sofala. The Angoche Islands were particularly active in this clandestine commerce. In 1513 the factor at Sofala tried unsuccessfully to impress upon the Lisbon court that the supply of gold was not as great as had been imagined, that its sources were scattered over a wide area and so did not provide a sufficient output for the Arab and Portuguese markets, and that, finally, trade with the frequently warring peoples of the back country was an uncertain business at best. Such negative reports, however, were not especially welcomed in Lisbon and not always heeded. Later in the century, when the Portuguese penetrated the interior up the Zambezi valley, trade in gold, silver, and ivory showed a relative increase, and many of the spices sent from the East were paid for in African gold, but even then the amount was disappointingly small.

There were good years and bad at Sofala, and fortunes were made by various Sofala captains during the sixteenth century. Had the Portuguese followed the advice of António Fernandes, who had explored gold-producing areas on two trips early in the century and had gone up the Save and Lundi rivers to establish there a factory directly on the edge of the gold country, the flow might have been increased. But there was no penetration up the Save, except for occasional expeditions like those of Fernandes, and Portuguese penetration when it came was up the Zambezi. The only useful purpose that these isolated journeys served was some centuries later to bolster Portuguese claims to priority in south-east Africa.

That part of Moçambique visited by António Fernandes and the lands north to the Zambezi were inhabited by the Maka-langa, a people of the Shona stock, who had come south from the Zambezi in about the twelfth century to occupy roughly what is today Southern Rhodesia and to make their capital at the site of Great Zimbabwe. Although there is no evidence that the Portu-guese visited the great walled city, they were aware of its exist-ence, and chroniclers of the age refer to its grandeur. Over the tribal confederacy of Makalanga, the Monomotapa, a paramount chief, exercised a power which, while somewhat less than that attributed to him by the Portuguese, was still considerable. The chiefs of the various tribes in the region acknowledged a limited suzerainty of the Monomotapa, but they were far from being his vassals. At the date of the Portuguese arrival, the area was engaged in a series of factional strifes into which the Portuguese were later drawn. But in the early years the Portuguese were content to trade and carry on a modest missionary work.

Although Sofala, until the emergence of Sena on the Zambezi in the 1530s, was the nearest port to the most productive region in that part of Africa, Moçambique island quickly became the centre of Portuguese authority in East Africa. It seems one of the anomalies of Portuguese overseas history that the town of Moçambique should have maintained itself for so many centuries as the isolated capital of the colony, but reasons for its import-ance in the sixteenth century are obvious: the island was a favoured port of call for Indies shipping and it occupied a half-way position between the gold country to the south and the Swahili city-states to the north. In 1507 construction was begun on a factory, a fortress, and a hospital for the sick arriving on the trans-ocean carracks. Moçambique became the most important point of call between Lisbon and India. Through the port passed viceroys, convicts, poets, stray foreign visitors, all drawn east-ward by the lure of fame and sudden fortune. A few stayed in Moçambique, some to die of malaria and others to swell the European population, which came to leave its impress on 'this most Portuguese of colonial cities'. As investment in the East prospered, so did Moçambique, which became the centre of a local trade from which Portugal often derived more profit than she did from the commerce between the East and the metropolis.

The captaincy of the island fortress was one of the plums of the colonial service; in his three-year term of office, the captain stood a good chance of making considerable gain. Originally all trade was handled by the factor, who controlled the customs-house, but later the captain received privileges of trade in certain products or areas not reserved by the Crown, and finally the whole area of Zambezi trade was delivered over to the captain at Moçambique for a certain (usually substantial) sum on his taking office. In return the captain assumed responsibility for the administration and maintenance of the fortress and the protection of its people. This leasing of the trade monopoly (at times the treasury reverted to its former practice of working exclusively through the factor) resulted in considerable scandal and charges of corruption, but such charges of dishonesty were common-place, and frequently false or exaggerated. Apart from his commercial dealings, the captain at Moçambique had a series of checks on his authority. He held office under the Viceroy of India, to whom he was obliged to submit reports, which also went to the Indies Council in Lisbon. His political and military powers were outlined in the *regimento*, and he was obliged to make certain decisions in consultation with the *ouvidor* (magistrate), the judicial authority on the island, and the king's factor. Generally the captains were chosen from among men with years of military or administrative experience in the empire.

By the middle of the sixteenth century the island town of Moçambique had achieved such importance that a decision was made in Lisbon to build a massive fortress there. During the next forty years the great solid structure of the *fortaleza* São Sebastião was devised and armoured into the impregnable bulwark that withstood the Dutch attacks of 1607. Still in use today, the bulk of São Sebastião hovers in isolation from its low white coral reef over the peacock sea. By 1600 the Portuguese population had grown to perhaps 400 men, a figure multiplied many times over when a large Indies fleet wintered at Moçambique. The Portuguese, undismayed by fevers, food shortages, scandals, intrigues, and complaints, made Moçambique town a rich bustling replica of a metropolitan Portuguese town.

The Failure of Imperial Exploitation ✓

In an effort to speed up the export of gold, the captain at Moçambique in 1531 founded a Portuguese fair at Sena, where there already existed a small Swahili trading settlement. The town, now only a place-name on the banks of East Africa's greatest river, prospered intermittently but surely, and in the next 200 years became the centre of trade, plantation life, and colonization experiments along the Zambezi. A few years later the town of Tete was built farther up the river, some 250 miles from the sea. In closer contact with the lands of the Monomotapa and the gold mines of Manica and Mashona, the two towns supplemented with moderate success the trade in gold that trickled into Sofala. At Massapa, south-west from Tete on the Mazoe River and the site of mine workings, a Portuguese adventurer set himself up about 1550 as a free-lance trader and adviser to the Monomotapa. Taking advantage of his presence, the viceroy conferred upon him the title Captain of the Gates (the gates being figuratively those to the gold fields), making him a royal factor and his representative at the African court. António Caiado was one of the first in a long line of frontiersmen who found it possible to live and prosper independently among the Bantu peoples of Africa, the most famous of the breed being the nineteenth-century explorer and merchant in Angola, António da Silva Porto. Caiado's success drew several countrymen to take up residence with him, and the office of Captain of the Gates was passed down to numerous successors before it died out altogether.

Still other small centres of trade, some ephemeral, others more permanent, came into existence during the century. At Quelimane a factory was founded; up the Púnque and Buzi Rivers, the Portuguese established occasional fairs. In 1544 Lourenço Marques skirted the coast south of Sofala to Delagoa

Bay, where he made arrangements with the local chief for regular visits by Portuguese coasters to buy ivory. In like manner a desultory commerce at Inhambane was effected.

Because of the commercial nature of the first sixty-five years of Moçambique's history, neither the captain at the island nor the traders along the coast and in the interior received any instructions other than to respect the rights of the African rulers. The reality of Portugal's power away from the island carried more weight than royal instructions, to be sure, but the interest of the Crown was still manifestly clear: to trade and live in peace with the Africans. Then in 1568 Sebastião, moody, devout, and headstrong, ascended the Portuguese throne at the age of fourteen. He conceived a Rhodesian vision for southern Africa, the creation of a vast domain stretching inland hundreds of miles from the Indian Ocean – a proposition which encountered serious opposition from a minority within the king's council who saw no reason to abandon a traditional policy of relatively peaceful trade. The main goal of the expedition that the king contemplated would be to gain control of the gold mines and see that they produced as the Portuguese thought they should; secondary goals were the expulsion of Arab traders from the area and the provision of free access for Portuguese missionaries.

In 1569 the first African army, 1,000 volunteers under a former governor-general of India, Francisco Barreto, took its thunderous leave from Belém bound for Moçambique. From the beginning, the expedition was plagued by bad luck and the bad judgement of its leaders. After a needlessly long delay at Moçambique, Barreto and his men went up the Zambezi in the November of 1571, the beginning of the rainy season. Sena, which boasted only ten Portuguese inhabitants, was unable to supply and feed the visitors. After more than a year of scuffling with several local tribes and inconclusive negotiations with the Monomotapa, less than 200 men were evacuated in 1573. Barreto died of fever and exhaustion a few weeks before the departure down-river. His aide-de-camp, Vasco Fernandes Homem, returned a year later with 400 men to seek out the mines. This time the expedition went in-country from Sofala. After several skirmishes, the Portuguese penetrated the land of Manica to a point near the present city of Umtali; here for the first time they ascertained the actual gold-producing possibilities of the area. Their conclusion, substantiated in later years, was that, without machinery and a supervised labour force, the output would continue to be small. From Sofala, Homem went north to the Zambezi and up to Sena, where he decided to track down the rumoured silver mines of Chicoa up the river from Tete. Again the mines failed to come up to the usual naïve expectations. Homem had a stockade built along the river where he left about 200 of his men, all of whom were destroyed in an African assault while Homem returned to Moçambique island. In the face of these disasters, the Crown put aside its plans for Zambézia. Then, as later, the difficulties of terrain and disease defied the best efforts of Lisbon planners.

Life on the Zambezi reverted to its normal course in the late sixteenth century, at least until 1592, when a force of Zimba warriors ravaged the region. João dos Santos, a Dominican missionary in Sofala who travelled in Zambézia, has left in his *Ethiopia oriental* (1609) a wonderfully coherent source of the life and customs in Moçambique. Sena he describes as the centre of Zambezi trade, boasting a fort, warehouse, church, and a population of perhaps 50 Portuguese and 750 Indians, half-castes, and African slaves. Tete was almost as large. Zambézia was divided into four tribal domains, usually at war with each other. To the chiefs of these kingdoms the Portuguese paid tribute or duty on goods. Thus the captain at Sena was obliged to give a supply of cotton goods and beads to the embassy from the Monomotapa, which visited the town every three years. At Tete the factor enjoyed the protection of a Bantu guard of honour, 2,000 soldier-slaves presented to the fort by a generous Monomotapa after a victory over a neighbouring tribe. Dos Santos also gave a sketchy mineral survey of the territory in somewhat less enthusiastic terms than those which Goa and Lisbon liked to hear.

In 1608 the Portuguese garrison in the São Sebastião fortress withstood the second siege in two years by a large Dutch fleet under Pieter Verhoeff. In the same year Philip III, deluded by a recent sample of ore of high quality from Africa, decided to organize another expedition to the silver mines of Chicoa. The enterprise seemed sensible enough, if one overlooked the empty consequences of the Barreto-Homem expeditions. Certainly the moment was auspicious. For fifteen years the Makalanga had been embroiled in dynastic struggles during which much of the Monomotapa's power had been eroded, and the paramount chief had come more and more to rely on the assistance of the Portuguese at Tete and Sena. Against this background Philip reorganized the colonial administration, creating the office of 'Captain-General of the Expedition', who would supersede the captain at Moçambique island. The captain-general was to seek out gold and silver and refrain from getting involved in African politics. But neither Captain-General Nuno Alvares Pereira nor his field-officer, Diogo Madeira, captain at Tete, could prevail against the intrigues of the captain at Moçambique island, resentful of his lost prerogatives, of the merchants at Sena and Tete, who saw their private trade being undercut, or of the vacillating Monomotapa, who chose to play Portuguese animosities against each other. After more than a decade of fruitless journeys up the Zambezi and into the interior, often in the face of armed African opposition, the project languished.

Moçambique was not prepared for imperial exploitation on a grand scale. Malaria, African unrest, dispersal of authority, and the essential poverty of the region conspired to thwart all ambitious plans for its development. The most that the Crown could hope for were the gains from commerce along the coast and up the Zambezi and from the sale of offices. On a modest scale the colony could prosper. The island was in 1625 the most important Portuguese town in Africa, with a Christian population (white, black, and brown) of several thousand and a steady traffic through its port. Sofala had now entered the long twilight of its decline. Up-river, life began to take on a somewhat different complexion with the rise of the *prazo*, or plantation, system and the periodic influx of missionary priests. Sena had four churches and about fifty Portuguese inhabitants; Tete had twenty men in the shadow of its fort and a great many more scattered on the surrounding estates. Up and down the river and in the lands of the Monomotapa, traders, soldiers, and priests carried on a solitary existence. A fair estimation of the size of the Portuguese population at this period would be 1,000 people, a figure which did not grow much until the twentieth century and even declined from time to time.

Lisbon was not content with moderate profit, and throughout the seventeenth century the Crown tinkered with ideas of opening up all of Zambézia to more or less free trade. Neither Moçambique nor Goa was enthusiastic about the proposals, and it was not until 1680, when the economic decline of the colony had set in, that the region permitted free trade to all Portuguese subjects. The results were not those anticipated. A number of Indian traders, generally referred to as Banians or Canarins, when not called harsher names, were attracted to Moçambique, where they gained a stranglehold on local commerce. Within eight years the Portuguese merchants faced extinction, and the decree of 1680 was cancelled, although by now a new and aggressive element had been introduced into the population. In the 1690s efforts were directed toward the formation of an East African Trading Company to be partly subsidized by the Portuguese government, but the company, with an undersubscription of its shares and an over-accumulation of commitments, collapsed, and in 1700 the government again took over African commerce.

Native policy in Moçambique – if the standard instructions in most *regimentos* on how to deal with African princes may be considered policy – took a slightly different turn in Zambézia during the seventeenth century, under the impact of a larger number of Portuguese settlers and missionaries with ideas of their own on how to treat the African and manipulate his leaders. Although the Portuguese were in no numerical position to dominate the area, they were numerous enough to increase the friction between European and African. The *prazero* demanded labourers or slaves for his estates and the missionary sought converts among a people not particularly receptive toward either institution. The number of armed conflicts up the Zambezi increased markedly. Had not the African princes dissipated their strength quarrelling among themselves and had not the converted Monomotapa given away his lands and people, it is not likely that the Portuguese could have survived the seventeenth century in the interior. That they did is better evidence of their tenacity than of their tact or the success of their colonial policy.

The whole population of Zambézia – trader, settler, missionary – was involved in the disputes of 1628. On the death of the Monomotapa in that year, a son particularly hostile to the Portuguese attained the chieftainship. When he declared an embargo on trade and attacked several garrisons, the Portuguese settlers and officers banded together their private armies and drove the new ruler deep into his kingdom. A more tractable member of the family took his place. The new Monomotapa, Manuza, or, after his conversion, Filipe, pledged vassalage to the King of Portugal and promised the Dominican missionaries and the Zambezi settlers and traders everything they wanted. For the first time in the history of the colony, the Portuguese had achieved an uneasy dominance over a large part of the Makalanga people. The first practical results of having a puppet as Monomotapa were a vigorous expansion in mission work and the breakdown of African resistance. Individual Portuguese, through gift or purchase – but also through bribes and threats – were able to gain possession of vast tracts of territory along the Zambezi, which they ruled much in the manner of the lesser African chiefs whom they had supplanted. During the rest of the century the Portuguese more often than not had a malleable Monomotapa; but these puppets commanded a diminishing loyalty among the other chiefs of Zambézia, and the period was marked by frequent disturbances and, on occasion, as in 1668, open warfare between the Makalanga and the powerful Portuguese land barons. Gradually the African population was scattered and demoralized, the majority either succumbing to slavery or withdrawing to parts of the country beyond Portuguese penetration.

By 1700 Moçambique province was beyond its apogee of influence and importance. Sofala was abandoned, the flow of trade through the island greatly reduced, and Sena and Tete survived in isolation, dominated by the splendidly barbaric *prazeros* who often recognized no law but their own. In 1752 the administration of the colony was finally separated from Goa, and Francisco de Melo e Castro became the first governor of Moçambique, Zambézia, and Sofala. The gesture meant little in terms of political consequence; neither Melo e Castro, an energetic man, nor later vigorous and ambitious governors, could bring a renascence of Portuguese fortunes to Moçambique. This would only come, and briefly, in the first half of the nineteenth century, when the slave-trade grew to Angolan proportions.

Missionaries and Prazeros

In Moçambique mission work ran parallel to the political course of the colony, although in the period of decline the clerical population suffered more acutely than the often opulent semi-independent *prazeros*. From the beginning of the sixteenth century, Portuguese priests were established in the fortresses of Sofala and Moçambique and followed the steps of traders into the interior. In 1541–2 St Francis Xavier spent six months on the island preaching and assisting in the relief hospital. In 1560 two Jesuit fathers and a lay brother arrived in Moçambique. One of the priests was Gonçalo da Silveira, destined to become the most famous of Catholic missionaries in southern Africa. One of the most eloquent of Lisbon's preachers, his evangelical zeal led him to the East where the opportunities in the spiritually desolate lands of the Monomotapa seized his imagination. By the end of the year Silveira had gone from Quelimane to Sena and Tete, and then beyond to the Monomotapa's capital in Manica, where Captain of the Gates António Caiado welcomed him. Gaunt, fever-ridden, driven with messianic intensity, the Jesuit father set about his work. After a month of training in the Catholic faith, the Monomotapa, his favourite wife and sister, and 300 relatives and counsellors were all baptized. But his success with the royal family led jealous Swahili traders at the court to denounce Silveira as a spy and evil magician. Variable in his new faith, the Monomotapa had Silveira strangled in his sleep and his body thrown in the river. The Barreto expedition was intended in part to avenge his murder, and the Jesuits did not return in force to Moçambique until 1607.

By then the Dominicans dominated mission work in the colony. From the middle of the previous century they had moved through Moçambique with great speed and energy, spreading faith and empire. Whenever they could, the Dominicans adopted the tactic of working with the African chiefs; they tried to make each conversion a permanent one and to this end tried to educate the Africans in the faith they were to accept. They early entrenched themselves at the court of the Monomotapa, into whose lands they sent a steady flow of missionaries.

The impetus of the 1570s and 1580s was lost in the early 1590s, with the general collapse of Portuguese authority on the Zambezi during the raids of the Zimba, and it was never quite regained. The Dominicans, however, returned, and with the Jesuits were chiefly responsible for the work of evangelization. They were aided by secular priests. While the Jesuits either concentrated their efforts on the island or in the remote interior, where they performed feats of exploration unequalled in Portuguese missionary history, the Dominicans worked along the river and in the court of the Monomotapa, from which they drew a number of African youths to be prepared for the priesthood at the Dominican seminary in India. Some of these men remained in Goa or Cochin; some returned, although they did not, judging by contemporary reports, contribute notably to the spiritual progress of the land. Occasionally Capuchins, Augustinians, or friars of the order of São João de Deus served in the colony, principally in the capital.

By 1650 the missionary campaign in Zambézia was in trouble. African hostility, disease, and moral corruption had begun to take their toll. Many of the Dominicans arriving in the colony were Goan priests who did not always exhibit a complete dedication to the cause. In the midst of the uncertainties of life, the

Dominicans, like the Portuguese residents, sought security in the accumulation of property. In the eighteenth century the Dominicans – and the Jesuits – had come to own vast tracts of land, which they administered like any *prazero*, collecting head taxes and dealing in slaves. Other missionaries responded to the mood of the times. The Dominicans were under almost constant attack for their 'scandalous behaviour'. The Church in effect was now confronted with a moral crisis in Moçambique; the occasional pompous processions which dazzled the Africans only revealed that the missionary spirit had been replaced by material values. The tumble-down churches at Sena and Tete and Quelimane attested not only to decline in missionary work but to the disappearance of its inspiration.

Towards the end of the eighteenth century, an ecclesiastical census of the colony revealed the following: the island had a cathedral, one parish church, two chapels, and two monasteries, with a clergy of six priests and five lay brothers; Mossuril across the bay had three parish churches and two priests; Sofala, one church and one Dominican; the parishes of Quelimane and Sena, six churches and three priests; Tete, three churches and two clerics; Manica, a parish church and a chapel entrusted to two Dominicans; Zumbo, Lourenço Marques, Querimba, and Amiza each had a church and a priest. Nor did the spiritual influence of the church extend far beyond these points. An estimate of a few years earlier had put the total number of Christians in Moçambique at 2,141, a figure which decreased each year, since priests were baptizing only those Africans in mortal danger. Not even the slaves on the estates were being indoctrinated.

If mission affairs were bad in the eighteenth century, they were even worse in the first half of the nineteenth. Along the Zambezi only a vestige of Christianity remained, and on the island the situation was not much better. In 1825 the number of priests in the province was ten, seven of whom were Goan. The Liberal government's decree of 1834 which abolished religious orders had little meaning for Moçambique, since these were by then virtually extinct. The lands of the Dominicans, who had more *prazos* than priests to manage them, were confiscated by the island government.

Another aspect of Portuguese life in Zambézia, the *prazo* system, was more resilient than the church. Whether the *prazo* was responsible for the ruination of the Zambezi area, or whether it was only through the *prazo* system that the final threads of Portuguese attachment were retained, is speculative. Certainly, for all its inherent evils, the *prazo* régime had a curiously vital history which extended right up to the 1880s and influenced, directly and indirectly, the formation of the three great land companies in Moçambique.

In the middle of the seventeenth century, the alleged golden age of the Portuguese occupation of Moçambique, the lands within the area determined by drawing a line from Quelimane to Chicoa and from Chicoa to Sofala, could be found divided into great estates, ranging in size from three or four square leagues to eighty or even ninety square leagues. The most prosperous were those bordering the Zambezi from the coast to Tete. The owners of some of the *prazos* were powerful and independent men who either lived on their lands in great luxury and splendour or who, especially in the eighteenth century, were absentee landlords, residing in Goa, Lisbon, or Moçambique island. Theoretically responsible for the development of the land and the protection of its inhabitants, the *prazeros* in reality were most of the time indifferent to any profitable enterprise except the collection of taxes and fines. A trickle of quit-rent ran into the royal treasury.

The Moçambique *prazo* originated in the late sixteenth century, when individual Portuguese soldiers and merchants infiltrated to the interior up the great river. They found an African society superficially not very different from the semi-feudal society of Portugal. The lands of the Monomotapa and of other leading princes were governed by lesser chiefs, whose allegiance to the supreme ruler took the form of tribute, military assistance, and a declaration of fealty. Under such a system, white adventurers with ambitions and strong constitutions prospered. By helping the Monomotapa or other great leaders in their innumerable small wars, they received grants of land and authority over the inhabitants. Having taken African wives, and acquired personal armies, these men frequently expanded the limits of their grants.

When in the seventeenth century the Portuguese government seriously attempted to extend its administrative jurisdiction over the region, it was confronted with conditions it had no choice but to acknowledge. It recognized the rights and privileges that the pioneers had received from the Monomotapa or taken for themselves, and sought only to give juridical form to an existing organization. At the same time the Crown divided the captaincy of the Rivers of Sena, mostly lands on the south of the Zambezi, issuing *prazos da coroa*, or Crown grants, to those of its subjects who had given distinguished service. The concessionaires were to receive not more than three square leagues of land, were to reside in the province, marry Europeans also residing in the province, and to cultivate and colonize the *prazos*. Not many of these stipulations were kept: the *prazos* usually swelled to tremendous proportions impossible to cultivate or to people, and the concessions often fell into the hands of speculators. There was no one on the Zambezi to enforce the terms of the grant.

On his lands the *prazero* was absolute master. He established the tribute, a modified head tax, to be collected from the petty chiefs residing on his lands. In default of payment in goods (usually ivory) of the head tax, slaves were accepted. The *prazeros* had taken the original powers of the local chiefs and increased them. Acting together they were the strongest force in Moçambique, able to contain the Monomotapa and to bend Portuguese captains to their will. Their great deep-walled residences attracted the admiration of visitors. The cool rooms were furnished with oriental luxury. Tables were set with imported delicacies, and scores of slaves served the white lords and their guests as the *prazeros* tried to outdo one another in displaying their munificence.

In the latter part of the seventeenth century complaints from missionaries and administrators, emphasizing what was called the state of barbarism in the Zambezi valley, moved Lisbon to try and check the excesses of the *prazeros*, many of them by this time a mixture of Portuguese and African and often Indian ancestry. To introduce fresh Portuguese blood into the region, by which it was hoped that the white population might be stabilized, the government devised the plan whereby the inheritance of the Crown *prazos* would pass to the eldest daughter, to be retained by her only on the stipulation that she marry a Portuguese subject born in Portugal. The government also gave *prazos* to a scattering of orphan girls as dowries, with such grants made subject to the same matrimonial stipulations. These measures, however, did not have wide application and enjoyed only limited success.

Constantly decried as a vicious régime, the *prazo* system persisted without serious modification. The *prazero* defended his own against his neighbours, African tribesmen, and legislation from the metropolis. The majority of resident *prazeros* by 1800 were only distantly European. A steady infusion of Goan and African blood had created an ethnic blend of uncertain proportions, a condition no more unique in Moçambique than in Brazil, India, or West Africa. The opulence of *prazo* life had largely disappeared, and the classic report of Villas Boas Truão, Captain of the Rivers of Sena in the first decade of the nineteenth century, describes the stagnation of the area. He pointed to the excessive size of the *prazos*; the lack of security for person and property; the flight of the African *colonos* from the slaving practices of the manor lords; and the collapse of Portuguese administration. Religious morality was non-existent, he claimed; education, commerce, and industry were not to be found. Other reports during the century echoed the familiar charges.

The Portuguese government outlawed the system in 1832. The legislation, however, had no more practical result than did subsequent decrees in 1838 and 1841 and the elaborate diploma of 1854 which proposed fundamental changes. At the same time, indeed, the government found it necessary to use certain *prazeros* for maintaining a semblance of Portuguese authority against African invasions from the south. Various *prazeros* were named captains of fortresses, given elaborate titles, and even decorated for their services to the realm. It seemed that the feudal order could only be abolished by force, and in this cause the various expeditions of convicts and African soldiery sent up the river from Moçambique island were singularly unsuccessful. The *prazero* was neither a rebel nor a revolutionary; he fought only in defence of his own. He refused to submit to an arbitrary distant power, and in his resistance he was joined by other *prazeros* and Zambezi adventurers. Against this array the colonial government could do little. Portuguese authority, after almost 200 years of neglect, could not be restored so easily on the turbulent estates of the Zambezi, and it was not until 1890 that the *regime dos prazos* was broken – or better, modified to serve the purposes of a developing provincial economy.

Supply and Demand in the Slave-Trade

In the first half of the nineteenth century the *prazos* were the reservoirs for much of Moçambique's suddenly increased slave-trade. The traffic in slaves, of course, antedated Portugal's arrival in East Africa, for the Negro was a standard commodity of Swahili trade. And, from the days of the Sofala captaincy, Portuguese ships carried slaves to India and even in small numbers to West African ports and Portugal itself. The main trade was mostly eastward. Moçambique was too distant and the Cape passage too hazardous to make East African slaves an economical proposition in America. Only in 1640, with the relaxing of certain restrictions on Indian commerce and the temporary loss of Angola to the Dutch, did the area become important; but neither then nor in the eighteenth century was there any question of Moçambique's competing with Angola and the Guinea coast. There was no systematic exploitation of the interior as in Angola. Governor Lacerda was pleased to note in the 1790s that slave-dealers made no money on their ventures, which, he observed, must have been punishment from the hand of God for making slaves of men created in his image.

Although slaves did make up the bulk of Moçambique's

exports by 1800 – not a surprising situation given the perilous state of the colonial economy – slavery as a domestic tradition was more important here than in Angola. The *prazero* had his army of slaves, for the more slaves a man owned the greater his prestige in the Zambezi community. There was still in 1800 an academic distinction between slave and *colono*, the latter being an African who dwelt on the *prazo*. Allegedly a free man, the *colono* paid a head tax, was obliged to work without pay, and was subject to his landlord's caprice. In reality the difference between the two categories was indistinct and often non-existent. In the bustling period of the nineteenth century, most *prazeros* did not examine too closely the legal condition of the Africans they sold down the river.

The nineteenth-century boom in the Moçambique slave-trade was the usual result of supply and demand. The Congo and Angola were not sufficient for New World needs, and East Africa was called upon for larger quotas. It is estimated that from some 10,000 slaves exported each year, from 1780 to 1800, the figure rose to over 15,000 a year and soared upward to 25,000 a year for a decade before spiralling downward after 1850. The commerce had a distinctive international flavour. For goods of British and American manufacture, Portuguese, Arab, Banian, and half-caste traders purchased African slaves in the interior, to ship them on Spanish, French, Brazilian, and American vessels, mostly of American construction, to various parts of the world. Although most of the population was involved, in one way or another, a few merchants, the contractors, and key officials garnered the profit.

The abolition decree of 1836 had a reception in Moçambique similar to the one it received in Angola: consternation, resentment, and a grim determination not to comply. Governors and captains of fortresses, ill-paid and often corrupt, felt that they had nothing to lose by permitting the practice to go on, and those officials who made efforts to curb the traffic found the means at their disposal pitifully inadequate. Only the strong intervention of England in the 1840s, pursued with the full cooperation of the Lisbon government, had a material effect in reducing the number of slaves shipped out of Moçambique. After 1850 the Atlantic trade passed its peak, to die out completely in the next fifteen years.

But the trade itself took another direction. For fifty years French ships had, openly and secretively, been acquiring Moçambique slaves for shipment to the New World or to the French island possessions in the south-west Indian Ocean. By the 1850s the French came to rely heavily on Moçambique for its island labourers – genially called *émigrés*. Africans were brought from the interior, in most cases by the same merchants and land agents who had formerly supplied the slave-ships, crammed in barracoons until the arrival of a French vessel, hauled aboard and asked if they were willing to serve as voluntary workers on Réunion and the Comores for five years. The ceremony was a farcical formality, and the practice nothing less than slaving. The main ports in this infamous traffic were Ibo, Delgado, and Quelimane. Portugal made several efforts to curb the clandestine trade – to the extent of a serious diplomatic crisis with France, in which England failed to support Portugal – but it was not until 1864 that Napoleon III abolished the system by decree, and even then rapacious slave smugglers sailed the coast for another fifteen years.

The implications of the trade in slaves and the latter-day traffic in *émigrés* went beyond Moçambique. English humanitarian opinion which had first been directed against the Angolan trade now centred on Moçambique. The East African colony had in an earlier century survived Dutch attacks, ousted a handful of Austrians from a factory at Lourenço Marques in the late eighteenth century, and by good fortune avoided a French invasion in the early 1800s. But English philanthropic and imperial interests in the area were not so easily blunted, and during the nineteenth century an attitude toward the Portuguese presence in Moçambique progressively hardened into policies which were to have disastrous results for Portugal in 1890. It became the fashion for England to view Portugal's occupation in Moçambique as the relic of a barbaric and backward age, and any diminution of her authority or territory as a triumph for enlightenment.

In the 1820s Commodore Owen, who on a coastal survey had raised the Union Jack across the river from Lourenço Marques, roundly condemned Portuguese practices in Moçambique and accused residents of the colony of selling free men as slaves. English accounts in the 1850s made corrosive accusations. Moçambique was presented as a degenerate backwater of cruelty and corruption. Livingstone, who had praise for the Portuguese in Angola, had few kind words for Moçambique. Ruin and immorality were rampant. All was desolation. The panacea, of course, was free trade and free labour – proposals to which the Portuguese were about as receptive as was Livingstone to the slave-trade. The missionary doctor wrote:

Let the pathway into the interior be free to all, and instead of wretched forts, with scarcely an acre of land around them which can be called their own, let real colonies be made. If, instead of military establishments, we had civil ones, and saw emigrants going out with their wives, ploughs, and seeds, rather than military convicts with bugles and kettledrums, one might hope for a return of prosperity to Eastern Africa.

Ominous words which foretold the end of an era in Moçambique.

Part 2: The Years Between

4 Discovery and Diplomacy

David Livingstone's two expeditions into Portuguese territory, the transcontinental journey and the Zambezi exploration, and the abolition of slavery, all three occurring within five years of each other, mark the beginning of the end of a particular period – the romantic period, as one Portuguese historian put it – of Portuguese African history. Isolation and a discredited way of colonial life were now, gradually, to be sure, disappearing, and Portugal would be obliged to confront the realities of the modern and progressive – to use the language of the day – period of African colonialism. Livingstone's scorching condemnations of Portuguese rule in Africa pointed the way to troubled days ahead. Reginald Coupland has written:

Portuguese ministers need not have been very conscience-stricken nor very faint-hearted to dread the passionate philanthropy of Britain, once it was on fire – they had felt its heat before – nor need they have been over-cynical to suspect that British philanthropy might be more fierce and predatory than it had ever been if it were now united with British commercial and colonial schemes and interests.

The immediate task was to defend and extend Portuguese priority in Africa; afterwards, it would be the task of diplomacy to protect those lands in Africa which Portugal had so long been innocently accustomed to consider her own, if only by forfeit of competition.

The first response to Livingstone's scornful rejection of any substantial Portuguese penetration of central and southern Africa was made by Dr José de Lacerda, a name now unfortunately found only on the margins of African scholarship. As in his way David Livingstone represented a particular and dominant attitude in the mid nineteenth century toward Portuguese enterprise in Africa, an attitude still widely held, so Lacerda's response constituted in its way a classic mould by which defences of Portugal's role in Angola and Moçambique seem still to be shaped. *Exame das viagens do Doutor Livingstone* (1867) is an angry, dense, and dignified reply to *Missionary Travels* and *Narrative of an Expedition to the Zambezi*: its anger proceeds from an injured national pride; its density from a 300-years' accumulation of detail; its dignity from a sureness in its cause. Although implicit in the *Exame* is Lacerda's suspicion that Livingstone was essentially interested in doing Portugal out of trade and territory in a part of Africa rightfully hers, he neverthe-less met the issues squarely. On the priority of exploration in central Africa, Lacerda produced extended documentation to prove that the areas visited by Livingstone had been explored or were known to Portuguese subjects. Barotseland and Makololo-land were familiar territory to ivory and slave merchants. As for the crossing of the continent, Lacerda not only defended the *pombeiros* as Portuguese citizens, but suggested several other transcontinental journeys. The lands of Kazembe were recon-noitred by Francisco de Lacerda e Almeida and again, fifty-odd years later, by Majors Gamitto and Monteiro. The Shire high-lands and the lands around Lake Nyasa were also scenes of Portuguese penetration. To defend Portuguese contributions to the Africans, he cited the history of the Jesuits and Dominicans, and produced impressive statistics to demonstrate Portugal's commercial activity. If, in spite of Lisbon's stringent decrees, slavery was still being carried on, such was the reality of African life, and Portuguese *prazeros* and settlers were only conforming with the demands of that reality. And, as Livingstone himself had admitted, no European people had better relations with the African (although Lacerda was not concerned to any great extent with native policy as such, some of his remarks in this regard are significant as being among the first specific elaborations of a Portuguese native policy).[1]

1. The extended controversy and its results and significance I have discussed at some length in my *Portuguese Africa* (Harvard University Press and Oxford University Press, 1959).

Exploration from Lacerda to Carvalho

With the atrophy of Portuguese prestige in Africa by 1850, it was difficult for Livingstone to know the extent of historical exploration in the interior. The Portuguese were at that time unquestionably the foremost explorers of a continent which other Europeans had only begun seriously to penetrate sixty years before. It is not romance but geographic fact that the administrative limits of Portuguese Africa had been established for centuries by the line of forts through the interior of Angola and into Zambezia and the realm of the Monomotapa. Beyond these limits, traders and freebooters and priests and campaigners had gone to dwell or preach or fight in distant African communities, sometimes to return and sometimes not. Many were isolated examples, still not clearly recognized, for the Portuguese, like Livingstone, were at their best in acts of individual exploration. These scattered enterprises reveal a greater activity in the interior of Africa than the improvident condition of the colonies indicated in the 1850s. There is as much truth as exaggeration in Léon Cahun's remark made in 1883 – 'Comparing a map of Africa, made in 1850 . . . with a map at the end of the sixteenth century . . . one may see that the interior of this continent was less well known thirty years ago than it was 300 years ago' – and it is a great pity that there is still no detailed and detached examination of Portuguese exploration in Africa.

It is practical here only to mention those official expeditions which shortly preceded and followed Livingstone's journeys. The three pre-Livingstone journeys were those of Governor Lacerda to the lands of Kazembe, the crossing of the continent by the two *pombeiros*, Pedro João Baptista and Amaro José, and the expedition by Gamitto and Monteiro, again to the kingdom of Kazembe. Perhaps the most important was that made by the Governor of the Rivers of Sena, Dr Francisco Lacerda, in 1798, to the kingdom of Kazembe in the Luapula valley – roughly, the territory between Lakes Mweru and Bangweulu. Its purpose was to open a commercial land-route between the two coasts. Lacerda was a kindred spirit to Livingstone. An anti-slavery advocate, the Brazilian mathematician believed that, by promoting trade, the benefits of European civilization could be brought to central Africa. Lacerda was also a remarkable visionary, rightly predicting that the British occupation of Cape Town in 1795 foreshadowed the movement of Britain into south and central Africa, and therefore the perpetual division of the two Portuguese colonies. With some twenty Portuguese and half a hundred native soldiers, Lacerda made his way to the Kazembe's kraal on the shore of Lake Mweru, where he died in October 1798. The expedition did not continue across the continent, but returned to Tete. Little commerce with the lands of Kazembe ensued, but Lacerda left behind a map of the area and a significant diary of the expedition's progress and tribulations.

The lands of Kazembe figure in another journey made several years later by two half-caste *pombeiros* from the Cassange district of Angola. Departing in 1802 (the more generally accepted date, although some authorities give 1801, others 1804, and still others 1806), Pedro João Baptista and Amaro José came to the Kazembe in 1806, where they were detained by the great leader Kazembe IV for four years. In the following year they reached Tete, thus completing the first authenticated journey by a Portuguese subject (a distinction Livingstone refused to accept) across the southern heart of Africa. Again the expedition was a solitary episode of Portuguese exploration, since no Portuguese trade-routes were established in the following years. In 1831–2 the Moçambique government sent Majors José Correia Monteiro and António Pedroso Gamitto to Kazembe, to explore the headwaters of the Zambezi and the possibilities of commerce with the Kazembe. The expedition suffered severe hardships, and its memorandum argued that trade with the barbarous and unreliable people of Kazembe was neither profitable nor desirable. With that, any consistent Portuguese penetration of the deep interior lapsed for almost forty years, and by then it was a matter of too little too late.

No man in the history of Portuguese Africa comes closer to filling the role of folk-hero than António Francisco da Silva, invariably known as Silva Porto. A pioneer in the grand manner –

generous, shrewd, sentimental – his personality dominated the interior of Angola for almost fifty years. He lived in that patriarchal relationship with the Africans of Bié, the characteristics of which the Portuguese have most in mind when they speak of their ability to get along with the African. Silva Porto arrived in Luanda in 1839; in 1841 he was in Benguela; a few years later he was in Bié, where he built his home and stockade at a village that he called Belmonte, less than a mile from the modern town which bears his name. From Belmonte he traded through the countryside, establishing a new route of commerce from Bié to Benguela by way of Bailundo and Chisanji.

Although full of uncertainties, commercial life in the plateau country of the Ovimbundu had existed for more than a century. *Pombeiros* and Portuguese traders dotted the area up from Benguela and out from Caconda with tiny forts and trading stations from which they extracted ivory and slaves. With the abolition of the slave-trade, and the cessation of the Crown monopoly in ivory, commerce blossomed in this region of Angola. New Portuguese merchants took up residence in the Bié highlands, and the Ovimbundu came into their own as the most important African traders in the southern half of the continent. With the opening of the ports of Benguela and Luanda to foreign ships, trade with the outside world took the encouraging upturn which so impressed Livingstone.

Few, if any, Portuguese have known the interior of the colony as well as Silva Porto. His presence there and his repeated warnings of its importance to Portugal helped keep a wavering colonial policy from entirely neglecting the hinterland during the crucial middle years of the century. In 1852, after several Swahili traders from Zanzibar appeared in Benguela, Silva Porto began a journey across the continent; on this journey, which carried him to Barotseland before he decided not to continue, Silva Porto met Livingstone, then on his way to Luanda. (Livingstone dismissed Silva Porto as a half-caste trader, while Silva Porto regarded the Englishman as an inquisitive, somewhat quarrelsome intruder.) In the later years of his life, Silva Porto was captain-major of Bié, and his warnings to Lisbon grew ever more acute. He saw that Livingstone's visit had broken Angola's long isolation and that the days of considering coastal occupation as tantamount to possession were numbered. Missions, trading routes, railroads, capital investment, and settlement in the interior were indispensable. His suicide in 1890 was an eloquent conclusion to a now embittered life. Having failed to negotiate a truce between the *soba* of his region and an armed Portuguese column sent to annex Barotseland, Silva Porto wrapped himself in a handmade Portuguese flag and ignited a dozen kegs of gunpowder at his feet.

Silva Porto's contemporaries in Angola included explorers and naturalists. Joaquim Rodrigues Graça in 1846–8 travelled to the headwaters of the Zambezi and the territory of Lunda bordering Kazembe, obtaining treaties of friendship from various African *sobas*. From 1852 to 1861 the Lisbon government commissioned the Austrian naturalist Friedrich Welwitsch to make a botanical survey of Angola. Welwitsch travelled extensively throughout the colony, collecting new and valuable botanical specimens. For the rest of the century, another naturalist, José Alberto de Oliveira Anchieta, intermittently patronized by his government, wandered up and down Angola collecting material for Lisbon museums and his own macabre laboratory at Caconda.

Neither Angola nor Moçambique was as lacking in explorers and prophets as Livingstone had supposed, even though both colonies presented a discouraging countenance to Portuguese and foreigners alike. As Portugal moved into the critical decade of the 1870s, however, it became apparent to statesmen in Lisbon that a larger, more concerted effort would have to be made in Africa. João de Andrade Corvo, a one-time history professor and journalist who served on and off in these years as Minister for Navy and Overseas and as Foreign Minister, defined the demands of a practical colonial policy. About 1875 he wrote:

> We can no longer continue to live isolated, as we could when our African colonies were no more than parks for the production and creation of slaves. Today the world is one of work and not indolence; the earth is for men, and no one can keep civilization from it.

In a speech in the Câmara dos Pares in 1879 he said:

In my opinion, our country's interest urgently demands the development of our colonies. Only through these colonies will Portugal be able to take the place she deserves in the concert of nations; only on their preservation and prosperity does her future greatness depend.

Andrade Corvo and the scholar-diplomat Luciano Cordeiro were among the founders in 1875 of the Geographical Society of Lisbon, which made decisive contributions to Portugal's colonial cause in the next quarter of the century. The Society, through a special African Committee, undertook the task of invigorating an African consciousness in Portugal by sponsoring scientific exploration of the colonies and the publication of texts illustrating Portugal's historic role in Angola and Moçambique. The Society's work did far more than legislation and speeches to dramatize the presence of Africa, and helped restore natural pride in the traditional abilities of Portugal's explorers; in a smaller way it became an effective force in helping to combat the prevalent attitude in Europe toward the Portuguese occupation, or non-occupation, of Africa.

The most famous exploration promoted by the Society was the Capelo-Ivens-Serpa Pinto expedition which, though prepared in haste and possessed of an uncertain purpose, was the most significant Portuguese geographical journey since Lacerda's trip to Kazembe. Hermenigildo Capelo and Roberto Ivens were young navy officers, while Alexandre Alberto da Rocha de Serpa Pinto, the striking personality of the group, was an army major. The men sailed for Luanda in July 1877, intending to make a hydrographic survey of the Congo and Zambezi headwaters and to chart the territory lying between Angola and Moçambique. But Andrade Corvo had given the explorers generous latitude in their decisions, and after arriving in Angola the men were obliged to change their plans in favour of penetrating the back-country of Bié. From Belmonte, Serpa Pinto, whose personal relationship with Capelo and Ivens was not good, struck out on his own across the continent. Following the Portuguese trade-route into Lealui in Barotseland, Serpa Pinto then headed south, eventually reaching the Indian Ocean at Durban. His spectacular crossing achieved an immediate response in Europe; in Portugal he was fêted as a hero, the equal of Stanley and Livingstone.

The journey of Capelo and Ivens, less sensational though more painstaking, did not arouse the same popular enthusiasm. From Bié the two officers travelled in a northerly direction for two years, to Cassange and Malange, then along the upper reaches of the Cuango, and from there to Luanda. The expedition produced the first thorough survey of this part of the province and a notable journal, *De Benguela as terras de Iaca*. In 1884 the government again called on Capelo and Ivens, this time to lead an expedition to Moçambique, ostensibly to map the Cubango basin and investigate the commerce of the interior. Fundamental to their exploration, however, was the discovery of a trade-route between the two colonies, a route with which Portugal could establish a sufficient connexion to justify her claims for a corridor across the continent. From Moçâmedes, Capelo and Ivens followed the by now familiar route to Lealui, then north into the Katanga and south to Zumbo and down the Zambezi to Quelimane.

Two expeditions even more plainly designed to strengthen Portuguese sovereignty were the Niassa explorations of Serpa Pinto and Augusto Cardoso and the Cassai journeys of Henrique Augusto Dias de Carvalho. Conceived by the ambitious Overseas Minister Pinheiro Chagas as further demonstrations of a Portuguese renascence in Africa, neither expedition was in any large sense one of geographical discovery. Such African political excursions by the middle 1880s were generally explained as expeditions of scientific or commercial inquiry, a sacrosanct explanation which may have fooled some scientists and businessmen, but which had a more cynical significance for certain of Europe's statesmen. The Portuguese realized that, if they were to salvage the country east of Lake Nyasa and south of the Rovuma, more persuasive arguments than ancient maps were needed. Accordingly in 1884 Serpa Pinto, now consul at Zanzibar, was asked to lead the expedition. When Serpa Pinto fell ill his associate Augusto Cardoso continued to the lake, where he raised the flag of Portugal and obtained signatures of fealty to Portugal from various local chiefs. Dias de Carvalho journeyed to the heart of modern Katanga with the same purpose. He got the signature of the Mutianvua, the great chief of Lunda, to the standard contract that every European explorer seems to have carried in his boots on the off chance of running into an African leader not signed to a rival company. By the time that Carvalho got to the Mutianvua's capital beyond the Lulua River in 1886, however, the diplomats at the Berlin Conference had among themselves already disposed of this part of the world. But the expedition was not entirely in vain. The occupation stations established by Carvalho helped to push the eastern frontier of Angola to the Kasai River, a formidable achievement if one considers that these territorial inroads were made into the private lands of that most rapacious humanitarian, King Léopold of Belgium. (In fact, if the partition of Africa had been made purely on the basis of exploration, the boundaries of Angola and Moçambique would without doubt be very different from what they are today.)

The Consequences of the Berlin Conference

The Berlin Conference of 1884-5 hardened European attitudes toward Portugal's position in Africa into policies. The conference itself had developed out of the abortive Anglo-Portuguese Treaty of 1884 regarding sovereignty over the Congo basin – it was the Lisbon Foreign Office which had first proposed a meeting of colonial powers – and it began a series of events, few of them favouring the Portuguese, which extended to 1914. Of the major colonial powers taking part in the conference – France, England, Germany, Belgium, and Portugal – only the last failed to gain some sort of advantage; though Portugal, the European nation with the longest and most valid colonizing record in Africa (such a statement has value only in a comparative sense), was fortunate, in the view of some dispassionate observers, in not losing more than she did in the years after 1885. Portugal's reputation in Africa was not good at that time, in spite of recent stirrings in Angola and Moçambique, and the centuries of neglect and slaving cost her dearly.

In this troubled period Portugal had special need of her

ancient ally England, but the English government's attitude toward Portugal in the nineteenth century could at best be considered pious hypocrisy, and it was a tricky problem for Portuguese statesmanship simultaneously to maintain a useful alliance and to keep England from abusing it. Andrade Corvo defended Portuguese–English friendship as an absolute necessity for his small country. England, however, had made the mistake of submitting the Delagoa Bay squabble with Portugal to arbitration and seen President MacMahon of France in 1875 acknowledge the legitimacy of Portuguese claims. She had not found Portugal altogether amenable on other issues involving her African possessions. And the predominant attitude toward colonial Portugal in English public opinion, which had its repercussions on the Foreign Office, was of a backward if not degenerate dominance in Africa which should be abolished and entrusted to the forces of progress and enlightenment.

For years England had refused to recognize Portugal's authority over the Angola coast north of Ambriz, although in the treaties of 1810 and 1817 on control of the slave-trade, England seemed to acknowledge Portuguese dominion. Portugal had constantly protested the English position and refused to yield her claims to both banks of the Congo. In 1882–3 France's manoeuvring in the Congo basin gave both countries new grounds for discussion: Portugal saw that she might shortly lose territory she had been accustomed to regard as her own, while England feared that as a consequence of France's high-tariff policies, the great river might be closed to international traffic. In the draft of the Anglo-Portuguese treaty of 1884 England at last recognized Portugal's position. In return for recognition of her claims to both sides of the river about fifty miles up to Noqui, Portugal acceded to freedom of navigation on the river, an Anglo-Portuguese commission to control traffic, and a maximum duty of ten per cent *ad valorem* on goods entering the area, with Britain receiving a most-favoured-nation treatment.

A treaty which gave, as it seemed, commercial advantages to England in the Congo basin and which placed control over the lower banks of the waterway in the hands of Portugal, regarded by her few friends as incompetent and by her many enemies as isolationist and backward, was bound to meet with opposition. In Europe opposition was virtually unanimous, while in England a considerable segment of parliament reacted against giving the delta to a power whose 'moral title was certainly no stronger than the legal title ... whose customs were such as to fetter the activities of trade with shackles of a truly medieval type'. In the midst of delicate negotiations, Portugal suggested that a new basis for the treaty might be reached at an international conference. When Germany seized the proposal as an opportunity to take the initiative away from Britain, the Berlin West African Conference of 1884-5 was born.

At Berlin, Portugal lost half of what she had sought to keep, and had it not been for the skill of her diplomats, who played the animosities of France, England, and Germany against each other, she would have lost more. In the early weeks of the Conference she stood firm on her 'historic rights' in the lower Congo. Gradually these 'rights' were whittled away: first, control of the river; then her claim to land on the north bank (with the exception of the Cabinda enclave); next her claims to lands on the southern bank beyond Noqui. At the end of the conference Portugal held Cabinda, the southern shore up to Noqui, and from there inland along the latitude of Noqui to the Cuango River, whose southern course was to form the boundary with the Congo Free State. The final Angola–Congo Free State frontiers were fixed by treaties in 1891 and 1894, but not before the indefinite nature of the boundaries had caused several incidents. Portugal's claims were again extensive and based on historical contact; but, with the dissolution of her trans-African dream, these lost much of their significance. (In 1890, for example, the two nations discussing territorial rights in the Katanga, where the Portuguese had been the first to trade and explore, were England and the Congo Free State.) The frontier established by these treaties is the one, with small modifications, separating Angola from the Congo Republic today, with the southern courses of the Cuango and the Kasai forming the main lines of demarcation.

What perverse fortune drove Portugal in 1886 to attempt to reassert the trans-African schemes of Manuel, Sebastião, and Sousa Coutinho? Fifty, thirty, perhaps ten years earlier she could have claimed and occupied much of the land lying between Angola and Moçambique without fear of grave reper-

7. Portuguese-controlled territory south of the equator in Africa, c. 1880

cussions, but such a move in 1886 was an invitation to disaster. Many factors, some rational, some emotional, precipitated the plunge. There was the very sound suspicion that the English would drive up the continent from the south. Portugal may mistakenly have thought that the articles in the General Act of the Berlin Conference which referred to the establishing of authority back from the coast applied to minor colonial powers. Pique and vanity also helped turn the heads of Lisbon statesmen. Portugal considered herself humiliated at Berlin, and in an effort to boost national confidence decided to try the same blunt tactics of Bismarck which appeared to obtain such impressive results. Portugal, who had the year before quibbled endlessly over a few acres of territory, now prepared boldly to embrace a piece of the continent larger than the accepted areas of both Angola and Moçambique. The only two flaws in her ambitious project were Portugal's own unhappy reputation as a colonial power and Cecil John Rhodes. The intervention of Rhodes was perhaps difficult to foresee in 1886; but her own fatal mistake was not to have realized that the distrust she inspired as mistress of African colonies was a pervasive and influential prejudice of English public opinion.

The proposition was not altogether a fanciful blunder, however, and Portuguese diplomats were not entirely ignorant of African politics. If Germany, seconded by England and associated powers, legalized Léopold's empire in the Congo, why couldn't Germany and France do the same for a trans-African Portuguese empire? Accordingly, from May 1886 to July 1887, omnibus treaties were signed and ratified with these two countries to cover various mutual frontiers in Africa. Portugal was obliged to sacrifice several claims along the west and east African coasts, but in return she obtained recognition of her privilege to exercise her 'rights of sovereignty and civilization in the territories which separate the Portuguese possessions of Angola and Moçambique, without prejudice to the rights which other powers may have acquired there'. The following year Foreign Minister Henrique de Barros Gomes presented to the Portuguese parliament the famous rose-coloured map which swathed the interior of the continent approximately between the twelfth and eighteenth parallels in bright rose-pink.

England refused to recognize the transcontinental sections of the treaties; Lord Salisbury argued that Portugal did not occupy the territory claimed and was not able to protect foreign life and property there. Barros Gomes replied that the General Act spoke only of coastal occupation, and that, if it were to concern occupation of the interior, German and French possessions, Léopold's holdings, and even parts of the British protectorates in Africa would be invalidated. He referred to 'spheres of influence' and summed up Portugal's historic claims in Africa. But while Barros Gomes spoke of ancient treaties with the Monomotapa, ruined forts and factories in Mashonaland, mining expeditions to Manica, missionary work, traders, priority, the scientific journey of Lacerda, of Gamitto and Monteiro, and of Serpa Pinto, England needed only to speak of 'progress', the catchword of white imperialism, to eradicate all of Portugal's pretensions. The fundamental conflict between Portugal and England was between the past and the future. Portugal had not yet acquired the determination or sense of necessity to enable her to compete with other colonial powers. The rules of the game in Africa had been changed by the players who had entered the game late, and no accumulation of historic claims could prevail against Kiplingesque platitudes on progress and duty.

At several points in the tense and complicated negotiations which ensued, a compromise seemed at hand, but the intransigence of the British missionaries in the Shire highlands, Rhodes's gargantuan projects, and what Oliveira Martins called Portugal's 'stupidly patriotic insistence', frustrated any satisfactory compromise and brought on the British ultimatum of 1890. Barros Gomes learned that the use of forceful diplomacy presupposed an authority which Portugal did not possess. In the south, Rhodes ('the plateau for England, the lowlands for Portugal') was set on the expansion of British South Africa into the highland country between the Limpopo and the Zambezi. In Nyasaland, missionary and commercial interests, encouraged by Rhodes, were fearful of Portuguese expansion and their own complete isolation. In 1890 a conflict between a Portuguese column and Africans of the Shire valley brought British gunboats to Moçambique and an ultimatum. A lesser conflict in October of that year, between a private army of Rhodes's Chartered Company and a Portuguese volunteer expeditionary force, hastened the inevitable débâcle. Without any support from either France or Germany, Portugal was obliged to capitulate, and signed in June 1891 a treaty settling the major frontiers. All that remained of the rose-coloured map was a distressing jig-saw puzzle which, when finally put together, revealed a crimson strip of British territory running north from the Transvaal to Katanga and German East Africa.

But the disaster of 1890 did serve some practical purpose in Portugal, for not since the sixteenth century had the metropolis been made so vividly aware of the African colonies; the feeling that something had to be done temporarily united the many factions of Portuguese political life. It was commonly agreed that the miserable realities of Angola and Moçambique presented a challenge, since the threat of appropriation by other powers did not disappear with the treaty of 1891. It was apparent that exaggerated glories of the past, though admirably suited for speeches and for inspiring patriotic sentiments, and ancient documents would not be sufficient defence against another onslaught. For twenty years, Portugal was able to exploit the energies and anger stirred up by the ultimatum for the oc-cupation and development of her African provinces.

Throughout the 1890s Portugal was bullied alternately by England and Germany. The former clearly wished to strengthen her position against the Transvaal, while the latter was intent on obliging a bankrupt Portugal to borrow large sums of money – with the colonies as collateral. Although Portugal was in a very difficult position in Moçambique, she succeeded in keeping free from damaging commitments and discreetly avoided the too-warm embraces of both powers. In 1898 an Anglo-German agree-ment established, in a secret clause, the division of Portugal's colonies should 'it not be possible to maintain their integrity'; the German sphere of influence would then be Moçambique north of the Zambezi and southern Angola, while to England there would fall Delagoa Bay. But a year later, in October, when German pressure on Portugal had become extreme and England had begun to fight the Boer War, a secret Anglo-Portuguese pact (the so-called Windsor treaty) was signed, reaffirming earlier treaties of friendship and underlining the promise contained in a treaty of 1661, whereby England agreed to defend and protect Portugal's colonies. In return Portugal agreed to forbid the import of arms for the Boers through her territory and to permit England to make use of Moçambique ports for the landing of troops.

In 1914 Germany's ambition to annex parts of Angola and Moçambique was revived, and again she sought to establish with England respective spheres of influence. War broke out before these agreements could be terminated, and both Portuguese colonies were the scene of hostilities between German and Portuguese forces. But not even Portugal's participation in the Great War on the side of the Allies left her colonies safe. In the early 1920s there was renewed speculation on the partition of Angola and Moçambique, the heirs again to be England and Germany. But the aggressive tactics of the major colonial powers gradually softened, and with the growing reliance of England, Belgium, and South Africa on the rail and port facilities of Angola and Moçambique, relations grew increasingly more cordial. In the 1940s and 1950s the demands of self-preservation in Africa drew the various colonizing countries to find common cause against the challenge of African nationalism.

5 Promise and Disappointment

The ultimatum of 1890 ushered in a new and often turbulent period in the history of Portuguese Africa, a period of change and frustrated change, of realism and folly, of promise and disappointment. It was a period for Portugal of quickening interest in Africa, of attempts, given urgency by the political necessities of the hour, to carry out historic programmes of occupation and development. The problems which a new generation of soldiers and administrators had to face were chronic and not brought on by the events of the previous decade. Neglect and inertia could lead to further territorial spoliation. Occupation of the interior, a reorganization of the provincial administration, and a colonial policy consistent with current realities were the compelling requirements of the 1890s. Although one could not be separated from the others, the most pressing problem was the conquest and effective military occupation of the interior.

Not only did this first step promise to accomplish what apparently was meant by the article of the Berlin General Act regarding occupation, but in a number of regions a resurgence of African power was threatening Portuguese strongholds. A young officer summed up the condition of Portuguese East Africa when he said: 'The province of Moçambique belongs without question to the blacks who live in it.' The military and political value of campaigns in the two colonies was thoroughly exaggerated by popular sentiment of the day, which desperately needed a show of national heroics, and later by the Salazar régime, which found it convenient to consecrate a hierarchy of colonial heroes. Nevertheless, the psychological importance of Portuguese armed triumph over native forces cannot be minimized.

At home and in Africa these victories stood for progress and positive policies; they meant that Portugal could now hold her head on a level with other great colonial powers, who were busy implanting civilization in the hinterland with the end of a rifle.

Warfare Against the Tribes

Warfare with the tribes of Angola had gone on sporadically since the days of Paulo Dias de Novais, and in terms of ultimate pacification they served no very useful purpose, since in 1885 African hostility in the back country was as strong as it had been three centuries before. The two regions of most persistent opposition to Portuguese occupation were the Dembos and Congo regions in the north of the territory and the Cuanhama country in the south.

In the Humbe region it took Portugal twenty-five years to subdue the militant Cuanhama. Here Portuguese troops – the first columns were made up of convicts and African troops, neither of whom distinguished themselves – suffered several serious reversals until the establishment of a fort at Cuamoto with a large permanent garrison. Only in 1915 was the entire southern region of the Huíla plateau brought under Portuguese control. In 1902 the so-called Bailundo campaign was fought on the Bié plateau. Many factors, including forced labour and the demoralization caused by the rum-trade, brought the normally pacific Ovimbundu to revolt. For the Portuguese this was a classic native war: the punitive expeditions were organized quickly; the Africans fought bravely but foolishly; every Portuguese soldier was a hero; and, finally, thousands of Africans were killed while Portuguese losses were minimal. The Dembos-Congo campaign was the most difficult of all. Rain, heat, difficult terrain, and disease had made the area virtually inaccessible to any military expedition until 1907, when Captain João de Almeida made a remarkable march through the region, fighting a number of skirmishes and arresting or shooting opposition leaders. Within three years the Dembos region was pacified. A Bakongo uprising in 1913 and a campaign in the vicinity of Vila Luso provided the only other serious conflicts, and by 1920 the

Angola government could claim the subservience or allegiance of most of the African population.

The state of affairs in Moçambique was, if anything, less settled than in Angola – and politically far more dangerous, since during the 1890s the British South Africa Company still talked ominously of taking over what was left of Moçambique below the Zambezi. That Portugal enjoyed any prestige in the interior at all during the latter half of the century was due to several powerful *prazeros*, notably the Goan Manuel António de Sousa (usually known simply as Gouveia), who had resisted the invasion of Landin and Vatua warriors from the south and had extended their own influence over a good part of Zambézia. As late as 1890 most of Moçambique was almost completely innocent of Portuguese authority, and in 1894 Lourenço Marques suffered a serious assault by African warriors from the outlying area. But in the following year, after the arrival of António Enes and his brilliant young soldier-statesmen, Lourenço Marques district was pacified. In the same year the great Gungunhana, chief of Gaza, with whom Rhodes had been intriguing for five years, was captured by Mousinho de Albuquerque and shipped off to Lisbon, where in Roman style he was paraded through the streets before the admiring eyes of the populace. By 1900 the only area of dissent south of the Zambezi was in the Barué region, a haven for criminals, deposed chiefs, and resentful *prazeros*; and a major campaign in 1902 brought the area under control. North of the river, the Zambézia Company extended its influence beyond Tete and into Angonia toward the Nyasaland frontier. The last two districts of the province to submit were Moçambique and Niassa. From 1906 to 1910, in a series of small campaigns, the off-shore islands, the coast, and the near interior of Moçambique district were pacified. From 1908 to 1912, the Yao country of Niassa was progressively occupied by Portuguese forces. After that only an uprising in Barué in 1917, and the small revolts which followed in the wake of von Lettow's marches through Moçambique during the First World War, seriously disturbed the colony. The actual battles fought in Moçambique were, in terms of white casualties, more like election-day squabbles in Portugal, as High Commissioner Brito Camacho later remarked, but they unquestionably saved the colony from Anglo-German partition and they brought into the forefront of colonial affairs the famous generation of 1895, the circle of António Enes who served as Royal Commissioner of Moçambique in 1894–5.

The Generation of António Enes

It is almost impossible to overestimate the importance of that generation of colonial leaders. Although they had spiritual fore-fathers in Sousa Coutinho, Sá da Bandeira, and Andrade Corvo, they were set apart from the past, no matter how much their policies may have had roots in the Portuguese colonial tradition, by the ultimatum of 1890. Enes and his followers bore no responsibility for the decisions that had led up to that disaster, and they felt free to start the process of colonial rejuvenation with a clean slate. All, except Enes himself, were military men, and each found practical inspiration in António Enes's hard-headed policies and absolute dedication to Portugal's colonial affairs. For the next twenty-five years these men influenced and often determined Portugal's course in Africa. The policy that the generation stood for, with some individual variation, required: no politics or patronage in colonial affairs; a practical and profit-able colonial programme adapted to regional needs and con-ditions, even though this might mean free trade, foreign invest-ment in the colonies, and a systematic use of native labour; the setting of attainable goals; revision of the administrative appara-tus; and a tougher native policy. It is not surprising that when the Salazar government began to pay serious attention to the African colonies in the 1930s, it should have returned for inspiration to the deeds and writings of the generation of 1895.

Who were these men who went to Moçambique in the 1890s? Mousinho de Albuquerque, who succeeded Enes as Royal Com-missioner and wrote the classic study *Moçambique* (1899); Aires de Ornelas, Mousinho's chief of staff in 1896, governor of Lourenço Marques district in 1900, and Overseas Minister in

1906–7, during which period he was responsible for the Colonial Reform Act; Freire de Andrade, Enes's Chief of Cabinet and Governor-General of Moçambique from 1906 to 1910; Henrique de Paiva Couceiro, Enes's aide-de-camp, later the most vigorous governor-general of Angola since Sousa Coutinho, and author of two influential colonial tracts; Eduardo Ferreira da Costa, governor of Moçambique district in 1896, of Benguela in 1903, and governor-general of Angola in 1906, an administrative philosopher whose works were key-texts in the new colonial ideology; Pedro Francisco de Amorim, campaigner in the interior, governor-general of Angola in 1910 and of Moçambique in 1918.

António Enes himself was the dominant and moulding force of the new men. A romantic turned positivist, Enes was during his career a journalist, polemicist, deputy, and for a brief period Minister for Navy and Overseas. From 1890 he was an agitator for colonial change. He was sent to Moçambique in 1891–2 on a special mission to determine administrative reforms. His bristling report, *Moçambique* (1893), is a basic document of Portugal's modern colonial policy. Enes's judgements were consistently pragmatic. For example, he defended the role of the Indian trader as a valuable agent in the occupation and commercial life of the interior. Foreign investment was to be sought. Foreign missionary societies, if closely supervised, could perform useful tasks in medicine and education. The *prazo* and the chartered company could serve the state in a profitable manner. Immigration of Portuguese peasants into Moçambique had to be curbed, and manual tasks reserved for the African, who was used to the climate and soil. Uniform legislation for all Portuguese colonies, or even for all parts of one colony, was an absurdity. With new laws should come new administrators, decisive, intelligent, zealous, and prudent men. On native policy Enes was a forthright racist and a partisan of forced labour:

> If we do not learn how . . . to make the Negro work and cannot take advantage of his work, within a short while we will be obliged to abandon Africa to someone less sentimental and more utilitarian than we. . . .

The importance of Enes is the importance of a doctrine. The importance of Mousinho de Albuquerque is the importance of a colonial hero. Quite apart from his dedication to the abstractions of faith and duty and his mystical nationalism, qualities which have endeared him to the Salazar régime, Mousinho was much more than a man on a horse. As a victorious campaigner against the formidable Gungunhana, he was for Portugal a living link with the nation's past, a figure from another, more brilliant century, who appeared miraculously in an age of Anglo-Saxon superiority to revive the historic Lusitanian values and to give his country an illusion of greatness. ('For us Portuguese the task in Africa was to retemper the national soul, to revive the spirit of "Awake, my steel," engraved on the Toledo blade.') Mousinho had few original thoughts on colonial policy. More conservative than Enes, he sought during his tenure as governor-general in 1896–8 to establish administrative authority, to divide the lands of the great chiefs into smaller regions, each ruled by a Portuguese puppet. Any notion of equality for Africans seemed to him nonsense. During his tenure as Royal Commissioner, Mousinho had constant quarrels with 'insignificant politicians' in Lisbon, and chose to resign his post in 1898. But he remained a hero with the Portuguese people until his suicide in 1902.

It was apparent to the generation of 1895 that, in order to civilize the African provinces, new administrative moulds were needed. Armed occupation had to be followed by civil government, the remnants of ancient captaincies and military commands in the interior had to be replaced by civil circumscriptions, and all entrenched colonial servants, as Enes wrote, had to adapt themselves to the spirit of reform or give up their posts. The first civil circumscriptions were established by Enes in 1895 around Lourenço Marques, but not until the years after 1907, with the publication of the Colonial Reform Act, were other areas of Moçambique organized into circumscriptions. The system was not fully implemented in Angola until after 1911.

The details of the proposed colonial organization were most

clearly defined in Eduardo da Costa's *Estudos sobre a administração civil das provincias ultramarinas*. His proposals, an elaboration of Enes's concepts, are largely the basis of present-day administration in Portuguese Africa. The major point of difference is that Costa, like Enes and Mousinho, argued the need for decentralization and greater autonomy for the African provinces. What Enes and Costa sought above all else was the authority to initiate policies and make major decisions on issues of local importance. This authority was to rest with the governor-general and his subordinates, who had to be well-chosen; a local assembly Costa regarded as a grave inconvenience.

But Costa's contribution was not his thoughts on decentralization; it was his perfecting of the circumscription into a workable unit of colonial government, since, with the serious occupation of the interior, the necessity for a firm control over native affairs was of first importance. Costa rejected any thought of equality for the African, observing that legal equality frequently produced the greatest inequality in practice. (It is on this point that the generation of 1895 differed most with nineteenth-century Portuguese colonial thought.) There had to be two administrative codes, one for Africans and another for Europeans, and the African code was to vary, if need be, from district to district. Each district of the province was to be divided into a varying number of circumscriptions, and their Portuguese administrators were to constitute for the native peoples all administrative, judicial, and military authority, since the savage mind, in Costa's view, did not accept any division in supreme authority. The *administrador* – a sort of modern projection of the *paterfamilias*, embodied in men like Silva Porto, the seventeenth-century *prazero*, and the responsible captain-major – was a typically Portuguese creation; he was in effect a paramount white chief over the lesser chiefs and villagers in the *circunscrição*. Costa's policy implied no encouragement of tribal government; on the contrary, it envisaged its own eventual disappearance in the emergence of a single Pan-Portuguese community. The administrator was to be a more authoritarian figure than the British District Officer. In Costa's words:

His purely administrative functions are very different from those of a metropolitan administrator, because, in addition to police and civil services, he is charged with an important political mission, which is to maintain good relations with the native chiefs of the circumscription, to assure their obedience and tranquillity, to intervene in their disputes over boundaries, rights of succession, and other complaints, in brief to acquire over his charges a dominating and respected influence.

In theory, anyone contesting the administrator's decisions had appeal to the district or the provincial governor, but the almost absolute local power wielded by the Portuguese proconsul made such appeals impractical. That the proposed system was despotic, Costa admitted, but only in this way could it provide 'a just, humanitarian, and civilizing tutelage' for the conquered tribes of Portuguese Africa.

Gradually the new administrative procedures replaced the old captaincies in Angola and Moçambique. Only in a few places, around the larger towns of the provinces, was there a sufficiently large white or civilized population for the *concelho*, or council, system of government by local officials to be used. Not even the Republic's colonial legislation of 1914 and 1920, which made extensive grants of autonomy to the colonies, altered the fundamental context of the 1907 reforms. The administrator and his assistant, the chief of post, were powerful men, with an infinite opportunity for good and for harm in those critical years. Vigorous governors like Paiva Couceiro and Norton de Matos saw the circumscription as an opportunity, with the appointment of qualified and sympathetic administrators, to introduce Portuguese cultural values into the tribal life of the colony and to facilitate the co-existence of the two peoples. A strong governorgeneral sometimes imposed his own order and incorruptibility on the entire colonial administration; but usually the *administrador* was distant, a white chief with great power who more often than not followed the easygoing ways of his predecessor, the captaingeneral. Life in the bush of Portuguese Africa usually attracted neither the idealist nor the practical reformer in the early decades of the twentieth century.

Paternalism and Native Policy

Various governments, metropolitan and colonial, grappled with the problem of creating a native policy to accompany the new administrative forms. There was intense interest in the subject; colonial tracts discussed the problem at length, deputies made speeches, professors and journalists gave lectures; legislation was passed in Lisbon; decrees were handed down in Luanda and Lourenço Marques; and controversies raged. Through it all there were two points of fairly common agreement: the African was to be obliged to work, and was to be inoculated with Portuguese cultural values if possible. There was not much new in these proposals, for such had been Portugal's policy in Africa for centuries, although there had probably been a little more emphasis on labour than on assimilation in the years before. Nor was it hard to concoct legislation that seemed to bring these two aspects of native policy into fruitful balance. And it was easy for Norton de Matos to issue his demonic decrees urging his subordinates to get out of the contract labour business and start instead the work of acculturation. But nothing much happened. The only native policy that functioned in Angola and Moçambique was tradition.

How much of Portugal's consistent failure to pursue an enlightened and productive native policy, how much of her inclination to issue improbable decrees and evolve a meaningless colonial mystique, has been founded not only on poverty and confusion, but also on an unconscious desire to perpetuate the past in the present? Was it not easier in 1910, in 1915, and in 1920, if not to exploit the African further, to exploit the suppressed state in which he still existed? Contrary to their many pronouncements on the subject, the Portuguese have never made great efforts to understand the African or his cultures. And at no time was this more evident than in those years of possible change in the early twentieth century. What a Portuguese professed to understand was only his own image of the African and his culture, an image which summed up the African in paternalistic platitudes and made native problems less complex and burdensome. His culture was relegated to the limbo of *curiosa* and folklore. The Portuguese found it simpler to accept the African than to understand him.

If at the core of Portuguese paternalism there rested a belief that the infantile capacities of the Negro made the task of civilization a slow one, so at the core of the slowly formulating policies of assimilation lay the reality of miscegenation (although this was not a characteristic of Portuguese behaviour in Africa particularly attractive to the white-supremacy disciples of Mousinho). The colonialist Vaz de Sampaio e Melo wrote, for example, in 1910:

> For Portugal the problem of miscegenation in her colonies cannot fail to have the greatest importance, especially if the colonial system we adopt is one of political assimilation. . . . Miscegenation is the most powerful force of colonial nationalism. Given equality to the European under the law and admitted to administrative, religious, political, and military positions, the mulatto comes to adopt exclusively the customs and languages of the conquering nation, and they [mulattos] constitute the most profitable and appropriate instrument for the spread of those ethnic characteristics in the native society. . . .

In a strict sense, *mestiçagem* never became a colonial policy, but it was a fact to which Portuguese statesmen found it increasingly convenient to give moral dignity and egalitarian significance.

It is true that the short-lived Portuguese Republic (1910–26) tried to evolve a series of programmes which would meet the requirements of the African provinces (i.e. guarantee a supply of labour) and work toward attainable goals (i.e. the assimilation of a modest number of Africans). Both Enes and the venerated Liberal traditions had their influence on the legislation of 1914, which was to be the basis for the Native Assistance Code of 1921. It defined the civilized African, who could consider himself a fully-fledged Portuguese citizen, as one who could speak Portuguese, had divested himself of his tribal customs, and was regularly and gainfully employed. This constituted one of the earliest formal definitions of the *assimilado*. The rest of the African population were regarded as charges of the government for whom special laws and regulations were to be devised. An

Office of Native Affairs was set up in Lisbon to administer these wards of the state. And so the egalitarian concepts of the 1830s were reversed. At the same time, however, the Republic sought to protect and assist the African population. African workers were to be secured from exploitation by both the state and private employers. Infirmaries were to be established in administrative centres and medical posts in the large villages. As a part of the over-all programme of cultural assimilation a system of public instruction was to be established. Education for the student was to be practical, training in the crafts for men and in domestic science for women. Administrators were to encourage native agriculture by providing seeds and technical advice, and by seeing that the farmer received a fair price for his crops. On the basis of a modified free-labour system, medical and educational assistance, and the opportunity for the African to advance beyond what the Portuguese government considered to be his backward heathen state, the Republic rested its native policy.

Legislation like this was not much less enlightened than that being promulgated at this period in the British, French, or Belgian colonies. But the history of Portuguese Africa often seems to consist less in what *was* than in what *might have been*. Between the thought in 1914 and the act in 1921 Portugal was distracted by the First World War, and the momentum for colonial reform was lost. After the war, new goals, economic and material, took precedence over programmes of African assistance, and it seemed that the colonies could expand and prosper only by continuing to exploit the African. So what might have been once again turned out to be what was not.

Apart from the modest benefits rendered by missionary hospitals and doctors, health services in the interior remained non-existent. Erratic attempts to promote a diversified African agriculture came to nothing. The want of trained personnel in the colonies made any advance in these two important segments of African life virtually impossible. Nor were various decrees much more effective in curbing the sale of spirits. Although a 1902 law prohibiting the sale of rum to Africans had some positive results, the sale of fortified wine went on. Since wine was the principal import into each colony and the principal export of the metropolis, no draconian prohibition could be expected, while the various restrictions on its sale in the evenings or on Sundays were largely ignored. In many areas of Angola and Moçambique, alcoholism was widespread.

Education was only a little less of a failure in spite of the Republic's good intentions. At the beginning of the century the few schools existing in Angola and Moçambique were almost exclusively run by missionaries, and a substantial portion of them by various Protestant mission societies – notably the Swiss Mission in Moçambique, and the joint American Board of Commissioners for Foreign Missions in Angola – which had settled in Portuguese Africa toward the end of the nineteenth century. Their efforts, reinforced by those of other Protestant missionary societies and those of the Catholic Church, provided the major educational facilities for Africans during the early decades of the twentieth century. The task was enormous. Although the Liberal régime had made the usual elaborate plans for colonial education, the performance had been pitifully inadequate, and in 1865 the Minister for Navy and Overseas regretfully concluded that 'local difficulties, negligence, and imperfect organization annulled or paralysed' the government's attempts to establish a colonial educational system. In 1873, 456 boys and 33 girls, black and white, were enrolled in all of Angola's schools; in the same period, there were an estimated 400 in the schools of Moçambique.

Improvement in the early twentieth century was slow and unsure. Throughout Moçambique in 1909, in addition to the several trade and agricultural schools, there were only forty-eight primary schools for boys and eighteen for girls. Mulatto and African attendance had increased only slightly from the 1900 figure of 1,195 (146 in government schools, 412 in so-called municipal schools, 30 in private institutions, and 607 in missionary schools). In Angola the increase from 1900 to 1908 totalled 15 students, from 1,845 African pupils to 1,860, who attended sixty-nine schools. Although the few schools in the municipalities were open indiscriminately to African and white students, the one million potential students in the interior were un-affected. The reports of the African Education Commission, which visited Angola in 1921 and Moçambique in 1924, gave a generally dismal picture of conditions in the provinces. The reports noted the hostility toward Protestant missions, the practice of excluding native languages from instruction, mis-understanding and apathy in government circles, lack of funds, and the failure to encourage African teachers. Not only was the state of education backward, especially in comparison with several other colonial areas, but 'observations in Portuguese Africa . . . offer practically no basis for hope of any essential improvements in colonial policy'.

In the absence of action, there was considerable discussion on African education. What education should the African be given, and why should he be educated at all if he was to be only a worker? (According to Governor-General Freire de Andrade, the only education to give him was 'one which will make him a worker'.) How could the African be civilized without education? Should Portuguese or the Bantu tongues be the language of instruction? What were the roles of the state and of the mission-ary societies? Most of these questions are still to be answered today. Then, as now, there was no real conviction among the colonial administrators of Angola and Moçambique that educa-tion for Africans should rank very high in the order of colonial development.

The Principle and Practice of Forced Labour

But could any programme of assistance for the African popula-tion – arguing that Portugal was both capable and really desirous of doing as much or more than the European colonial conscience of the age permitted – take effect in colonies where the over-riding concept of the African was that of a working hand? This concept, which went beyond the limited vision of African intel-lectual capacity, was deeply rooted in the tradition of slavery and all of its casuistical justifications. It is a concept which, far more than the poverty or the scant potential of colonial Portugal, is responsible for the ignorance and isolation to which the African has been seemingly forever condemned in Angola and Moçambique. It is a concept which has led to the final collapse of Portugal's policy in our own day. The entire history of Angola and Moçambique is in large part the history of a ruthless exploitation of the Africans through the practice of slavery or forced labour.

Aware that little was being done in Portuguese Africa to prepare for the end of slavery (to take place in 1878, according to the 1858 decree), Lisbon in 1869 made all slaves *libertos*, slaves who would be paid and treated like workers until the moment of freedom. It is possible that the equivocal status of the *liberto* planted in the official mind the seed of the idea that a slave could be a slave in the absence of slavery, for this was certainly the concern of all subsequent legislation, which sought simultaneously to guarantee to the African his independence and to the European his necessary supply of labour. (For the rugged colonists of Angola and Moçambique, such legal sophistication was not needed, since most of them continued to ignore all native labour legislation.)

In 1878 the first real native-labour code for Portuguese Africa, the *Regulamento para os contratos de serviçais e colonos nas provincias de Africa*, became law. The Regulation was an advanced milestone in Portugal's native policy which has not been reached again. It flatly abolished forced labour and endeavoured to replace it with a system of free labour instead. It was designed to protect the rights and interests of the African and to guarantee for him a basic human standard. Impractical possibly, but any labour policy which did not sanction slavery was impractical in the African colonies. Enlightened for its age, the Regulation is one of the refreshing moments in a colonial policy which all too often seems to have been characterized by an intent to exploit the Negro in Africa and to confuse Portugal's critics abroad.

There were two flaws in the *Regulamento*, which would not have had such grievous consequences had the new code fallen on receptive soil. It did not, however, and African–Portuguese relations continued to rest on hypocrisy and injustice. The flaws were a specific vagrancy clause, similar to that contained in the metropolitan penal code, and the general supposition that a labour contract between worker and employer would benefit each mutually. What ensued could have been easy to predict. Many masters simply kept their slaves under the pretence of contracted *serviçais*. Slave-traders in the interior operated much as before, with the slight difference that, instead of buying prisoners or subjects from a chief, they contracted for them. The vagrancy clause was exploited to the hilt. In many areas Portuguese officials, including the *curadores*, whose office it was to supervise contracts and protect the African interests, declared all Africans not under contract to be vagrants and forced them into five-year contracts. In practice, free labour did not exist in the colonies. The employer felt less obligation to his contracted labourers than he had formerly felt to his slaves. The *serviçais* were often maintained at virtually a starvation level of existence. Thousands of Angolan workers were shipped off to the cocoa islands of São Tomé and Principe, never to return. Driven to desperation, many villagers fled into the deep interior or formed themselves into fierce small bands of warriors.

The state of affairs in 1898 should have given the Overseas Ministry pause when it appointed a committee to study the problems of Portuguese Africa. But the climate did not encourage the growth of humanitarian considerations in Africa, and the principle of forced labour, denied in the Regulation of 1878, was the heart of the report submitted by the commission, whose recommendations were incorporated into the stringent Regulation of 1899, the most complete native-labour code until 1928 and the inspiration for much of the Salazar government's African policy. The committee was dominated by António Enes, who had scorned the previous code and was determined that muddled liberal ideas should not be the basis for another one like it. Portugal had to develop her colonies, and this development rested on the Africans' shoulders. Lest the bald implications of forced labour again draw the fire of humanitarians – and because they themselves believed that what they said was sociological law – members of the committee defined their suggested repressions of the African by proclaiming that it was the duty of Europe to promote the African's advancement into civilization:

> The state, not only as a sovereign of semi-barbaric populations, but also as a depository of social authority, should have no scruples in *obliging* and, if necessary, *forcing* [the italics are the committee's] these rude Negroes in Africa . . . to work, that is, to better themselves by work, to acquire through work the happiest means of existence, to civilize themselves through work. . . .

Thus the first article of the Regulation of 1899 states:

> All natives of Portuguese overseas provinces are subject to the obligation, moral and legal, of attempting to obtain through work the means that they lack to subsist and to better their social condition. They have full liberty to choose the method of fulfilling this obligation, but if they do not fulfil it, public authority may force a fulfilment.

The obligation was considered fulfilled by those Africans who had sufficient capital to assure their means of existence or those who had a paying profession; by those who farmed on their own account a suitable plot of land or by those who produced goods for export in suitable quantities; and by those who worked in return for a salary a minumum number of months each year. Exempt from the obligation were women, men over sixty, boys under fourteen, the sick and the invalid, sepoys, policemen, chiefs, and locally prominent Africans. 'All others who do not fulfil voluntarily the obligation to work . . . will be compelled by the authorities to do so.' To make sure that sufficient employment opportunities were available for dilatory Africans, the law permitted their services to be requisitioned from the provincial government either by government agencies or by private individuals and companies. To protect the worker, the Regulation specified that the employers were to provide adequate salaries and look after his health and living conditions. The law forbade the employer to hold back any salary or to oblige the worker to buy from the employer's store.

The regulation of 1911 preserved almost intact the provisions of the 1899 code. It limited the term of the contract to two years and provided additional penalties for employers who administered corporal punishment to their workers. Three years later, the Portuguese Republic issued a decree revoking all previous labour legislation and replacing it with an extensive document designed to correct abuses. The new code was a little softer around the edges but just as hard at the core.

> Every sound native in the Portuguese colonies is subject under this law to the moral and legal obligation of providing, by means of his work, his sustenance, and of progressively bettering his social condition.

Many provisions of the new code were intended to regulate the conduct of employers and of labour recruiters; but the law did not abolish the colonial government's role in the recruiting process, nor did it effectively control the abusive practices of the labour recruiters. Between them, the administrator and the recruiter promoted something very akin to slavery in Portuguese Africa. The new code also stressed the increased obligations of the employer in matters of transport, medical care, maintenance, salary, and instruction, but it provided no effective guarantees that these requirements were to be met. And inevitably they were not.

Nor was the reality any improvement over the ideal, although labour conditions in the first quarter of the twentieth century were a little better than they had been throughout the nineteenth. There is often a generous sensibility present in the Portuguese character, and in the face of the intolerable reality perpetuated – even encouraged – by restrictive labour codes, a number of provincial governors, men like Norton de Matos in his first term as governor-general of Angola, strove to prevent excesses, while citizens of both provinces made repeated protests in the African's defence. The tragedy was not only that the primary purpose of native-labour legislation was pursued with a vengeance, but that its positive side, which did possess a modicum of social justice and promised some small advance to the African, was neglected. There is little evidence that the African was 'civilized through work', while there is abundant evidence that he was degraded and exploited. That a similar exploitation took place in other parts of colonial Africa should give small comfort to the Portuguese and even less to their foreign critics.

The São Tomé Scandal

The continuation of a neo-slave-trade in Angola during the late nineteenth and early twentieth centuries, and the official sanction that this activity seemed to find in the labour code of 1899, involved Angola and Portugal in a controversy which has not yet been forgotten. This was the São Tomé contract-labour scandal which grew out of the Nevinson and Cadbury reports. Once again a number of influential and vocal Englishmen took up the cudgels against their country's ancient ally, this time over improper labour practices in Angola and São Tomé.

The São Tomé scandal had been simmering for forty years before it boiled over. As early as 1865 British members of the English–Portuguese Mixed Commission on Slaving had protested that Negroes were being shipped to the cocoa plantations of São Tomé and Principe. For the rest of the century complaints trickled into London of contract labourers dispatched in large quantities as steerage passengers. During the same period various Portuguese governments and newspapers demanded investigations and corrective action, and the most pointed condemnation of the process was not written by an Englishman, but by a governor of Portuguese Guinea, Judice Biker. In an article published in 1903, Biker documented the whole sordid procedure: the workers were purchased in the interior of Angola, brought in chains down to Benguela or Novo Redondo, registered by the *curador* as contract workers, and sent off to São Tomé. The contract was for five years, but at the end of the period no one ever returned. Biker described the long working day, the moist climate of the islands, the high mortality rate, the poor diet, and the cruel treatment often endured by the workers. The export figures from Angola ran from 2,000 to 4,000 people a year.

Henry W. Nevinson in *A Modern Slavery* (1906) did nothing more than elaborate in cold and angry detail the substance of the charges made by Biker and by other Portuguese and foreign critics. The difference was that Nevinson, one of the most famous correspondents of his time, had a larger, more receptive audience. Commissioned by *Harper's* to undertake an 'adventurous journey' for them, Nevinson, after talks with leaders of the Aborigines Protective Society and the British and Foreign Anti-Slavery Society, set off for Angola. And Nevinson himself was not, as the Portuguese have claimed, a trouble-maker or an international carpetbagger or a hired hand of the anti-slavery forces. He was a journalist first and foremost, and he was a good one. He got his facts right. *A Modern Slavery* has been denounced, but never satisfactorily refuted. Nevinson traced the guilt to where it belonged: with the minor official, with the chief who sold his people, with the brutal contractor, with the callous slave-driver, and with the selfish plantation men of the islands. The work was not built upon generalizations and innuendo, but it *was* calculated to shock, for Nevinson wrote with passionate purpose. Of a young African mother trying to scramble up a swaying ship's ladder from a lighter loaded with *contratados*, Nevinson wrote:

At last she reached the top, soaked with water, her blanket gone, her gaudy clothing torn off or hanging in strips, while the baby on her back, still crumpled and pink from the womb, squeaked feebly like a blind kitten. Swinging it around to her breast, she walked modestly and without complaint to her place in the row that waited the doctor's inspection. In all my life I have never heard anything so hellish as the outburst of laughter with which the ladies and gentlemen of the first class watched the slave-woman's struggle up to the deck. It was one of those things which made one doubt whether mankind has been worth the travail of our evolution.

In England, Nevinson set off a storm of controversy in a series of lectures and several articles for the *Spectator* and the *Fortnightly Review*. He found support from eminent Englishmen like Ramsay MacDonald, H. G. Wells, Gilbert Murray, and John Galsworthy, and from long-term Portuguese and foreign residents of Angola who wrote that he had understated the case. Nevinson urged his own government to make representations to the Portuguese government and suggested that chocolate manufacturers in England initiate a boycott of São Tomé cocoa. Cadbury Brothers as early as 1901 had called attention to labour conditions in São Tomé, and in 1903 William Cadbury had gone to Lisbon where the São Tomé Planters' Association and the Minister for Navy and Overseas had made light of the matter. Then Cadbury sent his own agent Joseph Burtt to Portuguese Africa in order to ascertain the facts. Burtt and Cadbury then went again to Lisbon, where the Overseas Office was sympathetic. Nothing resulted, however, whereupon the open-minded Quaker went to the Portuguese colonies himself. *Labour in Portuguese West Africa* (1909) is the account by Cadbury and Burtt of their visits and conversations with Portuguese officials. In 1909 Cadbury, two other English manufacturers, and a German firm began a boycott of São Tomé cocoa.

The controversy fed on itself. Missionary Charles Swan in *The Slavery of Today* (London, 1909) gave the results of an inquiry he had conducted – at the request of Cadbury – into forced labour in the interior. In 1913 the most scalding condemnation of all, John Harris's *Portuguese Slavery: Britain's Dilemma*, was published. Citing priests, officials, and Angolan newspapers, Harris made dramatic reference to skulls by the side of the old slave-trail, shackles, murder, and a devastated land. He stated that 70,000 to 100,000 Angolan workers had been shipped to the cocoa islands before 1908 and that not one of these had been repatriated.

In the meantime diplomatic pressure from England, the need for labour in Angola itself, and the action of colonial officials in Lisbon and Luanda had its combined effect. By 1917 almost every Angolan worker was being repatriated, and Joseph Burtt could write 'a great human drama has been acted, and it has ended happily'. But the passions aroused had left their mark. Nevinson is still the *bête noire* of Angola, a representative of what Portuguese polemicists call 'sickly English humanitarianism'. And that liberal segment of English popular opinion, long hostile to Portugal, had been reinforced in its outraged contempt for Portugal's 'slave colonies'.

Although the neo-slave-trade to São Tomé had been curbed,

labour practices in Angola remained unchanged, and the Ross Report set off another controversy. Edward Alsworth Ross, a sociologist from the University of Wisconsin, visited Angola for several months in 1925 and collected his observations in his *Report on Employment of Native Labour in Portuguese Africa*. Ross referred to work-cards with thirty-six-day months, labour stealing, senseless road-building projects, oppressive hut taxes, empty villages, and the violent corporal punishment of workers. Ross gave his Report to the Temporary Slaving Committee of the League of Nations, where it was given a careful rebuttal which argued in essence that Portuguese native policy was excellent and that Ross had been misled by prejudiced Protestant missionaries.

Moçambique at the turn of the century became an even more important source of migrant labour, although not so scandalously. The burgeoning Transvaal mining industry found in Portuguese East Africa an abundant source of cheap labour, and through various conventions between the Union of South Africa and Moçambique, the supply was regulated in return for a certain guaranteed percentage of Transvaal traffic through the port of Lourenço Marques. Thus the convention of 1928, for example, permitted the agents of the mining companies to recruit up to 80,000 Africans a year in Moçambique, and established that 47·5 per cent of Transvaal traffic should pass through the capital of Moçambique in return. Recruiting after 1903 was entrusted to the Witwatersrand Native Labour Association, the celebrated W.N.L.A. Recruiting mainly in the country below the twenty-second parallel (workers from farther north were found to be susceptible to tuberculosis in the mines), W.N.L.A. maintained a number of stations and some 250 recruiters in the colony. Working with representatives of the colonial government, W.N.L.A. was responsible for recruitment, transportation, maintenance, and repatriation.

The arrangement proved to be one of the financial supports of the colony. Not only did the traffic help make Lourenço Marques into a major port, but the colonial government also collected a fee for each labourer, who in turn brought back his wages to be spent in Moçambique. Set against these advantages were a number of drawbacks. Early in the century the mortality rate in the mines was high at 67·6 per 1,000 (one report states that from 1905 to 1912, 87,000 out of 418,000 workers, or some twenty per cent, did not return for one reason or another). There were many abuses connected with the recruitment: Portuguese officials were bribed to produce workers, as were the village chiefs. Frequently the worker's salary, much of which was withheld to be paid by the government's agents on the worker's return, disappeared.

Within Moçambique itself, a long dispute raged between the colonists who saw the province's labour-supply diminished in some areas by over fifty per cent and those administrators who defended the over-all value of the system to the colonial economy. The drain on Moçambique's labour-supply was serious, but it is difficult to believe that this labour would have been very productively employed within the colony under the exploitative labour codes of the period. Another argument held that the Portuguese African was corrupted in the mines, which allegedly did not offer the same civilizing values as did the plantations of Moçambique. Professor António Mendes Coreia, for example, asked whether it was really right for the Portuguese Negro to waste his vitality in digging gold for a handful of capitalists instead of using it at home to benefit humanity.

In no sense was the recruitment of labour in Moçambique the degrading spectacle that produced the São Tomé scandal in Angola. But almost equally disturbing was the recognition implicit in the terms of the Convention that Portuguese administrators regarded the African as a commodity, no longer to be sold as a slave, to be sure, but still to be exchanged in the market of material values. The Convention did not provide for the voluntary emigration of the worker from Moçambique into the Transvaal; in fact, it sought to prevent any such initiative by a series of controls. Nor, as Mendes Correia suggested, could the classic excuse be made that through work the African was drawn into the Portuguese community. The Moçambique–South African Convention was an international projection of contract labour, and as such it was the step-child of a centuries-old policy in Portuguese Africa which, stripped to its essentials, regarded the African as a working hand, call him slave, *liberto*, *contratado*, or what you will.

Industry, Investment, and Settlement

Anyone familiar with the pride that the Portuguese have taken in their few material triumphs in Africa – the building of a bridge, the extension of a railroad, an increase in exports – knows that they would rather talk of financial success in Angola and Moçambique than of native policy. Only in the absence of continuing economic achievement have they been driven to emphasizing their moral contributions to Africa. While it is true that in parts of the two colonies astonishing gains were registered during this period, especially in comparison with development in the preceding century, neither became the spectacular success story which Portugal had been led to expect from glowing reports on its possibilities or from temporary upsurges in its economy. Capital was reluctant to invest in Portuguese Africa; mineral deposits eluded prospecting companies; the uncertainties of world trade seemed to make large-scale agricultural ventures too risky. Genuine progress was uneven, and although by 1930 the façade of both colonies had been changed by hundreds of miles of railroad track and by bright new towns like Lobito, Beira, and Lourenço Marques, which provided visible signs of physical development, Angola and Moçambique were foundering on the verge of bankruptcy.

Since the sixteenth century Portugal's optimism over the potential wealth of Angola and Moçambique had bubbled through even the most calamitous periods in the colonies' history, and with the beginning of a seemingly new era after 1890, hopes were brighter than ever for the discovery and exploitation of this wealth. All that apparently needed to be done was to transform a trading-post mentality into an agricultural and industrial one. The tariff system only had to be overhauled, white colonization sponsored, mineral surveys made, great land companies enfranchised, the Africans taught technical skills, ports built, and a network of roads and rail lines pushed into the interior. It all seemed simple and logical enough. Somehow, the theorists of the day were sure, financial marvels could be accomplished in the colonies by a nation whose government itself at this period was passing from one crisis to another. But the transition was slow. Apart from the monopolies, the great land companies – which did not flourish – and the transit traffic through the ports of Moçambique, colonial life retained many of its traditional characteristics: petty commerce in the hands of a few traders; subsistence native agriculture; and isolated communities of Portuguese farmers and fishermen.

After the founding of the Republic, the campaign in the colonies for economic independence intensified. In 1920 a new, more liberal régime was introduced in Angola and Moçambique. No longer did the national treasury control all colonial expenditure and income. Now the provinces could administer their own finances, subject only to general supervision from Lisbon. Each colony was permitted to retain any yearly surplus in its budget and contract loans for development schemes. This last item was the more important, since the colonial income (mainly from customs duties, various stamp taxes, and the native hut tax, which alone sometimes constituted fifty per cent of the annual income) just managed to cover the costs of administration; for the number of people on the colonial payrolls – 10,000 in each colony during 1910, for example – was very large. In the early 1920s, both colonies borrowed extravagantly in order to pursue development projects. Both colonies began to run heavy trade deficits; locally-issued currency became worthless, and speculators helped destroy any confidence in the colonial economies. By 1926, Angola and Moçambique were tottering into bankruptcy, and only loans from Lisbon, which were accompanied by stringent controls over provincial finances, saved Portuguese Africa from chaos.

The colonies had attempted to go too fast on far too few resources. The only mineral deposits of importance in either territory were in the diamond mines of Angola's Lunda district. Diamang, the Companhia de Diamantes de Angola, began operations in 1920. Capitalized mostly by the Belgian and British interests of the Union Minière, it immediately became Angola's main financial support. Exempt from taxes and duties, and with the Lunda labour force at its exclusive disposal, Diamang was – and is – a small monopolistic empire. Gold and coal in Moçambique made insignificant contributions to the economy. All other mineral production existed only in the pages of reports from various survey committees. Sisal, sugar, and coffee were produced on European estates in Angola, and the fisheries along the southern coast prospered modestly, but none of these activities, nor, in fact, all of them together, could give Angola anything like a permanently prosperous outlook. In Moçambique estate agriculture was almost exclusively the business of three great land companies. Native agriculture in cereals and cotton did not expand.

Moçambique in these years was the more prosperous province, due in large part to the land companies, which made a direct contribution to the treasury and a larger indirect contribution through their paying for the cost of administering about two-thirds of Moçambique's total land area. The three chartered companies formed in the last decade of the nineteenth century were the Moçambique Company, the Niassa Company, and the Zambézia Company, the last of which did not hold a formal charter from the Portuguese government. The purpose of the companies was frankly exploratory, even speculative, as manifested by the meagre working capital in proportion to the great size of the territories granted. Their hopes lay in the discovery of substantial mineral deposits, the success of large-scale agricultural projects, and the letting of concessions within the territory. Portugal's hopes, of course, equally speculative in essence, were for the permanent occupation and colonization of the area.

The most important was the Moçambique Company, established in 1891. The company was given sovereign rights to exploit and administer the more than 62,000 square miles that made up the district of Manica and Sofala. The concession was limited to fifty years, but could be withdrawn at any time the company failed to fulfil the terms of the charter or became insolvent. Portugal received 10 per cent of the shares issued and 7·5 per cent of total net profits, in return for which she refrained from collecting taxes in the area for a period of twenty-five years. The company received a monopoly of commerce, exclusive mining concessions, the right to collect taxes (among them, the usual native head tax, the surest guarantee of a constant labour supply), sole rights of construction, banking and postal privileges, and the right to transfer land. At the termination of the contract, all land under cultivation was to remain the company's property. In return, the company committed itself to secure Portuguese interests, to protect the African population, to build schools and infirmaries, to employ Portuguese administrators, and to obey Portuguese laws.

In the same year the Niassa Company received a thirty-five-year charter for all lands in the province north of the Lùrio River. The terms were about the same, and what the English investors thought that they would get from this most underdeveloped region of the province is uncertain. They did not get much, nor did they contribute much. The third company, formed in the 1890s, the Zambézia, was the largest and the most profitable – mainly because it held some of the richest land in the colony (in the districts of Tete and Quelimane) and because it was not burdened with the political administration of its lands. The company made large long-term sub-concessions Most of the colony's sugar, sisal, and copra was produced on the lands of the Zambézia Company.

Although the *companhias majestáticas* ultimately proved a disappointment to their shareholders and even, in a lesser degree, to the Portuguese government, their contributions, especially those of the Moçambique and Zambézia Companies, were, during their short existence, of a greater significance for the colony than those of the *prazo* after three centuries. They initiated the transformation of the interior from a wilderness into a developing productive region – a process that is still in its early stages – and created conditions which permitted the slow settling of several areas by a white population. The benefits that the Africans have derived from their presence, on the other hand seem less than negligible.

Much of Moçambique's development was also based on two rail lines and two ports whose construction was for the most part carried out in the early twentieth century. Lourenço Marques, which had become the capital of the province in 1898, was transformed from a feverish little community into a modern European city with an international tourist clientele. Its deep-water berths, which made it one of the first ports in East Africa, served an ever-increasing traffic, most of which was destined for the Transvaal. Up the coast, Beira became, with the construction of a rail line into the Rhodesias and later up into Nyasaland, the principal port for these two regions of the continent. By 1915 Beira's port traffic had risen to 200,000 tons, and the small city had taken on that spacious Anglo-Portuguese air so startling to European visitors.

In Angola the transition was slower. Luanda was, in 1905, 'bankrupt and beautiful', while Benguela slept in memory of better days. The dramatic change in both cities has only taken place in recent years. In 1903 construction was begun on the most remarkable of African rail lines, the Benguela Railway. One of Rhodes's associates, Robert Williams, obtained a ninety-nine-year concession to build a line from Lobito to the Katanga frontier, where his Tanganyika Concessions held important mineral rights. For twenty-five years the attention of Angola was fixed on the progress of the line up to the Bié plateau and across Hungry Country to the Congo frontier. Eighty per cent of the cost of construction came from British sources. As a colonizing force, the Benguela Railway soon began to make its contribution with scores of small towns sprouting in the interior of the colony. It was to make Lobito the most important port in Angola. Elsewhere, a line was built from Luanda back into Malange, and a railroad begun from the southern port of Moçâmedes up toward Sá da Bandeira. Under the driving direction of Norton de Matos, thousands of miles of road were laid across Angola, giving reasonable access for the first time to most regions of the colony.

Portugal, however, had no more success in attracting immigrants to Africa than it had in attracting heavy capital investment. Plans, polemics, and promotion schemes all yielded the same empty results. The largest immigrant group remained the Thirstland Trekkers, some 300 Boers, under the leadership of Jakobus Botha, who arrived at Humpata on the Huíla plateau in 1880. The Portuguese government, traditionally sensitive to the presence of denationalizing forces in its African colonies, felt mixed emotions: it regarded the newcomers with natural suspicion but welcomed any useful allies in the work of developing the *planalto*. Some of the Boers became successful farmers around Humpata, others migrated up toward the Hungry Country and disappeared into the Belgian Congo, while others went down to the coast. As fighters in the wars of pacification and as wagon drivers, whose massive ten- and twelve-team oxcarts made some of the pioneer roads in Angola, they gave invaluable service to the colony. But the Trekkers were never really happy in Angola; their sense of isolation in a Catholic Portuguese-speaking community, and various governmental restrictions on their use of firearms, led many of them in 1928–9 to return to the Union.

The presence of the Boers led to an intensification in the 1880s of plans for direct settlement in southern Angola. Impoverished families of peasants and workers were recruited in all parts of Portugal and sent to Huíla to help insulate the Boer community. The indiscriminately chosen settlers were thereupon almost forgotten. The union between Portuguese and Boer never came to pass, but Huíla with time became itself the most Portuguese region of Angola, its small farms replicas of those in Portugal and Madeira. By 1913 an estimated 2,500 Portuguese were residing in the vicinity of Lubango (Sá da Bandeira).

From 1900 to 1930 Portugal failed in all efforts at enticing direct colonization, unable to divert the flood of Portuguese emigration to Brazil. In 1908, 36,262 emigrants went to Brazil and 15 to Africa; in 1912, 74,860 to Brazil and 90 to Africa; in 1920, 33,651 to Brazil and 1,153 to Africa; in 1925, 13,280 to

Brazil, and 290 to Africa; and in 1928, 27,705 to Brazil and 189 to Africa. By subsidy, by grants of land, and by publicity, the Overseas Council tried to coax at least some of these emigrants into Africa, but only a very few could be persuaded to face what they correctly sensed would be a rigorous life in Angola and Moçambique. The cautious Portuguese worker, though diligent, was neither imaginative nor adventurous, and of the handful who did go to Africa, most, confused and dissatisfied, returned home or went to live in Luanda or Lourenço Marques. The immigration figures are, however, somewhat deceptive, since they represent only the number of Portuguese citizens who directly migrated. Other Portuguese, Civil Servants, employees on construction and agricultural projects, and a few professional and businessmen, took up permanent residence in Africa. Of Angola's estimated three million inhabitants in 1929–30, perhaps 50,000 were white and mestiços. Of Moçambique's population of almost four million in 1928, some 35,000 were non-African (17,800 whites, 900 Chinese, 8,500 Indians, and 8,350 mestiços). Both provinces continued to be depositories for convicts and political exiles. That crucial segment of the white population, the Portuguese woman, showed a slow steady increase, but an equally vital segment, that of the teachers and doctors, remained pitifully inadequate except in the cities and mission centres.

During the first three decades of this century, the complexion of life changed, gradually, almost imperceptibly, for both the African and Portuguese inhabitants. Northern Angola and southern Moçambique still had untrammelled frontiers, but modern transportation and an expanding colonial administration made Angola and Moçambique semi-coherent units of government, where before there had been only patches of authority in the wilderness. Inevitably the colonies began to lose their romantic reality and to become white settlements, estates to be administered and exploited, not always efficiently, by European techniques for the advantage of the European population. The multi-racial myth now began to dissolve. The lines of contact between the African and the Portuguese, in the cities and in the embalas, now began to separate. Not only were Beira and Lourenço Marques

European cities, but in the interior the new little towns which sprang up along the rail lines had their own Portuguese communities. The African lived apart, in his village or in the city's sprawling slums. Still only a tendency at this period, this characteristic of life in Angola and Moçambique was to assume more definite racist shape with each passing decade. And beyond the points of social contact, the mass of the African population lived as it had done for centuries, in poverty, disease, and ignorance, its chief contact with the Portuguese world being the necessity to pay the white man his tax and to furnish his labour.

Part 3: The Present

6 Theory and Reality

The history of contemporary Portuguese Africa is as much a study of colonial philosophy as it is an account of administrative and economic action in Angola and Moçambique. Certainly no Portuguese government has worked as diligently as Premier Salazar's '*Estado Novo* – New State' in planning and publicizing its overseas policy and in creating a colonial mystique from the values of the past and the promises of the future. But from 1930, when the Colonial Act – a statement of policy by the New State – was published, until the mid 1940s, the principal concerns of the government were the stabilization of the national economy, the conflict in neighbouring Spain, and then the Second World War. During this period, the colonial effort was largely an attempt to revive an imperial consciousness, to bolster as cheaply as possible faith in the African colonies at home and abroad, and to make the colonies pay their own way. While many of the programmes evolved in those years had already been effected by the end of the 1940s, Portugal seemed rather to be laying the philosophic, economic, and administrative foundations on which to base the full-scale development of Angola and Moçambique in the 1950s. There has been a strong continuity underlying Portugal's colonial policies during the last thirty years, and the various laws and programmes devised in the earlier period were more than a prelude to action; they were an indispensable and integral part of Portuguese decisions in the last critical decade.

The Vision of the Third Empire

Paradoxically, at almost no time in their history were Angola and

Moçambique greater liabilities or greater assets to the metropolis. They composed one of the many problems that the short-lived Republic passed on to the dictatorship in 1926. (Salazar joined the government permanently in 1928 as Finance Minister, to become Premier in 1932.) They were liabilities because in these depression years they were a burden and drain on national energies, and assets because they were a living link with the past and formed the bulk of an empire which still made Portugal something more than an insignificant force in the world. No other aspect of Portugal's history offered such abundant examples of patriotic abstractions (Duty, Faith, and Humanity) to the country's nationalistic pamphleteers. A succession of colonial heroes from Prince Henry to Mousinho de Albuquerque, the Congo experiment, the work of the missions, and exploits of exploration and conquest, all contributed to the re-shaping of a colonial mentality. Angola and Moçambique were simultaneously live exhibits in a museum of memories and a direct challenge to the new government. Portugal was again determined to demonstrate – theoretically at first, through a barrage of legislation and publicity – that she was capable of re-creating what her spokesmen held to be the glories of her African past, capable of showing that the Portuguese colonial tradition was a vital and successful force in the development of Africa: Armindo Monteiro, Minister of Colonies, wrote in the early 1930s:

In Portugal we now feel that we are so much the legitimate heirs of a great tradition that the generation of today is entitled to invoke the past, not as a remembrance of dead things, but as a source of inspiration for the future.

The new imperial mentality was defined by Jorge Ameal, one of the New State's many publicists, in terms of three elements: geography, heroism, and trade. First:

. . . the notion of vast territories over which . . . our flag flies. . . . It is the knowledge that our sovereignty as a small European state spreads prodigiously over three continents and is summed up in the magnificent certainty that we are the third colonial power.

Then:

. . . the evocation of our epic as sailors and warriors . . . who, moved by a sacred impulse, carried to the ends of the world our ships, our dominion – and our faith. In this heroic element is contained the most noble sentiment of our mission as a chosen people, since the task of civilizing must have, above all else, a spiritual content.

And thirdly:

. . . the sum of our efforts and the hardships of our expeditionaries, to take from distant lands their hidden riches and the founding in remote lands of centres of production and profit.

As it had done for centuries, nationalistic sentiment found inspiration in Camões's *Lusíadas*, '. . . the symbol of the moral unity of the Empire, whose discovery and conquest for civilization it sings in imperishable lines. . . .'

In the fanciful elaborations of Lisbon colonialists during the 1930s, the terms 'neo-imperialism' and 'Third Empire' recurred frequently as definitions of Portugal's policies and possessions. Portuguese imperialism, past and present, was held to be different from the common or garden variety of European imperialism, since it was characterized not by 'exploitation, often iniquitous, by oppression of a vanquished people, or by systematic devastation, but by altruism, abnegation, faith, and a historic responsibility of civilization'.

At the same time, however, the Third Empire was not to be the muddled humanitarian creation of the nineteenth-century liberals.

Empire and Liberty were incompatible concepts. Empire means Authority – and there is no Authority where Power is divided and diluted. It is the duty of the New State to re-establish the force of Power. With it will be revived all the power-concepts of the Past. One of these power-concepts was the unity of territory and of the Grail, as though there were no seas or races separating the constituent elements of the national Whole.

So wrote another spokesman for the régime, Dr António Leite de Magalhães.

Of all the theories publicized by the Salazar government in

the evolution of its colonial mystique, none has been more consistently advanced than the vision of a Pan-Lusitanian community, geographically scattered over the globe but held together by spiritual bonds peculiar to Portuguese culture. As Dr Salazar put it:

> By the same national criterion . . . without distinction of geographic situation . . . we administer and direct the Portuguese colonies. . . . We are a juridical and political unity.

The idea of a Third Empire was mostly a paper concoction, useful for purposes of propaganda and prestige. But the government's statements on the sense of unity existing between the colonies and the metropolis did have some genuine foundations in past colonial policy and in the national psychology (the close sentimental ties which still bind the Brazilian republic to Portugal furnish perhaps the best example of this attachment to the metropolis). This aspect of the Portuguese personality was magnified, of course, to serve several political causes in the 1930s; emphasizing the spiritual cohesion of the colonies was originally an attempt to arouse interest at home in the overseas provinces and to convince the Portuguese overseas that the new régime did not consider them second-class citizens. It was also an argument advanced in compensation for the slow material progress of the colonies; it would be vigorously employed later to confront the advocates of African autonomy. There was not much evidence, however, that the native peoples in the colonies shared this psychic reality.

In trying to popularize its colonial ideals and to arouse Portuguese interest in Africa, the Salazar government was facing the same problem that other governments had faced in the 1870s. The impetus given colonial affairs by the nineteenth-century explorers, the English ultimatum, and the generation of 1895, did not survive the 1920s, and for most Portuguese the popular image of Africa was one of a far and dangerous place inhabited by Negroes and exiles. Statements that Angola and Moçambique were only distant fragments of Portugal were not always convincing. The new imperial consciousness could not be formed out of ignorance and a lack of interest. Street-names and commemorative stamps, celebrating ancient warriors or exotic butterflies, were not enough. In the words of Vieira Machado, Colonial Minister in the late 1930s, 'To colonize is, in the final analysis, to teach and educate.'

As one part of its campaign of education, the government soon began to subsidize a growing list of publications on the overseas world, some popular, some scholarly. The Portuguese Press, which did not have much interest in Africa, was persuaded to take a greater interest, and Portuguese journalists were taken on junkets to Angola and Moçambique. To promote a literature on colonial themes – historically one of the richest traditions in Portuguese culture – the colonial propaganda office (the Agência Geral das Colónias) began to offer annual prizes in order 'to stimulate those writers who dedicate themselves to the study of overseas problems and those writers whose works are printed in the colonies'. These contests, however, with others sponsored by colonial newspapers, failed to raise the level of colonial literature. A lack of interest in the colonies by Portuguese intellectuals, and the stultifying attitude of the Salazar régime itself toward artistic production, were two deterrents. A semblance of colonial literature did nonetheless come into existence, but it was largely an impressionistic fiction, lushly exotic – and erotic – to which a small number of mulattos and assimilated Africans made contributions.

The historical and scientific literature, directly or indirectly supported by the government and various quasi-official organizations, has been more significant. Many valuable scientific and historical publications on Africa have been subsidized during the last thirty years. Several of the authors have been graduates of the Escola Colonial Superior (now the Institute for Overseas Studies) which was consolidated with the colonial administration. The Escola had functioned desultorily since its founding early in the century, and now it became a centre for advanced colonial studies, to instruct the élite of the nation in the special methods of Portuguese colonial action and to prepare a cadre of young officers for overseas service. At the same time the New

State sought to produce in secondary-school and university students an awareness of Africa, out of which, the government hoped, there might come an increased immigration of educated men and women into Angola and Moçambique. In spite of indoctrination in the schools, however, a series of summer cruises to Africa for university students, and the 'challenge to the adventurous spirit of Portuguese youth', the campaign was not very successful.

As a final gesture of solidarity between Portugal and Africa, the Salazar régime began to send high government officials on visits to the African territories. The Colonial Ministers have paid regular visits; in 1938 President Carmona went to Angola, and a year later to Moçambique; and in 1954 and 1956 President Craveiro Lopes made the trip. These visits have all been well-arranged tours, not only emphasizing the oneness of the Portuguese world, but serving in addition as useful deadlines for the completion of major projects. Thus each important visit has been attended by the inauguration of a dam, an airport, a colonization scheme, or a school. *Vilas* have been raised to the rank of cities, colonial fairs and exhibits have abounded, and African delegations from every part of the colony have been rounded up to greet the distinguished guest with declarations of loyal solidarity. And, of course, there have been the inevitable speeches. With these words the Governor of Manica and Sofala greeted Craveiro Lopes at Beira in 1956:

Here we are after more than four and a half centuries, here we are engaged today more than ever on a great and successful task. Taming the wilderness, building towns and making them prosper, teaching, educating, and leading to a better life the rude mass of natives, disciplining their rudimentary instincts. . . . moulding their souls in the superior forms of Christianity, administering them justice with affectionate understanding. . . . A task, or I should say, a mission, vast, difficult, and exhausting, but noble and dignifying as few are. It is our historical vocation emerging once again. . . . Everything indicates that we are on the verge of a new era, a decisive phase of History, of our History, that we have ahead of us, a great, auspicious, and attainable future. . . . Everything is for the common good and aggrandisement of the mother country.

It is difficult to gauge the extent to which the New State's colonial mystique has been a logical projection of Portuguese attitudes and aspirations, for the Portuguese themselves are not the least nationalistic of peoples and it has long been their custom to use hyperbole when discussing their colonial empire. Unquestionably the government's propaganda has produced its fair share of nonsense and official cant, developed during the early 1930s, in which all linguistic contact with reality has been suffocated. But to isolate the genuine from the spurious, the traditional Portuguese colonial sentiment from the synthetic abstractions sponsored by the present régime, is a tricky task, for not only did the New State's mystique make its influence felt in all colonial legislation – it had its origin in the Colonial Act of 1930 – but it became the language of communication for most overseas administrators and influenced their conduct and thinking. In the popular mind, as well, much of the government's colonial credo struck a responsive chord, although there were old colonists in Angola and Moçambique who were cynical of a colonial administration which, in their regard, was more concerned with verbalism than practical achievement in the African provinces.

Administration under Salazar

The spirit of the Salazar government's neo-imperialism was not only present in speeches and programmes designed to whip up interest in the colonies, it also pervaded all overseas legislation dating from the Colonial Act of 1930; in fact, these laws were often the source for much of the theorizing on Portugal's role as a colonizing power. (Thus, in the preamble to one piece of legislation: 'The development of spiritual relations between the metropolis and the overseas provinces shall be promoted for their mutual knowledge and *rapprochement* in all aspects of intellectual life; thus all institutions diffusing Portuguese culture in the overseas provinces should be protected and subsidized'.) At the same time the colonial laws reflected the sternly authoritarian attitude of the government and were of a piece with the new Portuguese Constitution of 1933 and similar metropolitan legislation. It was logical that an administration which exalted morality, the family, and the privilege of the Portuguese majority to be poor, should have sought to disseminate the same virtues in the colonies.

The Colonial Act of 1930 was the work of Salazar, who served briefly as Minister of Colonies in that year, and his successor Armindo Monteiro. The Act set forth general principles for the conduct of affairs overseas. It provided for the unification of administration in the hands of the state; the normalization of colonial rule and the end of high commissionerships (the Republic's equivalent of governorships-general); and the nationalization of colonial economies. It prohibited the use of forced labour by private companies and reiterated the necessity for employers to pay the African for his work. Finally, it stressed the duty of colonial administrators to sustain the sovereignty of Portugal. The aim of the Colonial Act was to reverse the trend of the 1920s toward financial and political autonomy and to enable Portugal to put forth to the world the picture of a united imperial front. Most subsequent legislation, particularly the Organic Charter of 1933, was a definition of these general principles. The Act itself was modified in some detail in 1935 and 1945 and was, with further changes, incorporated in 1951 into the Portuguese Constitution.

For the defenders of the New State at home and abroad the Colonial Act appeared an inspiring affirmation of Portugal's destiny, the emergence of a New Rome, 'the calling of the colonies to closer communion with continental Portugal and a sternly vigorous declaration of Portugal's intentions to maintain and perpetuate the legacy of history'. The reaction in the colonies was somewhat more reserved, especially among the long-time white residents who took a more limited view of the Act and later legislation. Their argument was, and is, that the natural development of Angola and Moçambique had been curtailed and that the metropolis had returned to the traditional policy of milking the colonies for the profit of Portugal. To meet these complaints, a certain amount of administrative latitude has in recent years been given to colonial administrators, and the consultative authority of the provincial Legislative Councils has been increased.

Administrative divisions in Angola and Moçambique have undergone various changes since 1930; the purpose of the change has been to extend Lisbon's authority more effectively into the remoter areas of the territories and to expedite the transmission of that authority. The last important regrouping took place in 1956 – after the colonies had become overseas provinces again. The following are the districts (with their capitals in parentheses) of Angola and Moçambique:

ANGOLA

Cabinda (Cabinda)
Congo (Uige)
Luanda (Luanda)
Cuanza Norte (Vile Salazar)
Cuanza Sul (Malange)
Lunda (Henrique de Carvalho)
Benguela (Benguela)
Huambo (Nova Lisboa)
Bié-Cuando-Cubango (Silva Porto)
Moxico (Vila Luso)
Moçâmedes (Moçâmedes)
Huíla (Sá da Bandeira)

MOÇAMBIQUE

Lourenço Marques (Lourenço Marques)
Gaza (Vila João Belo)
Inhambane (Inhambane)
Manica e Sofala (Beira)
Tete (Tete)
Zambézia (Quelimane)
Moçambique (Nampula)
Cabo Delgado (Porto Amélia)
Niassa (Vila Cabral)

Each district is divided into a varying number of circumscriptions, each with its subdivision into posts, where the so-called indigenous element predominates, and into *concelhos*, where a civilized population predominates.

It was the New State's intention that the source of all important colonial authority should reside with three bodies in Lisbon: the National Assembly, the Council of Ministers, and the Colonial (or Overseas) Ministry. The Assembly has played a modest role in colonial policy, serving only to legislate the proposals it has received from the Overseas Ministry through the Council of Ministers and to review the colonies' yearly reports. Among its members are deputies elected from Angola and Moçambique, but since these men need not be residents of the colonies and have been candidates chosen by the government for election, their influence on colonial conduct is usually as negligible as that of the Assembly's other members.

The Portuguese government (i.e. the Council of Ministers) acts in a general executive capacity on overseas affairs: it may legislate by decree; it must approve the negotiating of colonial loans and foreign concessions; it appoints and dismisses colonial governors; it effectively controls, through various commissions and boards, the economic life of Angola and Moçambique. The Overseas Ministry is responsible for the administrative functioning of Portuguese Africa in most of its ramifications, such as native policy, personnel, police (though not military) authority, missionary affairs, and some juridical matters. It is the Overseas Minister who, theoretically, 'superintends, directs, orients, coordinates, and controls on the highest level all overseas administration'. The Minister may consult with the Overseas Council or the Overseas Governors' Conference, but their influence is not important. The Minister keeps in contact with the problems of each colony through a corps of inspectors without administrative authority.

The supreme authority in Angola and Moçambique is the governor-general, charged with representing and maintaining political unity. More often than not during the last thirty years he has been a military man. Appointed to a four-year term, the governor-general possesses extensive powers and responsibilities to administer the colony under the terms of the colonial laws. He is charged with the appointment and conduct of much of the colonial bureaucracy; he is the financial authority, controlling expenditures and preparing for Lisbon's approval the colonial budget; he is in a general way responsible for the care, protection, and guidance of the indigenous population. In practice the particulars of these tasks are delegated to three chief associates, the secretary-general and two provincial secretaries. He is obliged to consult twice a year with the local Legislative Council, the majority of whose members are elected from carefully prepared electoral rolls. (The Legislative Council represents many interests – the Church, labour, business – but not one member directly represents African interests.) In each district there is a governor whose authority and responsibility are the equivalent, on a smaller scale, of those of the governor-general.

The administrator of the circumscription is the most important figure in the local administration, except for the governor-general, 'representing, in the middle of the native population, the sovereignty of the nation, the authority of the Republic, the order, the dignity, and the justice of Portuguese civilization'. In less abstract terms he is still the white chief envisioned by Enes and Costa, for he, and his *chefes de posto*, are the officers in most immediate contact with the people who constitute more than ninety-seven per cent of the population in both colonies. He is registry officer, judge, tax collector, protector of the African, and, in many circumscriptions, native-labour coordinator and supply officer. To fill the positions of administrator and chief of post the Salazar régime attempted, as other governments had done, to attract men of zeal, honesty, and competence to the Civil Service. In this, the government has not been entirely successful, but it is generally agreed that the quality and efficiency of Portuguese administrators has improved over the past thirty years. Although lately several assimilated Africans have been moved into the middle echelons of the colonial bureaucracy, their number is very small.

Integrated into the administrative hierarchy as auxiliaries are various native officials, the sepoys who form an African police force, the interpreters, the counsellors, and the *régulos*. Completely subservient to the administrator, the *régulo*, or village chief, is supposed to maintain local order, keep the Portuguese apprised of village happenings, assist in the collection of taxes, and persuade his people to fulfil their labour obligations.

Through this formidable administrative service, the authority of the government extends directly from the Overseas Ministry to the individual African in the hinterland. In terms of native policy, this has meant that the activities of the African population have been under close control, if not actual surveillance; it was one of several reasons why the Portuguese could boast, until 1961, that their overseas provinces were the most peaceful and secure areas in the continent. In terms of colonial development, political and economic, this bureaucratic channelling of authority, with its checks on almost every form of local initiative, has been considered by many to be a discouraging and restricting force.

Equality, Race, and the Assimilado

Ultimately the purpose of the colonial mystique and the close administrative control of Portuguese Africa was to implement a native policy. Although in practice the New State has been primarily interested in the economic viability of Angola and Moçambique, and has spent the larger share of its budget and efforts on behalf of the white populations, in theory it has professed to be above all concerned with the welfare and the assimilation of the Africans. In the late 1940s and through most of the 1950s, the colonies became what Portugal had long wanted them to become, productive white men's colonies. But for Africans the change of government in distant Lisbon had small significance. Theory remained theory, while practice and tradition were dignified by being called policy.

Until 1930 native policy was only incidental to the administration and exploitation of Angola and Moçambique. The African majority was ignored, enslaved, or 'pacified', depending upon the necessities of the age, and Portuguese actions and attitudes were based on little more than expediency. But since the New State's total overseas policy was theoretically for the social, as well as the economic, integration of Portuguese Africa, a battery of philosophic precepts and administrative forms had to be devised to explain and, perhaps, promote the goal of cultural assimilation, advertised as the answer to Africanism and the ultimate hope for European colonialism.

The policy was alleged to have its roots in the colonizing traditions of the Portuguese in Africa. Looking back across the centuries, what *really* were these heralded traditions? They were not much more than the pattern of behaviour followed by a handful of Europeans who barely survived 400 years of African vicissitudes.

Survival resulted more from the ability of the white inhabitants to maintain an uncertain *modus vivendi* with the Africans than it did from any of Lisbon's efforts to transplant European cultural values. The condition of the colonies in the mid nineteenth century is sufficient evidence of Portugal's luck of success in expanding either her political or cultural authority over the Bantu peoples. Apart from Luanda and the town of Moçambique, administrative centres more or less constantly refreshed by contact with Portugal or other Portuguese colonies, no focus of white activity in 1900 could boast a continuous history of importance. The soldier or trader in the interior lived a precarious existence, subduing the nearby African villagers in good years and trying to trade or negotiate with them in bad, but almost always mingling his blood with theirs. (The history of the interior in both territories is as much the assimilation of the Portuguese by the Africans as it is the reverse.) While the Portuguese did not always accept the Africans with whom they came into close contact as equals, they were usually willing to accept them, to trade with them, and to allow them to hold minor administrative or ecclesiastical offices. This was the assimilated element, and very small it was; the rest of the population, the almost total majority, was simply viewed as a potential commodity or labour force. This is the essential reality of the native policy practised by the Portuguese in Africa. It is all which properly lends itself to transcendental discussions. All other talk of civilizing missions, or inappropriate references to Brazil, is sheer fantasy.

The New State's native policy apparently considered it necessary to reach the goal of cultural equality by establishing a régime of clear administrative inequality. A *régime do indigenato* was set up in Portuguese Guinea, Moçambique, São Tomé, and Angola. Article 22 of the Colonial Act provided:

Attention will be paid in the colonies to the stage of evolution of the native populations, and there shall be special statutes for natives, which under the authority of Portuguese public and private law, shall establish juridical reulations for them in keeping with their individual, domestic, and social uses and customs, provided these are not incompatible with morality and the dictates of humanity.

Thus the population of Portuguese Africa was divided into two judicial categories: the *indígenas* (the unassimilated native Africans) and the *não-indígenas* (whites and the assimilated African or mulattoes). In practice, a third category, that of the assimilated African, or *assimilado*, was commonly recognized if not legally sanctioned, although the assimilated African was supposed to be, and in terms of civic privileges was considered, 'non-indigenous'. For the vast majority of the Africans (about ninety-eight per cent) it was rule under the *regime do indigenato*; for the minority, there were the doubtful rights and privileges of citizenship in Salazar's Portugal.

Lest the bald implications of this crucial decision stand out too nakedly, colonial legislation was clothed in fine rhetorical silk. The purpose of the policy, it was explained, was to eliminate the *indígena* as a separate element in a colonial population which was to seek its ultimate identity with Portugal. As usual, the past seemed to offer abundant example. As Bahia dos Santos, a contemporary commentator on Portuguese colonialism, wrote:

> The traditional concern for the improvement of native peoples as a factor in the progress of the human condition . . . has always constituted one of the fundamental characteristics of our overseas policy. . . . Endowed by nature with exceptional qualities of sympathy and attachment for their fellow men, the Portuguese were fortified in these sentiments by the sublime doctrine of Christ. . . . The gradual integration, or assimilation, which today is said to have been the characteristic of Portuguese native policy in the earliest days of our overseas action, was nothing more, therefore, than a way of following the dictates of our moral and religious sentiments. It is a question then of a native policy more spontaneous than deliberate. . . . Only much later, in the face of techniques adopted by other colonizing powers, techniques which could not serve us as an example without going fundamentally against our characteristics of social behaviour, does this attitude arise as a body of doctrines which today is called Portuguese native policy.

Morais Cabral wrote in 1939:

> Our whole policy has been and continues to be to improve the cultural, economic, and social level of the Negro . . . to drag him from his

ignorance and backwardness, to try to make of him a rational and honourable individual, worthy of the Lusitanian community.

Protection of the African, a detached humanitarianism, or an anthropological interest in his customs was not sufficient justification for a native policy in the New State's view. The creative quality of Portugal's work in Africa was that it drew the African peoples into a modern Christian community, gradually replacing their tribal values with the more substantial ones (i.e. the importance of the Christian family and the dignity of labour) of Portuguese society. The insignificant trickle of Africans who had been converted or assimilated into Portuguese society in the past did not seem to colonial theorists a valid argument against the use of tradition as a foundation of native policy.

By assimilation, however, the New State did not originally mean, as government spokesmen pointed out repeatedly in the 1930s and 1940s, *assimilação uniformizadora*, the Liberal's nineteenth-century ideal of granting to the native populations legal status and protection as Portuguese citizens. Such a policy was regarded as hare-brained philanthropy, and much of the régime's early admiration for Enes and Mousinho was because they led resistance to such liberal colonial policies. But just as the New State had made 'colonies' into 'provinces' in 1951 by the stroke of a pen, so, in 1961, in the urgency created by the war in Angola, the government, as we shall see, was obliged to return to the much-scorned policy of general assimilation that had originated in the previous century.

Much of the legislation concerned with native policy has been a mere continuation of the *Estatuto político civil e criminal dos indígenas das colónias de Angola e Moçambique*. Drawn up in 1926 by Colonial Minister João Belo, an Enes admirer, the law, according to a colonial theoretician, J. M. da Silva Cunha, was dominated by two ideas:

> One is to guarantee the natural and unconditional rights of the native whose tutelage is confided to us ... and to assure the gradual fulfilment of his moral and legal obligations to work, to be educated, and to improve himself. ... The other is to lead the natives, by means

appropriate to their rudimentary civilization ... to the profitable development of their own activities and to their integration into the life of the colony, which is an extension of the mother country. The natives are not granted, because of the lack of practical application, the rights associated with our own constitutional institutions.

The Statute of 1926, a similar statute in 1929, the Colonial Act, the Imperial Organic Charter of 1933, and the Overseas Administrative Reform Act of the same year defined, and in some cases determined, Portugal's native policy until the early 1950s.

In stressing the traditional Portuguese sentiments of racial equality and at the same time devising a policy founded on theories of cultural inequality, the Portuguese government was walking a conceptual tightrope. In reality, it was temporizing. Although the administrative machinery of the New State made it possible to set up a fairly close control over the African population, whose customs the government professed to respect but whose local authority had been irrevocably broken, the task of educating, or 'civilizing', the Africans in Angola and Moçambique could only have been regarded as a near impossibility by the most optimistic colonialist. Quite apart from the grinding abuse of African labour, the poverty of Portugal, the economic backwardness of the colonies, the lack of minimal educational or medical facilities, and the absence of technical personnel all made the goal of assimilation in the 1930s and 1940s a legislative dream. Hence the reiterated precautions that the government had to proceed slowly, that the evolution of the African to a civilized condition was a process requiring centuries (the examples of other areas in the world notwithstanding), that native problems had to be studied and carefully considered before any constructive policy was implemented. Hence the emphasis on the spiritual, not material, values of Portuguese culture. Hence the safety-valve of individual or selective assimilation, which had served Portuguese interests so well in the past. The purpose of colonial legislation and its often eloquent defences was really nothing more, in spite of its humanitarian language and its proposals for social and economic services, than an attempt to maintain the *status quo* of centuries.

To obtain the status of *assimilado*[1] (i.e. to be certified as 'civilized' or 'Europeanized', and thus to become a Portuguese citizen), the African had to measure up to difficult and stringently applied standards. The applicant had to be eighteen years of age and prove his ability to speak Portuguese. He had to demonstrate that he earned sufficient income for himself and his family. He had to be of good character and possess those qualities necessary for the exercise of the public and private rights of the Portuguese citizen. He had to submit a birth certificate, a certificate of residence, a certificate of good health, a declaration of loyalty, and two testimonies of his good character. In addition he had to be able to pay various fees and petty taxes which amounted to from ten to twenty pounds. The wife and children of the *assimilado* could also acquire citizenship if they spoke Portuguese and could demonstrate their good character. These formalities could be waived and the *bilhete de identidade* issued to any African who exercised a public charge, who was a member of the colonial administrative corps, who had a secondary-school education, or who was a licensed merchant or certified businessman. The *assimilado* was freed from the restrictions besetting his unassimilated neighbour. He could travel without permission; he did not have to pay the head tax; he was exempted from contract labour; he could, theoretically, receive the same pay as a European in the same government position; he could vote.

The 1950 census in Angola recorded some 30,000 *assimilados* out of a population of four million people; Moçambique's population of 5,733,000 contained 4,353 *assimilados*. (São Tomé and Principe, however, had more than fifty per cent of the island's 60,000 listed as 'civilized' and in 1953 the *regime do indigenato* was abolished with the mission declared accomplished.) Over the last ten years there has been no significant increase in these figures.

1. In 1953 the status of *assimilado* was abolished, although the term is still widely used, and the benefits of full Portuguese citizenship granted to assimilated Africans. At the same time, however, the new statute allowed for the revocation of citizenship granted to Africans should they fail to comport themselves in a manner deemed proper by the authorities. This left-handed gift naturally aroused many suspicions in the minds of would-be *assimilados*.

A system as selective as assimilation, which in a period of thirty years affected the legal status of less than one half of one per cent of the African population, had little to recommend it as a goal of native policy – unless the purpose of the policy was to maintain the degraded status of the greater part of the population. These embarrassing figures and the division of the colonial population into the categories of *indígena* and *não-indígena* obviously gave an altogether too accurate appearance of cultural racism and inequality, and gradually in the 1950s the ground was prepared for the time when pressures from outside the colonies would force a seeming revision of Portugal's native policy, with the abolition of distinctions which clearly contradicted Portugal's affirmations of cultural unity. Speeches in the Assembly, the transferring of some colonial authority from the Overseas Ministry to other Ministries, small changes in colonial laws, the increase in the number of *concelhos*, and much theorizing over the transition stage from tribalism to civilization made it clear that the Salazar government was leading up to its 'momentous' decision of 1961.

Law and Administrative Control

To assimilate the rest of the African population of Angola and Moçambique, and to raise the standard of living to a level where the process would involve the largest number of the provinces' inhabitants, the New State evolved a series of programmes designed to affect every aspect of African life. To a large extent these programmes were a continuation and intensification of previous efforts, and they demonstrated again the difficulty that Portugal has always had in obtaining positive material results from her specific policies in Africa.

The judicial system under the *regime do indigenato* is one of the least-well-defined aspects of Portugal's native policy. In the absence of native legal codes, and any satisfactory compilations of customary law, a makeshift arrangement has come into being under which the administrator or the chief of post acts as a sort of justice in all civil suits between Africans. (In civil suits between an *indígena* and a *não-indígena*, Portuguese civil law generally applies.) In his mediations the officer is assisted by one or two Africans, usually clerks or policemen, who act as interpreters and give advice on local traditions. On this basis the officer should try to make a judgement consistent with custom and Portuguese policy.

Portuguese law applies in all criminal cases, and the metropolitan penal code, with small modifications, operates for the whole population of Portuguese Africa. Minor crimes, either civil or criminal, are usually punished by correctional work sentences or by the *palmatório*, a beating on the palms of the hands, since, consistent with their concept of the African as an occasionally unruly child, Portuguese officials believe in the use of corporal punishment. For more serious crimes Africans are sent to penal camps or exiled to remote parts of their own or another province. Often they are severely beaten. Sometimes the prisoner, particularly if his alleged crimes have been of a political nature, simply disappears. These were the procedures generally followed in the quieter years before 1960.

The inadequate legal apparatus has never implied any lack of control over the indigenous population. Through an administrative system which has usually functioned quite efficiently on the native level, through native labour laws, and through the necessity for every male *indígena* to possess a *caderneta* (a passbook), a fairly close surveillance has been kept over the peoples of each province. In each village the Portuguese have usually had an informer. The most effective control was established through the *caderneta*, which contains the tax and labour record of the bearer as well as the names of the members of his family, with photographs and fingerprint identification. The bearer must show his *caderneta* on demand to officials and must have it appropriately stamped before he moves from one part of the province to another. Should he lose his papers or should they fail to be in order, the African may be sentenced to correctional labour. The repressions associated with the *caderneta* have been one of the causes of the considerable migration of Africans from Angola and Moçambique into neighbouring territories.

Any organization of Africans has been regarded with

disfavour by the colonial administration, although the government has sponsored certain social societies and agricultural cooperatives. But any organization with political or tribal overtones has been quickly suppressed and its leaders arrested. The only Africanist newspaper, *O brado africano* of Lourenço Marques, has had its political substance diluted. In large urban areas, where thousands of rootless Africans exist in poverty and filth, and the crime-rate constantly increases, the colonial government has been doubly careful to ferret out the beginnings of dissent. Luanda and Lobito, ports enjoying contact with free African countries, have been regarded as particularly dangerous.

The Realities of a Rural Society

It was with the countryside, however, that the Salazar government rightly realized it would succeed or fail in the African colonies, and although the rural problems were not in the 1930s of pressing importance, plans were gradually formulated for the ultimate social transformation of Angola and Moçambique. In neither colony did the best land rest exclusively in the hands of white plantation owners. In 1901 all land not privately owned had been declared the property of the state, and subsequent decrees set aside large tracts of land for the African population. Much of the land under white colonization, therefore, was the property of the government, leased on concessions which could be revoked with satisfactory indemnification. In theory tribal lands belonged to the Africans, although there was no very clear notion of the boundaries and size of their properties. Article 38 of the 1955 Native Statute for Angola and Moçambique reaffirmed this: 'Natives who live in tribal organizations are guaranteed . . . the use and development, in the traditional manner, of lands necessary for their villages, for their crops, and for the pasture of their cattle.' This guarantee has been largely kept, in spite of criticism from Portuguese settlers that 'the best and largest areas of land have been reserved for the natives and closed to occupation and exploitation by European capital'. Some native lands, however, have been taken over, without really satisfactory recompense, for the cultivation of coffee in northern Angola and for the sugar estates of Mocambique.

What the long view of an emerging New State sociology projected was the creation of a modern peasant society in Angola and Moçambique. It was Salazar's belief that any attempt to advance in a single step from a tribal way of life to a modern industrial society (even should conditions permit in Portuguese Africa a transition which had not yet taken place in the metropolis) was sociological madness. Thus an agrarian society was to be achieved through the settlement of Portuguese peasants in government colonization projects, in some of which the African was to participate, and through the establishment of African agricultural colonies which would create conditions favourable to the native's economic and spiritual assimilation. What the policy really envisaged was the creation of a semi-literate population of Africans and Portuguese holding rural Portuguese values, industrious, dedicated to the land, and politically conservative. Presumably such a society would absorb or divert the energies of the emergent African and at the same time not be a threat to the large European estates, the main economic props of both colonies.

After twenty years of study – and the failure of several pilot schemes – the government began to take action in the early 1950s. In south-central Angola, at Caconda, a native *colonato* had started operation with 20 families in 1948, and by 1952 the number of families had increased to 730, a total of 3,484 Africans. In that year maize, beans, rice, wheat, and peanuts were being cultivated on 2,250 hectares. In 1957 official figures announced 750 families in the Caconda *colonato*, and, in 1960, 700. A second *colonato* was started in Damba (in the Congo district) in 1950, and 234 families were settled there in 1954, since which time the number has not increased appreciably. Cultivated land totalled 4,500 hectares. Two other *colonatos* were planned for Bembe and Loge, both in north-east Angola.

The *colonatos* are directed by an agronomist and a farm manager. They are intended to be model paternalistic societies. Each village has its own farm buildings and implements, with production goals assigned. The government supplies land, seeds, and technical assistance, and livestock is provided through instalment purchases. These latter-day re-creations of the Jesuit work farms have not been spectacularly successful, and they are relatively expensive.

In Moçambique the emphasis has been placed on agricultural cooperatives somewhat similar to the Angolan *colonato*. (There are some African farmers at the predominantly white Guija settlement on the Limpopo.) In the three circumscriptions of Zavala, Chibuto, and Vila de João Belo, a number of cooperatives were promoted by the colonial administration in the 1950s. Each participant farms his own plot of land; he buys and sells through the cooperative, whose native directors are elected by its members. The cooperatives are directed by a Portuguese agronomist. The German economist, Ralph von Gersdorff, paints an optimistic picture of the prosperity enjoyed by the cooperatives' members – several of whom own tractors and Land Rovers – and of its financial stability. He believes that the institution points the way to the future in Moçambique and that the self-administration and democratic rule learned in the cooperative can be an important first step 'to the replacement of the paternalistic government in Portuguese Africa'. In 1960 the seven cooperatives in the circumscription of Zavala had 1,242 members and a total population of 6,195 people; there were perhaps as many in other circumscriptions in the district. The present African population of Moçambique is about six million people. By generous estimate, therefore, cooperatives in Moçambique have had a direct influence on about one-twentieth of one per cent of the native population.

African agriculture in both colonies is subject to a series of controls exercised by various agricultural and trade boards. The most successful African farms have been the handful of small coffee *fazendas* in north-east Angola and in the Cabinda enclave. The great bulk of African agriculture is the subsistence farming of maize, manioc, beans, rice, and peanuts. In Angola the principal village cash-crop is maize, for which there has been in recent years almost no market value. Nor have the colonial governments provided incentives for increased production. Prices are usually fixed to benefit only the Portuguese middlemen. A case in point is cotton production in Moçambique. Cotton is exclusively an African crop – as it is in Angola – and, since it constitutes the colony's largest export commodity, the Portuguese government has claimed great success for cotton-production campaigns. Marvin Harris, in *Portugal's African 'Wards'* (1958), describes how success was achieved in the cotton lands north of the Zambezi.

> In this modern serfdom the role of the medieval lord is exercised by twelve private Portuguese companies, each of which has received monopolistic concessions over cotton production in vast areas of Moçambique. *Indígenas* within the concession areas of each company are assigned cotton acreage by the administrative authorities. They have no choice in the matter and must plant, cultivate, and harvest cotton wherever they are told. Then they must sell the raw cotton to the concession company of their areas at prices which are fixed by the government far below those available on the international market. . . . In 1956 there were 519,000 African cultivators participating in the cotton campaign . . . the actual number of men, women, and children being forced to plant cotton [on acreage taken out of food production] probably exceeds one million. In 1956, the 519,000 sellers received an average of $11·17 per person as their family's reward for an entire year of work.

By conservative estimate, the state-controlled cotton programme in Moçambique has had a direct and often disastrous effect on fifteen per cent of the native population.

'To Christianize and Educate, to Nationalize and Civilize'

Hand in hand with the New State's plans to improve the material existence of the African went the Portuguese missionary effort to improve his spiritual and intellectual life. The Colonial Act simultaneously provided for the freedom of conscience and the freedom of various religions and for the special protection and assistance of the Catholic mission programme. (By contrast, for a brief moment the Portuguese Republic, after sharply curtailing the work of Catholic religious orders in the colonies, had offered to subsidize Protestant missions.) Once again the state recognized the rights and special functions of the Church 'to Christianize and educate, to nationalize and civilize'. The Catholic missionary programme in Angola and Moçambique is governed by appropriate provisions of the Constitution, the Missionary Accord of 1940 (which developed the principles contained in the Concordat of 7 May 1940 between the Vatican and the Portuguese government), and the Missionary Statute of 1941.

Both the colonial and metropolitan governments have subsidized the Church's missionary programme. Foreign Catholic missionaries are permitted in the colonies only after fulfilling certain conditions. Both Angola and Moçambique have over one hundred mission and parish churches, served by secular priests and fathers of various orders including the Franciscans, Dominicans, Benedictines, Lazarists, and those of the Holy Ghost Congregation. In 1959 the number of priests in Angola was 431 and in Moçambique about 240, a small percentage of whom were African. The Catholic population of the two colonies did not exhibit, in the 1950 census, a similar proportion: 1,500,000 in Angola (almost certainly an exaggerated figure) and 210,000 in Moçambique.

Under such favourable conditions the Church, while perhaps not thriving, at least not in Moçambique, has prospered moderately. Among its most important activities are 'the founding and directing of schools for European and African students, elementary, secondary, professional schools, and seminaries . . . as well as infirmaries and hospitals'. The Catholic missions have been entrusted by the government with much of the educational programme for African students. And as the number of Catholic converts increased, the state began to use conversion as a yardstick for the success of assimilation. During a speech he delivered in July 1960, on overseas reform, Adriano Moreira, then Under-Secretary of State for Overseas Administration, pointed out that, while the number of *assimilados* was insignificant, the number of African Catholics was nearly two million. He emphasized that although 'political loyalty does not depend upon Christian qualifications . . . Catholic missionary activity is inseparably linked to patriotism', and that the formation of Christian qualities leads to the formation of Portuguese qualities. In the developing struggle between nationalism in Angola and the government, Portuguese Catholic missionaries have generally supported the government, although the Bishop of Luanda has spoken out for social and political changes in the colony, and the Bishop's secretary was expelled in 1959 for alleged nationalist involvement. The African members of the clergy and a number of foreign Catholic fathers are known to support nationalist aspirations in Portuguese Africa. The Church is finding itself faced by a very awkward situation in Portuguese Africa.

The recent troubles in Angola have led to an intensification of the strongly anti-foreign sentiment in Portuguese Africa, and the Protestant missionary societies have begun to suffer serious reprisals where formerly they had been subject only to harassments. Since 1640 foreign missionaries have been suspected of 'denationalizing the natives' and acting as advance agents for foreign governments. When these missionaries are Protestants as well, fears and resentments are multiplied. For twenty years the Protestant mission effort in Moçambique has been hampered and sometimes thwarted by a powerful combination of Catholic clergy and officers of the provincial government. In Angola the official reception of the Protestant was more moderate, and sometimes even cordial. In 1961, however, the Protestant societies were turned upon with particular violence, and their future became questionable. All the same, the Protestant missions have solidified their position in Portuguese Africa, especially in Angola, during the Salazar régime. Their schools and hospitals have made striking contributions to African welfare. Some of the clergy, African and white, have been the leaders in the campaign against Portuguese repressions. In 1960 there were over 300 Protestant missionaries in Angola, and about 200 in Moçambique. The 1950 census showed 540,000 Protestants in Angola (including about 2,000 Europeans, 800 mestiços, and 6,000 assimilados), and some 60,000 in Moçambique.

Education in the African colonies has been distinguished by

the official standpoint that education is important for promoting assimilation; by the perhaps unconscious sentiment that education for the mass of the population represents an implicit threat to Portuguese interests; and by the inability of both Church and State to create an educational system capable of serving more than a small percentage of the inhabitants of Angola and Moçambique. The problems have been, of course, enormous for a mother country with a forty-per-cent rate of illiteracy herself. As with its African colonization projects, the Salazar régime dithered and planned for twenty years before anything was done, and only in the last decade has the African illiteracy rate begun to drop slowly from a figure of about ninety-nine per cent.

The education system in Portuguese Africa illustrates once more the dual reality of the colonies. There are two systems: one for Africans, *ensino de adaptação*, and one for Europeans and assimilated Africans, *ensino oficial*. The purpose of the native system is, one might suppose, to speed the assimilation of the African population; according to Portuguese colonial officials, it is also to teach the Africans good working habits and prepare them for being future peasants and artisans. In Portuguese policy the two goals are totally compatible. *Ensino de adaptação* is officially the responsibility of the Roman Catholic missions, whose services are largely underwritten by the government. Principally, the Church is responsible for training teaching personnel. *Ensino oficial*, on the other hand, is a state education system, virtually a duplication of the metropolitan one.

Ensino de adaptação (called until 1956 *ensino rudimentar*, which was an attempt to adapt native education to local needs) composes theoretically a three-year programme. The first year is called the 'initiation class', during which the student is taught the rudiments of Portuguese reading and speaking. The second cycle, or next two years, corresponds closely with the first and second years of elementary schooling under the state system. The basic courses are reading, writing, and arithmetic, with a bit of history. Instruction is in Portuguese, which, whatever the assimilating purposes of the system may be, places an initial handicap on the student, and is by catechistic methods. If the student passes a government examination – set in the colonial capitals or in Lisbon and administered by a jury of teachers from the colonial district – at the end of the second cycle he may continue his studies by entering the third year of an elementary-school system. Although in theory the *ensino* is a three-year programme, in practice it is usually a four- or five-year one. Students cannot begin school until they are seven years old.

All teachers in the *ensino* programme are African. Until 1958 their required training as teachers was the satisfactory completion of the fourth, or last, year of elementary school, and the majority were trained at Catholic normal schools in Angola and Moçambique. Graduates of several Protestant schools also taught in the *ensino* system, although they were not officially accredited. During the last three years, however, prospective teachers have been required to finish the first cycle (the first two years) of secondary school as well and obtain a teaching certificate. Theoretically they cannot get this if they are not *assimilados*, although, again, special dispensation may be obtained. A major difficulty is that the would-be teacher must present his birth certificate, which in many cases is impossible.

Education for the African in the Portuguese colonies is progressively restrictive. In the first place, no legal provision exists for the student to go on to elementary school although, to be sure, there are practical provisions. In order to enter the third year of elementary school, the African must not be over fourteen years old, and this is a real impediment if the student's progress in the *ensino* has been delayed, as it so frequently is. Usually there are no elementary schools close at hand, and the student is obliged to board. State elementary schools exist *only* for white students, *mestiços*, and assimilated Africans. The majority are therefore obliged to go to a missionary school, either Catholic or Protestant, which is, by native income standards in Angola and Moçambique, difficult. Fees for the year, including room, board, and tuition, are around £6 10s., which seems absurdly low, but frequently constitutes one-quarter or even one-third of a family's total annual income. There are other reasons why the African student does not get far. Boys in their teens, for example, are subject to an indiscriminate labour draft. In the absence of any official encouragement, it is surprising that as many students endeavour to continue their studies as in fact do.

State elementary schools exist only in those areas of Portuguese Africa where there is a sufficiently large white or assimilated population to justify them. The rest are missionary schools. The elementary system comprises a four-year programme: the first two years deal with the *primeras letras*, while the last two include such subjects as geography and history. All examinations are state administered through an academic jury. Teachers in this system have to have taken five years of high school and further education studies available only in Lisbon. There are almost no African teachers in state elementary schools, and only a few in the missionary schools.

Government high schools are also for Portuguese and assimilated Africans alone, the former making up the vast majority. (In 1960, at the Liceu Salazar in Lourenço Marques, only 30 students out of the school's population of over 1,000 were Africans.) The difficulties which keep Africans out of elementary schools are multiplied many times when they are ready for the *liceu*. Protestant missions do subsidize and administer boarding-houses for the very few Africans attending the various high schools. In Angola there are five state high schools, at Luanda, Sá da Bandeira, Nova Lisboa, Benguela, and Malange; there are three in Moçambique, at Lourenço Marques, Beira, and Inhambane. There are also a number of private secondary schools and a small number of secondary technical, or trade schools, at none of which is there much of an African enrolment. The high-school course covers seven years; the offerings are fairly rich and varied, and the teachers are all university graduates.

There are no universities in Portuguese Africa, although there has been talk of starting several professional faculties in Luanda, and in October 1961 the Overseas Ministry announced that a university would be established in Luanda and another in Lourenço Marques. A few Africans do go to universities in Coimbra, Lisbon, or Oporto. The number is very small, of course, but it does comprise a larger élite than the Belgian

Congo possessed in June 1960. Some of these graduates remain in Portugal, others enter government service, and a very few return to their homes. Whether by this final stage of his education the African student has become totally assimilated is hard to say: some African university students have joined the opposition in exile, while others make speeches in Lisbon or Luanda defending Portuguese policies.

Education in Angola and Moçambique *is* selective. It has been said that in the last five years the colonial governments have taken important steps toward broadening the basis of popular education for the African and toward permitting him to continue his studies beyond the *ensino de adaptação* level. It has also been stated by Portuguese authorities that the illiteracy rate among the African population is decreasing at the rate of two per cent a year from its 1955 level of ninety-eight per cent. But there is usually considerable variation between Portuguese pronouncements about what is happening in the colonies and what is really taking place. Tables 1 and 2 provide some rough idea of the educational programmes in Angola and Moçambique during the last five years.

The sources for Table 1 provide no breakdown beyond the *adaptação* level on the basis of race, but it may be reliably assumed that the school population in the private elementary schools is predominantly African, and that in the state elementary schools it is predominantly Portuguese with a small admixture of *assimilado* or *mestiço*. Thus there were probably some 12,000 African students attending elementary school in 1959–60 and about 14,000 Portuguese students, though the Africans represent a total population of about 4,500,000 and the Portuguese a population of perhaps 160,000. Nor does the table reveal the high rate of students who do not finish their course. In 1954, for example, out of 35,361 African students enrolled in the *ensino* programme, only 959 passed the third-year examination; one can be quite certain that only a handful of the 58,000 in the 1959–60 programme will finish the third year. And one can only guess at the number of Africans in the academic and technical high schools. A very generous figure would be 100. The

Table 1

Number of Schools, Teachers, and Students Enrolled in
Angola, 1955–9

SCHOOLS	1955	1955–6	1956–7	1957–8	1958–9
Adaptação	1,003	1,050	1,088	1,015	1,066
Elementary (Private)	154	177	217	245	371
Elementary (State)	144	152	163	175	211
Secondary Academic (Private)	18	21	26	27	26
Secondary Academic (State)	2	3	5	5	5
Secondary Technical (Private)	5	5	7	4	5
Secondary Technical (State)	5	8	10	10	10

TEACHERS					
Adaptação	2,526	2,595	1,396	1,311	1,363
Elementary (Private)	316	267	435	490	676
Elementary (State)	304	323	257	360	467
Secondary Academic (Private)	145	147	172	172	219
Secondary Academic (State)	47	65	96	108	122
Secondary Technical (Private)	36	27	60	28	45
Secondary Technical (State)	77	117	162	208	227

STUDENTS ENROLLED

Adaptação	48,248	49,142	47,671	57,428	55,779
Elementary (Private)	7,564	8,324	9,193	11,166	13,226
Elementary (State)	11,132	11,292	12,350	14,466	16,771
Secondary Academic (Private)	1,610	1,899	2,034	2,248	2,355
Secondary Academic (State)	1,510	1,730	2,009	2,457	3,006
Secondary Technical (Private)	530	395	235	211	288
Secondary Technical (State)	1,300	1,812	2,104	2,526	3,074

TABLE 2

Number of African Students in Moçambique Schools, 1955–9

	1955	1956	1957	1958	1958
Ensino de adaptação					
Enrolled	240,813	292,199	340,027	370,013	391,134
Finishing Third Year	5,027	5,626	5,860	8,158	9,486
Elementary School					
Enrolled	3,729	4,034	4,468	5,197	5,397
High School					
Enrolled					
Technical	116	139	185	183	301
Academic	10	10	20	34	41
Seminary	105	94	102	166	169

sketchy figures for Moçambique reveal the same story: a sharply progressive decline in the African student population from the basic to the secondary-school level. One need only call attention to the enrolment and completion statistics for the *ensino de adaptação*. About one student out of forty stands a chance of completing the most rudimentary and inadequate training, that is to say, about one-fifth of one per cent of the total African population in Moçambique achieves a modicum of literacy each year.

The problems inherent in such an education system are enormous, and statistics do not tell the whole story. Missionary schools do not have the resources or personnel to accept with any chance of success the great responsibility placed upon them. The *ensino* schools often lack the basic equipment of instruction. Education for girls is more difficult than for boys (about twenty-five to thirty per cent of the *ensino* school population is female). The emergence of an élite, even a barely literate élite, is slow, and yet it is these Africans who must, if Portugal prevails in Africa, undertake the real task of assimilation, or who must, if Portugal does not prevail, shoulder the responsibilities for governing and administering an independent nation. It would be difficult enough for Portugal to accomplish the education reforms in Africa that she has not brought about at home. There is not enough money, not enough personnel, not enough interest. But there is a more important consideration, the aim of the Salazar government to ensure that the African majority does not become politically conscious. For the masses, a harmless dose of *ensino de adaptação*, a sort of general psychological assimilation, is sufficient; for the few, an intensive cultural and political assimilation which perhaps will convert them to the Portuguese cause.

As with the educational system, both the government and the missions collaborate on the medical and hygiene services available to the African population. The need for such services is more desperate than it is for education, and less adequately met. In the cities and larger towns, state and private hospitals serve the urban population, although they may be said to take care largely of the European residents, while great companies like Diamang, the Benguela Railway, and Sena Sugar Estates have hospitals for their employees. With few exceptions, these government and company hospitals offer the most obvious examples of racial discrimination in the colonies. Separate wards and operating rooms in the Luanda Hospital, for instance, exist for European and African patients. In the interior, the government has established a number of rural infirmaries, but these can take care only of minor illnesses and injuries. Small maternity hospitals are located in some circumscriptions, but they are insufficient to care for more than a very small part of the population. In Angola, for 1959, only 13,173 infants, African and European, were recorded as born in hospitals or infirmaries.

Compared with past performances, the present government has probably made modest advances. A modern large leprosarium has been built in Angola, near the Rhodesian frontier. Under the technical direction of the Institute of Tropical Medicine in Lisbon, research in tropical diseases, notably sleeping sickness, is carried out, and preventive inoculations have brought some small benefits to the native peoples. Statistics for Angola in 1959, however, reveal serious deficiencies in personnel and establishments. There were 226 government doctors in service (there were also perhaps over 100 private and missionary doctors in practice), of whom 72 were situated in Luanda province. There were 531 male nurses (204 in Luanda district), 6 visiting nurses, 48 midwives, and an undefined 929 other medical personnel. There were 15 state hospitals, 62 private hospitals, 67 health centres, one mental hospital, and 32 maternity infirmaries. There were 271 sanitary posts throughout the territory. During the year, the government health service gave 3,634,224 injections, vaccinated 1,022,523 people, performed 15,098 operations and 1,260,793 laboratory examinations, and took 33,810 X-rays. Other statistical information is so meagre as to be virtually meaningless. There is no satisfactory record of infant mortality, which for the African population in some areas of Angola and Moçambique reportedly runs to over fifty per cent. The total inadequacy of government records may be seen again in the Angolan statistics for 1959. The government health service registered only 75,289 cases – 417 fatal – of some 32 infectious diseases. One may reasonably assume that the majority of the population suffers in unrecorded misery.

'The Absolute Necessity for Work'

But the cornerstone of the New State's native policy has continued to be the African's obligation to work. If the goal of Portuguese policy was assimilation, its achievement was seen to lie in getting the African to put his services to profitable use – for the state, for private employers, for himself. Through the centuries labour had been the essential point of contact between the colonial administration and the native population; for the Salazar régime, this relationship has been complicated by economic pressures for the development of the provinces and by the need for defending Portuguese policy before the world. But these demands have not substantially altered Portugal's position, bluntly stated sixty years ago by António Enes, that the African had to be forced, by every means available, to work. All other attempts to raise the African's cultural and economic level, to assimilate him into a single Portuguese community, whether by education, administrative tutelage, missionary work, health programmes, or colonization schemes, have been peripheral to this over-riding obligation.

The belief in the African's obligation to work was a part of Portugal's vision of herself as a civilizing force in a primitive world inhabited by lazy children. Former Colonial Minister Marcelo Caetano, now Rector of Lisbon University, wrote:

The blacks in Angola have to be directed and indoctrinated by Europeans. . . . The Africans have not learned how to develop alone the territories they have inhabited for thousands of years.

For New State colonialists human progress rested on discipline and hard work, and the success of any native policy rested on inculcating the indigenous population with these virtues. Another of Salazar's Colonial Ministers, Vieira Machado, said in 1943:

It is necessary to inspire in the black the idea of work, and of abandoning his laziness and his depravity, if we want to exercise a colonizing action to protect him. . . .

If we want to civilize the native we must make him adopt as an elementary moral precept the notion that he has no right to live without working.

A productive society is based on painful hard work, obligatory even for vagrants, and we cannot permit any exception because of race.

The policy of assimilation which I conceive of must be complete. Therefore it is necessary to establish a rule of conduct for the black which exists for the white, making him acquire a sense of responsibility. It is to be an unenlightened Negrophile not to infuse the African with the absolute necessity for work.

First the Portuguese dictatorship in 1926 and then the Salazar government devised legislation to correct the most obvious abuses in the labour system. A decree of 1926 declared that forced labour could only be used in the public interest – which, as it turned out, included many private projects – and had to be remunerated. The Indigenous Labour Code of 1928, which, with some alterations, is still the law governing the African worker in Angola and Moçambique, defined the whole area of overseas labour relations, and in a series of specific articles sought to give added protection to the native worker. ('The Government guarantees to the natives of its colonies full liberty in choosing the work which best suits them. . . .') The Colonial Act of 1930 stated that 'the system of native contract labour rests on individual liberty and on the natives' right to a just wage and assistance, public authority intervening only for purposes of inspection', a clause reaffirmed in the Imperial Organic Charter of 1933 and the Organic Overseas Law of 1953. The 1954 *Estatuto dos indígenas das provincias da Guiné, Angola e Moçambique* declared:

The State will try to make the native recognize that work constitutes an indispensable element of progress, but the authorities can only impose work upon him in cases specifically covered by the law [Article 32].The Natives may freely choose the work they want to carry out, either on their account or for another. [Article 33] . . . The use of native labour by *não-indígenas* rests on the African's freedom of contract and on his right to a just wage and assistance, and must be inspected by the State through its appropriate organs [Article 34].

All this legislation was philosophically of a piece with the

Regulation of 1899. What the 1928 Code attempted to do was to check abuses of the system while maintaining the system intact. It accordingly reflected concern for the payment of wages, the transportation, the lodging and feeding of the worker, and the provision of health and educational assistance. Such directives had not been regarded before, and they were not to be regarded now.

All these issues were academic, for the law demanded that the African work, and as long as that law remained, a repressive exploitation of the worker inevitably resulted. The 1926 decree eliminated the vagrancy clause. Thereafter 'obligatory labour' was to mean only that *indigenas* could be compelled to labour 'on public works of general and collective interest ... to fulfil sentences of a penal character, and to fulfil fiscal obligations'. What this meant was (1) that the African could be obliged to work on allegedly vital local projects (roads and sanitation programmes); (2) that if the African male could not prove that he was gainfully employed, he could be legally forced to work for the State for six months; and (3) that he could be made to work for failure to pay the head tax.

All other labour was held to be free, and, by the definition of Portuguese law, almost all labour in Angola and Moçambique from 1930 to the present has been voluntary. Either the African has contracted directly with an employer, or he has been given the assistance of the State in signing a contract with an employer. Although there was no legal distinction, the former became known as *voluntários* and the latter as *contratados*. Both signed a six-month contract, although in some cases (as in the Angolan diamond mines and fisheries, and for work outside the colony) contracts up to a two-year period were permitted, and both were covered by the same provisions of the labour codes. Children under fourteen years, the sick, and the elderly could not contract for their services. All contracts were subject to the approval of the colonial administration, and an Office of Native Affairs was charged with the task of supervising contractual arrangements and working conditions.

All males between the ages of eighteen and fifty-five were liable to contract labour. To claim exemption, the African had to submit proof that (1) he was self-employed in a profession, commerce, or industry; (2) that he was permanently employed by the State or a private employer; (3) that he was gainfully engaged as a labourer for at least six months out of the year by the State or by a private employer; (4) that he had worked within the last six months in the Union of South Africa or the Rhodesias under legal contract; or (5) that he was a farmer who fulfilled the terms of various native farming statutes and sold a cash crop. Anyone who could not satisfy these requirements was to be conscripted into government service or assisted in the signing of a contract with a private employer.

Such was, and is, the intent and substance of native-labour legislation. Although these labour laws could hardly be called models of an enlightened native policy, they have borne little resemblance to the reality of the last thirty years. The recruitment and use of African labour has been pursued with much the same callous indifference for the law and for the welfare of the worker that characterized labour practices in all the years before 1930. The complaints have been many: illegal recruitment, miserable working conditions, violent treatment of workers, underpayment or withholding of payment, unlawful extension of contracts, the use of child labour on Niassa tea plantations and Angolan coffee farms, and even the failure to return workers to their villages.

The most persistent, or at least the most publicized, irregularities in the administration of the labour code have occurred, as always, in the actual recruitment of the worker. Recruiting practices have been somewhat more flexible and informal than the laws have foreseen, although the very existence of a six-month requirement to work is basically responsible for all the conditions of exploitation. Large estates and the fisheries need an assured supply of labour. Private certified recruiters are permitted to contract labourers for such employers under the State's supervision. The recruiter is paid a little over £14 a head for his work. In Angola, in 1959, recruiters were issued licences for a total of 180,000 men; in 1960, for 190,000 men. There is no reason to suppose that the recruiters contracted for fewer men than their licences permitted – past practice suggests that they probably recruited more – in view of the labour shortages in Angola. Yet official statistics for these two years put the number of *contratados* at about 125,000.

The labour supply of the interior is under the control of the administrator and his chief of post. Village chiefs are instructed to produce a certain number of 'malingerers' or tax-delinquents, whose contracts are signed and who are then sent off to work in various parts of the province. The possibilities for bribery, corruption, and abuse in such a system are immediately apparent. Periodic scandals with administrative transfers and demotions have occurred in both colonies, and it is possible that in the last few years a gradual moral improvement has taken place in recruitment practices. It is true also that as a result of certain local conditions, either the failure of crops or the persistent 'civilizing' campaigns of local administrators, there has been in recent years a marked increase in the number of *voluntários*. But these have not really been significant tendencies, and the economies of both colonies still rest largely on the supply of cheap contract labour. Certainly there can be no solution to this great economic and human problem for as long as Portuguese administrators and estate owners in Africa continue to think and act in the traditional manner.

It was as much to the economic aspects of contract labour as to its abuses that Henrique Galvão addressed himself in his now-famous 1947 report. Galvão was then a High Inspector in the Colonial Service and deputy for Angola in the Portuguese parliament. When his indictment of corruption, forced labour, and maladministration was ignored by the Colonial Ministry, Galvão delivered a speech in 1948 to the National Assembly. This act led to his downfall, and in 1952 he was arrested by the political police for attempting to organize an opposition group. The next seven years he spent in jail or hospitals, and only in 1959 did he manage to escape and make his way to Latin America.

The Galvão report contained little that had not been said before, but the author's authoritative position and his subsequent fate at the hands of the police gave it a particular distinction and made the author a spokesman for the silent millions of oppressed Portuguese Africans. Galvão's first concern was for the demographic sickness of Angola and Moçambique, which so restrained the economic development of the colonies: the debility of its people, who suffered from lack of medical assistance, undernourishment, and a forced labour régime; the destructive consequences of Portuguese occupation during the previous sixty years; and the migration of Africans into the Belgian Congo, the Rhodesias, and the Union. Galvão claimed that health services hardly existed in Portuguese Africa. He painted appalling pictures of working conditions, and claimed that the state was itself the most culpable in its treatment of contract workers. He attacked the government's despotic control over African agriculture, principally cotton production. He dealt in detail with the system of labour recruitment.

The problem is a very difficult one. No one denies it. Today it is more difficult than yesterday. Tomorrow will be more difficult than today. The fact is that we have known this for ten years, and that in these ten years there has not been a single effective measure to solve the problem.

No satisfactory solution was found during the 1950s. The now rapidly expanding economies of Angola and Moçambique, together with the influx of white labourers from Portugal, ensured that the African worker would be what he had always been – *mão d'obra*, a working hand. In 1955 Basil Davidson could write without fear of reasonable contradiction: 'Forced labour is the economic flywheel in Angola.' And Marvin Harris could safely suppose in 1958: 'All of the African male workers employed by European agricultural enterprises are *shibalos* (forced labourers).' The whole issue of contract labour has produced a fair amount of controversy in the colonies. On the one hand, there has been the line of argument, pursued principally by old colonists and estate managers, that the labour laws have not been sufficiently stringent to extract the maximum labour from the available supply. ('As long as the natives enjoy six months of holidays every year and can emigrate to the neighbouring colonies . . . the problem cannot be solved.') Another more progressive view has maintained, with many references to other European territories, that in the artificially controlled economy of Portuguese Africa, the low wages paid to the African for his labour (between two and three pounds per month) have destroyed all incentive and forced the government and private employers alike to resort to a system of forced labour. But, of course, no satisfactory solution *could* be found for as long as influential newspaper editorials, from which the following quotation is taken, could be written in 1956 to support the traditional Portuguese attitude.

But for all the effective resources of the overseas soil and subsoil to be exploited and developed . . . much work, much perseverance, much human effort is absolutely necessary. Translated into everyday speech, this means that an abundant, permanent, and very reliable *mão-d'obra* becomes fundamentally indispensable. Now, this labouring force can only be supplied by the native. . . .

It has been more than once demonstrated that the white man in Africa cannot carry out heavy tasks, which demand a fatiguing and exhausting human effort. . . . He may only be given the task of directing and of guiding. . . . Other tasks are naturally reserved for the Negroes, since they are the only ones capable of carrying them out, because of their physiological function and their ancestral adaptation to an environment which, though harmful to the European, is familiar to them. And one should not be amazed that this is what happens.

Henrique Galvão estimated that some two million Africans from Angola and Moçambique were working, and in many cases living, outside of the two provinces. Marcelo Caetano calculated the number at a million. A part of this migration has been regulated by various accords between the Portuguese government and the Union of South Africa and the Rhodesias. Harris has estimated that recruiting companies from these two neighbouring territories held about 350,000 African workers from Moçambique under contract in 1954. To this total he added 50,000 clandestine migrant workers, making a total of 400,000 Africans from a labour pool of not much more than 600,000 in southern Moçambique. A similar migration, most of it informal, probably poured into the Belgian Congo as well. These high figures have presented some embarrassment to colonial officials, revealing as they do some inadequacy in Portugal's African policies.

Another consequence of contract labour and African migrations has been the destruction of African village life. With most of the able-bodied men away part of the year, many villages have been left only their women, children, and old men. Even less happily for Portugal, according to Thomas Okuma in his recent book on Angola:

> The system of 'voluntary labour' has contributed to the spread of nationalism, due to the transportation of workers from the south to the coffee plantations located in the north and to the docks in the two coastal cities of Luanda and Lobito. Workers made contacts beyond their own tribal groups. Their common grievances of inadequate pay and bad working conditions have meant the beginning of a feeling of solidarity against their European employers.

Brotherhood for the Few

The realities of Portuguese Africa, and the harsh criticism they have evoked at home and abroad, are not unknown to the Lisbon government. But when in all matters of material policy Portugal has been found wanting, her spokesmen have had recourse to the traditional Portuguese acceptance of the Negro as a fellow human. Until 1961 this 'singular attribute' of Portuguese behaviour in Africa was held to account for the peace and harmony prevailing in the colonies. In 1959, Prime Minister Salazar said:

> We do not even think of denying the relative backwardness of some regions and the defects in our services. It is obvious that there are not enough roads and bridges, hospitals and schools, and even . . . police and defence forces. This being so . . . how is it that we can traverse all Angola and Moçambique with no other aid than the good will of the native, his brotherly help, fundamentally the fact that he feels himself to be Portuguese? Why does the native of Angola or Moçambique when abroad say that he is Portuguese?

And, in a speech a year later, Salazar observed that 'the idea of racial superiority is not ours, but that of human brotherhood certainly is'.

Asserting that their work of colonization in Africa is an affair

189

of the heart, New State colonists have pointed to their traditional tolerance of the African and their easygoing attitude to miscegenation. They have argued that they do not practise segregation in Africa, that there are no colour barriers. They have found reinforcement for their beliefs in the reports of many travellers who have remarked on the lack of racial tension in the colonies. The Brazilian sociologist Gilberto Freyre reported that, whenever the Cardinal of Moçambique visited those Africans subject to Portuguese influence, he was received with the greatest naturalness by people who called themselves Portuguese and Roman Catholics. Every high official to visit the colonies was met by seemingly enthusiastic native delegations, professing their Portuguese attachment. And so for thirty years, particularly for the last fifteen, the Portuguese closed their eyes to the dangerous racial situation developing in Angola and Moçambique. Founding their faith in equality and brotherhood on the doubtful associations of the white minority with an equally small black minority, they failed to see that the African majority remained unaffected by any aspect of the Portuguese presence except a sometimes negligent, sometimes oppressive native policy.

Even granting for a moment Portuguese assumptions, could miscegenation and a professed lack of colour prejudice provide sufficient basis for an African policy in the middle of the twentieth century ? Could those two forces alone create the conditions for the assimilation of some eleven million Africans into the Portuguese world ? Could they compensate for the lack of education, inadequate economic opportunities, and forced labour ? The New State brought to the colonies the ideological trappings of a pseudo-benevolent paternalism and a superficial prosperity, enjoyed in the main by a few thousand Europeans, but it did not break with the unrewarding traditions of the past. Instead it accepted them, used them whenever possible to practical advantage, and sought to create from them an intensely nationalistic colonial policy. It may well be true that the Portuguese have, as they themselves sometimes confess, the vice of history, for from 1930 to 1960 they have appeared strangely intent, in their dealings with the African population, on prolonging the past into the future.

7 The Death of the Dream

In 1951 the African colonies, by a stroke of the New State's legislative pen, ceased to be colonies and became once again overseas provinces. Another step was taken toward the integration of Portuguese Africa into the Lusitanian community. Angola and Moçambique were at last to be accepted as prosperous members of the family. The golden decade of Portuguese African history was at hand, a period of the most genuine prosperity and vitality that the colonies had ever known. Plans and projects were at last to leave the drawing-board. Under the impact of National Development Plans (the first, from 1953 to 1958, was immediately followed by an even more ambitious six-year plan), the countenance of the colonies began perceptibly to change, as roads, bridges, dams, high-tension wires, factories, colonization settlements, and new ports came into existence. Portuguese African products increasingly found their way into the world market as ships of many flags put into the handsome modern ports of Angola and Moçambique. The colonies provided an ever-larger market for goods of Portuguese manufacture. The centuries-old problem of attracting white immigrants to Africa was finally solved. There was talk in Angola of a new Brazil. While the fires of African nationalism blazed higher in the rest of the continent, Portuguese Africa seemed serene and safe, and Portuguese officials, referring constantly to the peace in the provinces, were confident that history was once more to demonstrate the uniquely creative quality of Portuguese policy in Africa.

Economic Development in the 1950s

One must remember the aborted hopes for the development of

Portuguese Africa during previous generations to understand the material accomplishments of the 1950s. In comparison with similar developments in neighbouring territories, progress was perhaps not so remarkable. Portugal herself enjoyed only a modest rate of economic growth (4·4 per cent) in this period, somewhat less than that of most countries in Western Europe and even of several in Eastern Europe. What is important to realize is that the development of Angola and Moçambique progressed at a fairly consistent rate, even in those years of unfavourable trade balances, so that it seemed that the two provinces had become what Portugal had always wanted them to be, productive European colonies. And it is important to realize too that much of the transformation was dramatically visible. Increasingly the territories, particularly Angola, made valuable contributions to the total Portuguese economy. As the successful growth of the colonies continued, practical arguments were added to theoretical considerations for drawing Angola and Moçambique more closely into association with the metropolis – in spite of the growing chorus of protests from colonial farmers and businessmen, who advocated greater economic and administrative freedom for the provinces themselves.

How much of the development of Angola and Moçambique since the end of the Second World War has been, in a sense, natural, and how much has been the result of the government's long-range plans for the colonies, it is difficult to say. Certainly private Portuguese capital cannot claim much credit. Always ultra-conservative about investing in the colonies, financial interests in the metropolis did not seek outlets in Africa except under near-monopolistic conditions. Nor, until very recently, was the Salazar government anxious to permit foreign capital to invest in colonial development. The Diamond Company and the Benguela Railway are, to be sure, dominated by foreign capital, while a number of smaller farms and estates are owned by foreign interests, but the general tendency of Salazarian economic policy in Africa was for Portugal to pay its own way and to pay as it went. In the last six or seven years, however, the government, excited perhaps over the economic potential of the colonies, began to change its rigid policies and to welcome, still under somewhat stringent restrictions, significant amounts of foreign capital. In Angola the exploitation of oil was entrusted to a Belgian firm. A £16,200,000 project to develop iron ore and manganese in Angola has been underwritten with German credit. Heavy-construction contracts have been regularly let to European firms, and much of the mineral prospecting in the two colonies has been carried out by foreign concerns. Behind the New State's decision to relax its opposition to investment from abroad was perhaps the thought that these foreign economic ties with Portuguese Africa might help to strengthen political associations in time of crisis.

In the late 1930s the New State undertook a series of minor development plans to strengthen the colonial African economy. These early programmes, some of which did not at first get beyond the planning stage, were financed from surpluses in the provincial budgets supported by loans from the National Treasury, and they were mainly concerned with expanding port facilities and transportation systems. In Moçambique over £10,000,000 were spent to improve transit communications, particularly the railway system. Then from 1953, with the inauguration of the first six-year Portuguese National Development Plan, in which Angola and Moçambique participated – although much of the financing in the colonies was drawn from local budgets (Angola drew ninety-five per cent from its budget surplus, while Moçambique used forty-two per cent from local resources) – the pattern of development became more diversified, with considerable attention now paid to colonization and hydro-electric schemes, and somewhat less to health and education programmes. From 1953 to 1958 more than £28,500,000 was spent in each province to carry out various projects. In 1959 a second National Development Plan was begun, with some £60,000,000 to be spent in Angola and some £38,000,000 in Moçambique. About half of each of these sums was to be provided by the metropolis and international financial organizations, while the other half was to be drawn from local sources.

In Moçambique in 1959 the following sums were distributed

during the first year of the new plan. These may be compared with the disbursement planned for 1961. (The figures are given in value of *contos*; the *conto* is worth about £12 10s. or $35·00):

	1959 (*Spent*)	1961 (*Disbursed*)
Communications and transport	265,870	246,000
Colonization	84,360	131,500
Development of resources	66,170	131,000
Education and health	15,000	90,000
Local improvement	5,000	20,000
Studies	8,109	14,500

To stimulate economic development at home and overseas, a National Development Bank was established in 1959 to make long-term loans for agricultural and industrial development. Whether the onrush of events in Angola and the threatening crisis in Moçambique will render the Bank's whole objective useless is a serious question. In 1960 Portugal joined the International Monetary Fund and the International Bank for Reconstruction and Development, although, again, it is doubtful whether these associations will very profitably serve the African colonies. Earlier in the 1950s Portugal received some financial aid from the United States to carry out a geological survey in Angola. Neither colony has been able to count on much assistance for development from local or Portuguese banking interests. In Angola, the monopolistic Banco de Angola (the bank of issue in the colony) has long followed a conservative course, and the newly formed Banco Comercial has only limited funds available for agricultural and industrial loans. In Moçambique the Banco Nacional Ultramarino has also been cautious in supporting private development schemes.

In the apportioning of development funds the emphasis has been placed on the economic, not social, progress of the colonies – apart from the construction of several imposing new high schools and hospitals. In Moçambique, the colony's greatest project has been the construction of a barrage across the Limpopo River to provide irrigation for the predominantly white *colonato* at nearby Guija. The Lower Limpopo Valley Scheme has as its goal the placing of some 250,000 acres of land at the disposal of some 10,000 families for crops and pasturage. In the same region the Limpopo Railway has been extended from Guíja to Pafuri on the Rhodesian frontier, so linking the Lourenço Marques system with the main Rhodesian line and siphoning off part of the Rhodesian traffic from Beira to the less congested wharves of Lourenço Marques. The ports of Beira (whose facilities and railway had been purchased by the colonial government from affiliates of the Moçambique Company) and Lourenço Marques have both been expanded and modernized to serve an ever-increasing traffic. The goods moved through Lourenço Marques rose from 4,446,000 tons in 1958 to an estimated 6,000,000 tons in 1960; in Beira, the weight of goods increased from 2,618,000 tons in 1958 to 3,209,000 in 1960. At Nacala a new port has been created to serve northern Moçambique from the coast to Lake Nyasa, and a railroad is being built from Lumbo and Nacala through Nampula to Malema and then up to Vila Cabral. About two-thirds completed, the new line, it is hoped, will help develop an underpopulated and potentially wealthy section of the country – much as the Benguela Railway did in the highlands of Angola. The construction of bridges and roads has opened up sections of the province to all-season traffic. A modern new airport at Lourenço Marques and lesser airfields at many towns throughout the province have made air services in Moçambique rapid and efficient. The colony's first hydro-electric plant was built on the Revué River to provide power for industrial and urban needs in the vicinity of Beira; surplus power has been sold to Umtali across the Rhodesian frontier. A similar hydro-electric plant, on the Movene River twenty miles from Lourenço Marques, is planned.

In the private sector of Moçambique's economic development, progress has been less spectacular, but it has been steady. Again, this progress may be seen in the centres of trade and commerce throughout the colony. Quite apart from Lourenço Marques and Beira, which have become international cities of obvious growth and prosperity, the smaller towns of Moçambique, like Quelimane (5,000 people), Tete (3,000), Nampula (2,500), and Vila Cabral (2,500), have grown and developed into replicas of

Portuguese towns. Trade and plantation crops compose the back-bone of the colonial economy. Sugar, sisal, copra, and tea remain the principal estate crops, while citrus fruits are grown on smaller Portuguese farms in the Incomati valley. Despite various surveys for suitable mineral deposits, including many years of oil-prospecting by Moçambique Gulf, virtually the only mineral activity remains the production of some 200,000 tons of coal a year up the Zambezi at Moatize. A promising growth and diversification has occurred in local industry, however, all of it for local consumption. A cotton-seed refining plant outside Nampula, a cotton-textile factory at Vila Pery (which costs much more to operate than similar plants in Portugal), cement and tile plants outside Beira, and soap, tobacco, and beer factories in Lourenço Marques, have come into operation in recent years.

The modest development of private industry and trade is consistent with the cautious economic programmes that the New State has followed in Moçambique. The colony suffers from a perennial trade deficit, as figures for 1958–60 clearly indicate. (The figures, again, are given in value of *contos*; see page 194.)

Imports from	1958	1959	1960
Portugal	932,000	889,000	1,055,000
Portuguese Overseas	160,000	171,000	202,000
Abroad	2,344,000	2,491,000	2,538,000
Exports to			
Portugal	910,000	900,000	1,008,000
Portuguese Overseas	72,000	87,000	66,000
Abroad	1,040,000	916,000	1,024,000

During the same period the quantity and value (in *contos*) of Moçambique's six principal export crops were:

Product	1958 Tons	1958 Value	1959 Tons	1959 Value	1960 Tons	1960 Value
Sugar	132,387	337,174	114,108	289,567	111,249	278,239
Cotton	35,974	549,073	35,051	540,622	44,398	681,531
Cashew nuts	95,973	253,317	61,903	176,969	55,848	199,915
Tea	6,904	145,650	7,987	154,485	8,066	176,420
Copra	44,368	189,323	37,639	211,045	40,753	194,333
Sisal	32,450	131,390	30,596	158,418	27,950	177,863

Moçambique has all the same continued to maintain a balanced budget and even contribute to its colonial development programmes. The two main sources of income which help the colony to meet its constant trade deficit come from the transit traffic of the Rhodesias and the Republic of South Africa which uses Moçambique's ports and railroads, and from the export of Moçambique's labouring force to neighbouring territories. For each labourer recruited under the several conventions, the Portuguese receive in the neighbourhood of £2. The worker's local taxes are also collected abroad. These contributions, which are paid in gold, with the remittances that the working force sends or brings back into the colony, raise considerably the income from abroad. Tourism is another significant source of foreign revenue.

For a number of reasons, commercial and plantation interests in Moçambique, as in Angola, resent what they feel to be the metropolitan government's rigid and doctrinaire controls over the local economy. They argue that metropolitan import firms are given privileged positions in major development schemes, to the detriment of local interests. They are not, as António de Figueiredo states, happy that,

while prices for raw materials and foodstuffs are officially kept below world levels, and some commodities, such as cotton and sugar, are sold exclusively to Portugal, imports are subject to protective policies, aimed at maintaining the market for Metropolitan Portuguese manufacturers where these would otherwise meet with foreign competition.

They have questioned the New State's claim of economic integration when they are still obliged to pay duty on Portuguese goods entering the colonies. And they maintain that the establishment of industries to meet local requirements depends on their ability to compete with Portuguese industry. The growing anger against Portugal's mercantilist policies in Africa is unquestionably one of the significant elements in the formation of a conservative white separatist sentiment in Angola and Moçambique.

Where Moçambique has had to be content with a comparatively modest growth, the emergence of Angola in the last fifteen, and especially in the last ten years, has been flamboyantly spectacular. Even though a small recession at the end of the decade and declining prices for coffee dampened the more enthusiastic spirits, the Cinderella Colony, the second Brazil in the dreams of Portuguese colonialists, seemed at last to have come of age. Few cities in Africa have had a more dramatic growth than Luanda, which doubled in size and number of inhabitants in the decade 1950–60. Lobito, Benguela, Nova Lisboa, Malange, Sá da Bandeira, Silva Porto, and Vila Luso have all developed into energetic and handsome towns. Lavish hotels, restaurants, cinemas, radio and sporting clubs, and even an occasional Sunday traffic-jam gave evidence of the new spirit of confidence in the colony and the hopes for its future. Needless to say, these were white men's hopes, just as these are white men's cities.

White colonization projects at Cela in the Amboim plateau, north-west of Nova Lisboa, and at Vila Folgares, near Matala, are being pursued in the government's view successfully. Populated by Portuguese peasant families, whose venture into planned emigration and settlement is supported by a twenty-five-year loan from the government to each colonist, these agricultural settlements are an important part of Lisbon's vision for colonial development. In 1943 Salazar remarked that

the rich extensive colonial lands, under-developed and sparsely populated, are the natural complement for metropolitan agriculture. . . . In addition they will take care of that part of the metropolis's excessive population which Brazil does not wish to accept.

Each immigrant family receives a house, livestock, seeds, and over one hundred acres of farming and grazing land. Whenever possible an effort has been made to re-create the life of the Portuguese countryside. At Cela over 300 families raise vegetables, rice, and fruit, and have begun dairy- and meat-cattle production. There has been no significant increase since 1954 in the number of families at this showplace of Portuguese planned colonization. For years, in spite of the government's mellow pronouncements, there have been evidences of discontent at Cela, while in the colony there has been much talk of money wasted on splashy projects. Some observers believe that Cela will gradually collapse. At Vila Folgares, some 200 Portuguese families raise tobacco, wheat, and vegetables. A third white *colónato* is being developed in the Bengo River valley, north of Luanda, there to grow produce and raise dairy and meat cattle for the capital's needs.

Under the two Development Plans, various hydro-electric plants were constructed in the 1950s. The first, near Mabubas, was finished in its first phase in 1954; its capacity is just sufficient to supply Luanda's demands. The Craveiro Lopes Dam at Biópio was completed in 1956, and presently supplies the Lobito–Benguela area. The new power station at the Salazar Dam on the Cunene River near Matala, which serves also as a bridge for the Moçâmedes railroad and provides irrigation for the Vila Folgares *colónato*, furnishes electricity for Sá da Bandeira, Moçâmedes, and the environs. A still larger project is under construction up the Cuanza at Cambambe. This £10,000,000 dam will furnish power for Luanda and nascent industrial sites near Dondo.

As in Moçambique, a great deal of attention has been paid to the transportation complex. About forty per cent of all development funds have gone into improving and constructing airports, railways, roads, and port facilities. The highway network in Angola totals some 22,000 miles of road, 5,518 miles of which are classified as first-class (only 435 miles are asphalted). Bridges are gradually replacing primitive ferries over many of Angola's rivers. A branch of the Luanda–Malange railway line, which has been widened to standard gauge, has been extended to Dondo, while in the south the Moçâmedes line has now reached 446 miles into the interior to Vila Serpa Pinto. It is unlikely now that the road will be pushed to the Rhodesian frontier, but a spur is to be built to Cassinga in order to carry iron ore. And the Benguela Railway plans to run a connecting line from Vila Robert Williams to the iron-ore deposits at Cuíma. Construction of a line from Luanda into the Portuguese Congo has only progressed eight miles, and the future of this development is at best uncertain. The three major ports, Lobito, Luanda, and

Moçâmedes, have all been improved. In 1959, a total of 1,434,865 metric tons passed through Lobito, 599,010 tons through Luanda, and 84,501 tons through Moçâmedes. It is hoped that a larger share of the mineral traffic from Katanga and Northern Rhodesia, much of which now goes to Beira, will pass through Lobito. Air services are of the same efficiency as in Moçâmbique, and the newly completed runways at Luanda's modern airport are capable of handling commercial jet traffic.

Although the backbone of the Angolan economy continued during the 1950s to be agricultural, principally coffee cultivation, Portuguese officials in 1960 spoke of the coming mineral decade. A geological survey was carried out in 1953–5 by the government, with the help of the International Co-operation Administration, and other surveys are constantly being undertaken. In 1960 diamonds and iron ore were the only minerals to make any sizeable contribution to the gross national product. Diamang, mining sixty per cent gem-stones and forty per cent industrial ones, plans to increase its production. (In 1959, the value of diamonds mined was some £7,500,000, and in 1960 some £6,500,000, constituting each year about ten per cent in value of total exports.) Iron ore was exported for the first time in 1957 by the Companhia Mineira do Lobito from deposits at Cuíma, Bailundo, and Andulo. Production in 1960 almost doubled the 1959 total of 350,000 tons. With the receipt of credit for some £16,000,000 from the German Krupp firm, the Companhia speaks of exporting up to four million tons a year. The Companhia de Manganês de Angola now produces about 200,000 tons from its deposits west of Malange. A small amount of manganese and copper has been exported in recent years, and Alumnio Português has announced plans for a plant at Dondo, to be completed in 1962. Oil production remains well below the 1955 expectations of an ultimate 500,000 tons a year. Crude-oil production in 1960 reached 66,848 tons, and Petrangol's refineries were processing mostly crude oil from Venezuela. Petrofina, the Belgian parent company, is not optimistic about recovering all of its almost £16,000,000 investment.

In agricultural production coffee, until the 1961 revolts in the northern Angola coffee country, was king, and provided much of the impetus for Angola's expanding economy. In the early 1950s coffee made up forty per cent of the value of total exports. In 1957 there were 250,000 hectares in production, four-fifths of these in European hands. The production of sisal has continued to increase, while sugar production has fluctuated between 30,000 and 40,000 tons for annual export, although production goals for the coming years have been doubled. Palm oil and citrus fruits have come to make a small contribution to the export economy. Local plantation owners feel that the various commodity boards, located in Lisbon, which have jurisdiction over the cultivation and export of certain crops, have had a restrictive influence on agricultural production.

The fishing industry, which in the early 1950s provided, behind coffee and diamonds, the colony's third largest export, has recently encountered difficulties which threaten its very existence. A shortage of fish, inefficient production, and a drop in world prices have brought the many once-prosperous fisheries of southern Angola to the brink of ruin. On the other hand, forestry and livestock production have registered significant increases. A jute and fibre factory has begun operation in Luanda, and a new cement plant at Luanda has been built to go with the older plant at Lobito. Alcohol, beer, and tobacco are now manufactured locally. A flour-mill has been constructed in Luanda. A cellulose plant has been completed, and a fertilizer factory is being planned to make use of phosphate deposits in northern Angola. These industrial developments are not yet important, but they reveal a growing self-reliance in the colony.

Although toward the end of the decade Angola suffered an economic recession, the financial position of the colony in early 1961 was basically sound, and the future looked comfortingly bright. Declining prices for agricultural commodities, mostly coffee, and the increasing expenditure on development, caused reserves, built up early in the period, to dwindle and lead to a deficit in the balance of trade. But strict trade controls over imports were expected to right the balance. The following tables for 1958 and 1959 show the trade situation in Angola. (Values are in millions of *escudos*, the *escudo* being worth about 3d. or 3·5 cents.)

EXPORTS

Commodity	1958	1959
Coffee	1,505	1,387
Diamonds	548	596
Sisal	214	290
Corn	218	215
Fish meal	289	205
Cotton	85	104
Iron ore	77	99
Sugar	87	77

IMPORTS

Commodity	1958	1959
Textiles	478	465
Wines	352	366
Industrial machinery	188	214
Railroad material	128	244
Iron and steel manufactures	147	140
Trucks	199	140
Medicines	83	80

Trade in the same two years and its percentage of the total was as follows (values again given in millions of *escudos*).

EXPORT MARKETS	1958		1959	
Country	Value	Percentage	Value	Percentage
United States	935	25·4	904	25·2
United Kingdom	600	16·2	657	18·3
Portugal	665	18·0	652	18·1
Holland	459	12·4	389	10·9
Germany	242	6·6	248	6·9
France	124	3·4	112	3·1
Belgian Congo	83	2·3	69	1·9
Belgium–Luxemburg	131	3·6	68	1·9

Source of Imports

Portugal	1,722	46·1	1,754	44·6
Germany	348	9·3	435	11·6
United Kingdom	435	11·7	360	9·6
United States	434	11·6	347	9·2
Belgium–Luxemburg	201	5·4	148	3·9
Italy	41	1·1	97	2·6
Sweden	42	1·1	67	1·8
Macau	48	1·0	65	1·7

It must be emphasized again that the recent growth in the prosperity of Portuguese Africa is only relative and that in addition to having raised the cost of living to roughly twice that of the metropolis – with all of the consequences of misery for the African population that this implies – economic progress has benefited only a handful of people, most of them white. But no matter what old colonists have said about Salazar's cautious economic policies, no matter what foreign economic critics have called a stagnant situation, and no matter that both colonies suffer from trade imbalances, the plain fact is that Angola and Moçambique have become more than psychic or historical appendages of Portugal. They have become profitable, and because they have become profitable they have given Portugal, and not only the government there, a positive sense of accomplishment as a world power. These were to be significant considerations in the decisions of 1961.

White Men's Colonies

Nowhere was the New State more successful than in solving the ancient problem of enticing Portuguese immigration to Angola and Moçambique (thus sowing the seeds for future discontent and perhaps revolt), if the government can claim credit, that is, for the conditions which created the migration to Africa. Poverty at home and exaggerated stories of prosperity in Africa succeeded where other persuasions had failed. Certainly life in metropolitan Portugal (whose *per capita* annual income of £70 to £84 has for long been the lowest in Western Europe), where overpopulation and unemployment prevailed, was enough to lead a number of cautious Portuguese workers to try their luck in Angola. Angola's white population rose from 30,000 in 1930, to 44,000 in 1940, to 79,000 in 1950, to 110,000 in 1955, and to an estimated 170,000 (some more liberal estimates put the figure at 200,000) in 1959. In 1960, for the first time in recent years, there was no large-scale immigration; in fact, more people in that year left the colony than entered it. Moçambique's growth has been as steady though less spectacular, from 18,000 in 1932, to 27,500 in 1940, to 48,000 in 1950, to 67,000 in 1955, and to an estimated 85,000 in 1960.

This migration has made its most striking impact on the cities and towns, where most of the new settlers seem to have concentrated. These towns have become white pockets in a black world, isolated, often insulated little communities, all bearing the uncompromising stamp of continental Portugal. Here the Portuguese cultural image has been re-created – in the architecture, in the cafés, in the formal little parks. Here perhaps one may measure at least one success in the New State's attempts to forge a single identity between Portugal and Africa, though in the process the Salazar government has contributed to freezing the frontier between two distinct worlds, one white and one black.

The New State's two-sided policy, which simultaneously proclaimed the ideals of non-racialism and pursued the most discriminatory cultural and political repressions, contained its full measure of racialism, but it remained for the influx of Portuguese peasants and workers to give that racialism real substance. Angola and Moçambique have become, since 1940, white men's colonies. With the growing Portuguese population has come a sharpened colour-consciousness; not only has the Portuguese immigrant – himself a labourer from an economically depressed country – sealed off the African's economic opportunities at the lowest level, but his own insecurities have led him to justify his privilege on the basis of his colour. Any notion of racial integration, of a new Brazil, in Portuguese Africa is fantasy. The white Angolan has probably never taken the New State's euphoristic statements on brotherhood seriously, and the savagery of white vigilante groups in Angola against innocent African villagers after the 1961 rebellion broke out is probably as good an indication of his real sentiments as the government's own eloquent pronouncements on Portuguese fraternal tolerance are not. But even before 1961 the colour line had been sharply drawn in colonial cities and towns – in the theatres, restaurants, hotels, stores, and on trains. Informal curfews were an accepted reality in Luanda, Lobito, Lourenço Marques, and Beira.

Portuguese artisans, skilled labourers, and even domestic servants have changed the total employment picture in the urban centres of Portuguese Africa. The African's economic mobility in these areas is small. The better-paying jobs in industry and the trades are filled by Portuguese. And, where the African does obtain work beside the Portuguese, his payment is from two to five times less than that of the Portuguese. In Luanda, an African painter, stone mason, or carpenter receives about half as much as his Portuguese counterparts, but in other districts the ratio drops to one-fourth or even one-fifth. Such has been the influx of Portuguese workers to Angola that in 1960 there were 7,000 unemployed white workers.

As a result of the political stability that the Salazar régime brought to Portugal and Africa, with the accompanying upsurge in the colonial economy, the Portuguese Africa of 1930–60 was no longer regarded with suspicion by her white neighbours. Angola and Moçambique became less often the object of sometimes ill-informed attacks on the backwardness of Portuguese policy. In addition to their need for Portuguese African ports for a large part of their trade, the Belgian Congo, the Rhodesias, and the Union of South Africa came to discover that their policies were not so very different after all from those of the Portuguese. And the discovery that they each shared a concept of white supremacy, whether called assimilation or apartheid, drew the countries of southern Africa into closer rapport. As the former Governor-General of South Africa, Dr Ernest Jansen, said during a state visit to Portugal:

By a happy accident we are neighbours. I believe that we should be grateful to history for this accident.

More than diplomatic courtesy, Dr Jansen's comment under-lined an awareness that the governments of the lands below the equator had a common cause – their survival.

With the independence of the Congo in 1960, the pockets of white resistance to African nationalism grew smaller, and the relations between the Welensky government, the Verwoerd régime in South Africa, and Portugal grew closer. The cere-monial visits between the Portuguese colonies and her neigh-bours have now reached a new tempo. South Africa and Portugal have allegedly signed a mutual defence agreement, and South Africa has apparently sent military advisers to Angola. Should an uprising occur in Moçambique, similar to the revolt in Angola, many observers believe that South African troops would assist the Portuguese army in the field, and there is further speculation that should such a situation in Moçambique ever reach danger-ous proportions, a union between South Africa and the southern half of Moçambique would become a real possibility.

World Opinion Hardens

But if Portugal has strengthened alliances with her immediate neighbours in Africa, her relations with much of the rest of the world have progressively deteriorated during the last seven years over her African colonies. In the 1930s and 1940s, Portugal avoided most of the humanitarian attacks from abroad. Occa-sional critics of her African policies were dismissed as Bolsheviks or international Jews, whose aggressive intentions 'only Hitler and Salazar know how to confront'. Skilfully moving Portugal from the Axis camp to the North Atlantic Treaty Organization, which Portugal joined in 1949, Salazar allied his country with those nations who could be reasonably counted on to defend her colonial position in Africa. Once again, however, British human-itarian opinion turned against Portugal as it had done before, and, although this opinion did not find diplomatic expression in Whitehall, it was effective in arousing other voices around the world against Portugal's presence in Africa. In the years 1955 to 1960 condemnation of Portugal mounted, in Europe, in Asia, in Africa, and in the Americas.

Once again the issue turned upon forced labour. Once again it was a British journalist who set the match to the fires of indignation. In 1954 Basil Davidson, who was in the Belgian Congo preparing a book, paid a visit to Angola. In *An African Awakening* (1955), and articles published in *Harper's* and the *New Statesman*, Davidson angrily established himself in the tradition of Nevinson, Cadbury, and Ross. He saw little change from the conditions that these men had described earlier in the century. Forced labour, economic exploitation of the African, brutality, unreasonable taxes, and racial discrimination were the hallmarks of the Portuguese occupation in Davidson's eyes. He drew attention to the Galvão report, and made Galvão a kind of hero to English liberal opinion. The *Observer* and the *Guardian* then took up the attack, in which they were joined by newspapers and journals in Sweden, France, the United States, and Brazil. In the United States, an anthropologist from Columbia University, Marvin Harris, published in 1958 *Portugal's African 'Wards'*, the first authentic criticism in thirty years of native conditions in Moçambique. Journalists at last began to include Portuguese Africa in their itineraries, and their commentaries on life in Angola and Moçambique did not always follow the Portuguese version of health and happiness. By 1960 the shroud of ignorance which had enveloped Portuguese Africa for so many years had been penetrated.

It was on these writings that Asian, African, and Soviet critics based their denunciations of Portugal in speeches at the United Nations. In the mid 1950s the controversy over Goa between the Indian and the Portuguese governments had already served to harden Asian and anti-colonial sentiment against Portugal. Portugal became a member of the world organization in 1955, but refused to furnish information on the colonies to the UN. Portugal argued that Article 73e of the Charter, which stipulated that members should furnish information on non-self-governing territories under their control, had nothing to do with her, since Portuguese Africa was made up of provinces which were in effect integral projections of Portugal. Although this defence hardly satisfied her critics, Portugal, with the aid of her allies, succeeded nonetheless in keeping the attacks within reasonable bounds until 1960. In that year, and in 1961, the crisis could no longer be postponed, and the United Nations in effect passed censure on Portugal for her African policies.

From the end of the Second World War, it must have been apparent to the Salazar government that the stronger Portugal's position in Western Europe and America became, the stronger would be Portugal's position in Africa itself. During the war the government had tempered its Fascist sympathies to the extent of permitting the United States to construct and maintain an air-base in the Azores, and it was this military association which was in large part responsible for the entry of Portugal into NATO. Portuguese diplomacy, of course, exploited this membership to the full in Britain and the United States. Britain once again became 'Portugal's oldest ally', while toward the United States Portugal put forth the face of militant anti-Communism in Europe and in Africa. Throughout the 1950s these tactics were successful. While a minority of opinion in both countries questioned the moral and political reliability of the Salazar dictatorship, the seeming necessities of the Western Alliance or of colonial policies in Africa obliged Britain, the United States, and, more often than not, France, in effect to dance to the Portuguese tune. Secretary of State Acheson held Prime Minister Salazar in considerable esteem; in 1955, at the height of the Goan controversy, Secretary of State Dulles referred to the 'Portuguese province of Goa'. In 1960, on a visit to Lisbon, President Eisenhower spoke warmly of Portugal's role in NATO. The attitude of the British government during this period was only a little less restrained.

Thus until late 1960 the Portuguese government could count on both military assistance, which, directly or indirectly, helped to strengthen her garrisons in Africa, and diplomatic support, which helped to control the mounting world-protest against her repressive policies in the colonies. And the Salazar régime's own position at home was unquestionably bolstered by such powerful alliances. African nationalism was assiduously converted by Portuguese statesmen into a Communist menace, against which the Portuguese colonies were represented as the last bulwarks of Western European civilization. The Azores and the possibility of using Portuguese African bases were carefully intruded into military discussions. A stable government in Portugal was presented as a vital necessity for the well-being of Western defence. For ten years New State diplomats manoeuvred with quiet and convincing skill. For five years at the United Nations, from the moment of her entry into the world organization in 1955 until 1960, Portugal, using her various friends and allies, succeeded in frustrating anti-colonial attacks upon her position in Africa.

On another front, Portugal made every effort to turn her sentimental association with the one-time Portuguese colony of Brazil into diplomatic advantage, and during the second half of the decade she could usually count on the enthusiastic support of Brazil and a fair number of other Latin-American countries. The Presidents of Portugal and Brazil exchanged ceremonial visits, and there was much talk of a Lusitanian community, a sort of cultural commonwealth of Portuguese-speaking lands. In 1960 a treaty of friendship and consultation was signed by the two nations. For Portugal the creation of such a commonwealth would have been a resounding demonstration of her claims for the spiritual unity of the Lusitanian world. Brazil, whose population is in the majority Negro or mulatto, had long been heralded as the success story of Portugal's overseas policies, and her formal association with Portugal in an amorphous union would have offered, Portuguese planners clearly hoped, a convincing argument against anti-colonial attacks. While for the moment the nascent commonwealth was exploited primarily by Portugal for diplomatic and propaganda purposes, it was probably intended to be Portugal's last trump in Africa; a commonwealth could have provided, it seemed as late as 1960, a framework in which Portuguese Africa could be granted limited independence. But the change in the Brazilian administration with the election of Jánio Quadros destroyed this contingency, just as the election of Kennedy in the United States and the increasing importance of the Afro-Asian states began to move the United States and

Britain away from their unquestioning acceptance of Portuguese policies in Africa. By January 1961 it was apparent that Portuguese diplomacy would need to redouble its efforts to prevent the gradual isolation of Portugal, if not in Europe, certainly in the larger arena of world opinion and politics.

The Beginning of the End

Midnight came for the Cinderella colony of Angola early in 1961. Before the year was out, it seemed clear that Portugal was engaged in a struggle which she could not win. Nor could the Salazar government be certain that policies which had so manifestly failed in Angola would succeed in Moçambique and Guinea, beyond whose borders militant African opposition-forces were gathering. The government hinted at liberal reforms in the colonies, continued to speak of multi-racial societies living in peace and prosperity – and diligently intensified its régime of terror. But, by the end of the year, the bonds of tradition which tied the past to the present and which the Portuguese had hoped would contain the future had frayed and broken. The dream had died.

From the shock and bitterness which the Angola rebellion aroused in the colony and in Portugal, it is apparent that both Portuguese settlers and the government were astounded by the events of mid March. The colonial administration in Angola was prepared for trouble, to be sure; for three years an increasing show of military strength had been made in Angola and every effort employed to subdue and scatter nascent African opposition. Portuguese officials must have assumed, however, that any native rising would be an isolated incident – a village demonstration, a strike, or a march of protest in Luanda – which could be ruthlessly and effectively suppressed. But this is not what happened, and for the widespread rebel attacks in the Angola coffee country which occurred in the week of 15 March, the colonial administration seems to have been virtually unprepared. To add to Portugal's chagrin, there were in Luanda at the time a large number of correspondents from various parts of the world, so that it was impossible for the authorities to stifle the story of the rebellion. Portugal's anger and embarrassment at seeing the carefully supported façade of a happy and peaceful colony so dramatically torn down undoubtedly contributed to the violence with which the uprising was met.

And it is obvious that many Portuguese had come to accept the myth of Portuguese Africa as true. They had only that vision of Angola which they chose and were encouraged to have – a colony where the benevolent ideals of a civilizing, humanitarian Portugal had so infused the native society that it had nothing to fear from the African nationalism already at its very borders. They believed, because a white man could reportedly travel alone and unharmed throughout Angola, that Portugal's mission in Africa had succeeded. They believed that paternalism was an acceptable alternative to freedom. They believed, because a few thousand Africans had become Portuguese citizens and the colonies themselves were called overseas provinces, that Portugal had found the answer to African nationalism. They believed that the only trouble besetting Portuguese Africa was caused by meddlers and Communists in the world outside, a notion that the government took the greatest care to nourish. They believed, all evidence indicating the contrary, that the Africans in their colonies would rather be Portuguese than free. They were wrong.

Bemused by the myth of Luso-African solidarity and confident in the prosperity of Angola and Moçambique, Portugal refused to heed the course of events in the rest of Africa and the stirrings of discontent within the territories. In May 1959, Dr Salazar spoke on the African problem:

It is the literal truth to say that Africa is afire, even in the neighbourhood of Portuguese frontiers. Why is Africa on fire? Let us not imagine that it is due to internal combustion, that is, the unavoidable force of a historical movement urging the populations on to revolt, sedition, forced dispersion, and independence. Africa is burning because it is being set on fire from outside. . . .

It is well known that the overseas portion of Portugal comes under especially sharp fire. Criticisms of our alleged incapacity for colonization, insufficient capital, lack of dynamism in production, slowness in the spread of education, the low wages paid, defective health-protection, and many other things of the same kind . . . are common. . . .

This fact [the alleged good will of the African population] shows the danger of trying to reduce the whole of the task of colonization to economic indices. It signifies that there is a work of human understanding and sympathy which from generation to generation builds up inter-racial contact that is invaluable. This is the basis for the solution of the problems of Africa, for without it they can have no lasting solution. This is more than our conviction: it is our way of being. . . . But we cannot neglect external circumstances, in so far as they may alter the calm of populations and order and work in the overseas portion of our national territory. These we must fight with all suitable weapons.

We are reconsidering the bases for the solution of these problems, taking into account present conditions and later needs. Although the surest defence is the reciprocal confidence and unity of the populations of the Portuguese world, we must be present as always and now more vigilant than ever before. The nature of events near in time and space may have destroyed some illusions, but it has not altered one fact we may consider to be permanent in our overseas history; in the absence of outside influences the Portuguese, of whatever race and colour, do not usually go astray, but go their way in peace.

In November 1960, President Américo Thomaz said:

We are not in Africa . . . like so many others. We will continue as always our policy of integration . . . to this end it is necessary for us to be what we have always been, and we will not change.

Dr Castro Fernandez, head of the National Union, Portugal's ruling party, put it even more bluntly: 'Portugal is in Africa and Portugal will remain in Africa.' In the face of such determined affirmations, African opposition-groups in exile, whose existence the Portuguese government acknowledged only with epithets, had but one choice.

In 1948, High Inspector Galvão warned his government of the consequences of holding to its policies of repression. In the same year, a minor manifestation in Lourenço Marques occurred; its leaders were promptly exiled. In 1953, a group of Angolans sent a letter to the United Nations documenting their protest against the misery and brutality in the colony. In 1953, on São Tomé, more than one hundred African farmers and labourers were killed by colonial police in a demonstration of protest against local authority. In 1956 portraits of Nasser and Pan-Arab pamphlets began to appear among the predominantly Moslem African peoples of northern Moçambique. The leaders of the government-sponsored Liga Africana, in Angola, a federation of indigenous associations, whose activities were supposed to be limited to the social sphere, began to dissociate themselves from the official policy and refused in 1957 to send a delegation to the United Nations to voice the Liga's support of Portugal. Small political groups in both colonies were secretly formed; African and Portuguese liberals began to speak, not always secretly, against Portuguese colonialism. Even within the Salazar government, and among its supporters, cautious voices urged changes, some of them drastic, in the authoritarian colonial régime. Principally these men advocated the giving of some reality at last to the fiction that the African populations of Angola and Moçambique were Portuguese. The support given in the colonies to Humberto Delgado, the opposition candidate in the 1958 elections, was yet another indication, although it came from a predominantly white electorate, of unrest.

As the crescendo of protest against Portugal rose in the outside world, particularly at the United Nations, and as the importance of several newly formed Portuguese African parties in exile began to increase, repression in the colonies mounted. In Bissau, the capital of Portuguese Guinea, a number of African strikers were killed by colonial police during a demonstration for higher wages. In Angola wholesale arrests of dissidents, real and suspected, took place. Forty-five Africans and *assimilados*, men and women, with seven Europeans, were arrested in 1959 and brought to trial the following year, in June, on a charge of subversion. Another fifty-two Africans, including the African Chancellor of the Archbishopric of Luanda, Father Joaquim Pinto de Andrade, were arrested in June 1960. The Portuguese Bishop of Beira spoke out repeatedly against repressive practices in Moçambique. Another among the Africans arrested in June' was Agostinho Neto, a doctor and poet and the President of the Movimento Popular de Libertação de Angola, a clandestine nationalist movement. Hundreds of villagers from Dr Neto's birthplace in Bengo and from the nearby small town of Icolo decided to march to the administrative centre of Catete to protest against Dr Neto's arrest. They were met there by Portuguese troops. Thirty of the marchers were killed and 200 wounded; the two villages were then destroyed by the soldiers, and more of their inhabitants killed or arrested. Once again the colonial administration was careful to prevent news of the incident from being broadcast abroad.

With the passing of the Congo from Belgian hands, it became apparent that the days of Portuguese peace in Angola were numbered. But the revolt against the Salazar régime took first a curious and dramatic turn, not in Africa at all, but in the Caribbean, where on 22 January, Captain Henrique Galvão seized the Portuguese luxury liner, *Santa Maria*. According to Galvão, in his recently published account, *Santa Maria: My Crusade for Portugal*, original plans were for the small band of Portuguese and Spanish rebels (twenty-four in all) to sail to the Spanish island of Fernando Po, gather reinforcements there and in Spanish Guinea, and then sail for Angola. Although Galvão finally brought the ship into the Brazilian port of Recife, he had nonetheless achieved a great deal: he had focused the world's attention on the Portuguese dictatorship and, indirectly, on the plight of the African colonies; he had driven a small wedge between Portugal and her NATO allies, who refused Salazar's request to treat the incident as piracy; he had caused the public separation of Brazil from the warm embrace of Portugal. Although neither then nor later did Galvão's cause or his views on colonialism coincide with those of the Portuguese African opposition, in retrospect the *Santa Maria* episode looms larger and larger as the symbolic beginning of the end for Portugal in Africa.

Whether the African rising in Luanda on 4 February was originally intended to coincide with the arrival of the *Santa Maria* is still uncertain. What is certain is that, driven to despair by the administration's refusal to heed either their pleas or their warnings, African leaders in Luanda decided to take direct action. On the evening of 4 February, the Luanda jail and two separated police barracks were stormed by African crowds variously estimated at from 200 to 500 people. At the funeral on 5 February for the seven policemen killed during the attack, rioting again broke out, and in the fighting, which continued for the rest of the day, Portuguese security forces killed twenty-four rioters, wounded over a hundred, and arrested another hundred. That was, officially, the end of the incident, held by the government to have been inspired by outsiders and Communists. The unofficial story must be pieced together, for following these events Portuguese censorship clamped down upon Angola, and, on 9 February, four foreign newsmen were asked to leave the colony. Reprisals against the African population went on for the rest of the month. The African slums were repeatedly raided by marauding white groups, who indiscriminately murdered and pillaged. Political prisoners in the Luanda gaol were executed and buried in mass graves. White hoodlums roamed Luanda's streets at night, beating, often fatally, any Africans they encountered.

No sooner had Luanda put its house ruthlessly in order and invited the international Press back to report on the harmony that prevailed, than northern Angola exploded into a scene of terror and counter-terror. The exact events of 15 March and of the following days are still difficult to establish. Either as a result of labour disturbances on a coffee plantation which set off a chain of spontaneous violence, or as a planned campaign of rebellion, African terrorists and workers attacked Portuguese settlers, often mutilating their victims. No matter what the original source of the rising, a leadership quickly asserted itself, and, during the following days, the bands of rebels, their numbers swelled by peasants and contract workers from the coffee estates, carried out organized attacks in this fertile coffee-growing area. Within a week Portuguese troop detachments had penetrated the area, a large part of the white population had been evacuated, and the war in Angola had begun.

From the beginning the Portuguese government offered simple and misleading explanations of the Angolan tragedy, explanations which revealed the depths of Portugal's self-delusion and an almost perverse refusal to face the necessities of political life in Africa. First, the government chose to emphasize the acts of atrocity committed by the rebels and to attribute them to a resurgence of tribalism – to, in the words of the anthropologist Dr José Redinha, Director of the Angola Museum, 'all the primitive atavisms, all the latent savage substratum'. In taking this line and carefully referring to another Mau-Mau terror, colonial propagandists sought to evoke at home and abroad what were essentially racialist sentiments – abroad, the image of Christian European Portugal confronting savage Africa; at home, and in the colonies, a bloody picture of the fate that awaited those who failed to stand firm in Africa. A popular nineteenth-century vision of Africa, with all its latent suggestions of tribalism, fetishism, cannibalism, and primitive savagery, was carefully reconstructed by Portuguese publicists. Thus the picture of the spear-wielding, blood-thirsty, *black* barbarian murdering and mutilating innocent *white* women and children. Thus the widely distributed photographs of grotesquely mangled corpses. Thus the repeated references to the savage beast, and the sanctimonious defence for what the Portuguese have openly called a war of extermination. No one will deny the awful violence that has been committed by both sides in the fearful Angolan struggle. One can only comment that if savagery and atrocities provide the index of tribalism, Portuguese soldiers and colonists are no less atavistic than their African opponents, while remembering that it is these same Portuguese who have repeatedly claimed that they were bringing to Angola the Christian brotherhood and the higher cultural values of Western civilization.

The second explanation offered by the régime was that the revolt in Angola was the work of outsiders. It is perfectly true that the guerrilla campaigns were organized and in part conducted by outsiders. But the outsiders were Angolans, not, as Portugal has repeatedly implied but never proved, men from other African countries. The guerrilla fighter in Angola was an outsider in the same sense that the Frenchman who returned across the Channel with the Allied armies in 1944 was an outsider. Certainly they were no more outsiders than the troops from Portugal confronting them. It is a curious commentary on the much-publicized tolerance and harmony of Portuguese rule in Angola that there should have been such a group of outsiders at all among the estimated one million Angolans living beyond the frontiers. Certainly, once in Angola they had been joined by men who were not outsiders, farmers and contract workers who had been carried to the coffee plantations of northern Angola from many parts of the country.

The third explanation for the revolt was that it had been inspired by Communists abroad and abetted by foreign meddlers within. In Angola, where the government could hardly admit the existence of a Communist leadership, Protestants served Portuguese purposes as well. White Protestant missionaries were accused of conspiracy, and some of them were gaoled. African Protestants were also gaoled, many were tortured, and some were murdered by colonial police. White vigilantes made African Protestants their particular target for brutal reprisals. The Portuguese were acting consistently. Through much of their history in Africa, they have revealed an extraordinary incapacity to accept responsibility for the results of their own actions or policies. Again and again they have blamed 'denationalizing foreign forces' for their difficulties. Had Communism and Protestant missionaries not existed, Portuguese xenophobia would have had to invent something else.

Communism was the most damning label that the Portuguese could attach to the Union of Angola Peoples (U.P.A.), the movement that had directed much of the nationalist activity in northern Angola, and such a tactic was clearly consistent with the anti-Communist image Portugal had been projecting to the world. The Salazar régime need not have been over-cynical to realize that in the Western world, especially in the United States, a cry of Communism is often sufficient to condemn. And for those people perplexed, and perhaps disturbed, by the startling emergence of African nationalism in recent years, the cry of Communism, coupled with tales of primitive savagery and the myth of a benevolent Portuguese rule, was often enough to explain untoward events in Angola. It did not matter that Portugal based its charges on innuendo, half-truth, rumour, and a few distorted facts. It did not matter that the U.P.A., and its leader, Holden Roberto, were essentially conservative men, that Roberto himself had steadfastly rejected Communist support for his movement. No less an authority on international Communism than the Central Intelligence Agency reportedly made an investigation of the U.P.A. and satisfied itself that it was an authentic African nationalist party, free from any Communist association. For the Portuguese, however, the measure of a man's Communism remained the extent of his resistance to the Salazar régime.

The Union of Angolan Peoples is the largest, the most moderate, and potentially the most effective of Portuguese African opposition groups. Organized in 1954, the Union has grown to an estimated membership of 40,000, and publishes a newspaper in four languages, French, Portuguese, Kimbundu, and Kikongo. Although its leader Holden Roberto and many of its members are Bakongo, and the Union has enlisted the support of Kasavubu's Abako, the tribal association does not seem to be dominant, and Roberto has rejected any possibility of union between the Portuguese Congo and the Congo Republic, although he fears that the Central Congolese government may well press for such a merger, especially in the event of any Angolan fragmentation. But the Union sees itself principally as a party working for the independence of all Angola, and during 1961 it took an increasing responsibility for directing and supplying the revolt.

The 1960 Declaration of the Steering Committee of the U.P.A., 'The Struggle for the Independence of Angola', is predominantly an exhortation to the African peoples to overthrow the ancient tyranny. It calls upon both Portuguese and Africans to join the cause and promises equal participation in national affairs to Portuguese residents of Angola. Its proposals are general:

Angola would form an autonomous state, establish its own democratic responsible government, conforming to the traditions and needs of the land – a government fully competent to direct public affairs, organize public services, national economy, education, public health, in the best interests of all its citizens and excluding all foreign interference.

Angola would appear on the international scene to participate in world government and in the building up of the United States of Africa in support of the resolutions of the Conferences of African Peoples held at Accra and Tunis.

So far, the U.P.A. has sought support from Western or neutral countries, and Roberto himself, who has spent some time in the United States, has already been attacked as a tool of American interests in Africa. The longer the struggle in Angola continues, however, the more difficult it will be for the U.P.A. to follow its essentially moderate course. Its leadership is even now being challenged by a perhaps more radical group, the Popular Movement for the Liberation of Angola (M.P.L.A.).

Although numerically inferior to the Union, the M.P.L.A. is a more cosmopolitan and seemingly better-organized group. It is one of the dominant forces in F.R.A.I.N., the African Revolutionary Front for the Independence of the Portuguese Colonies. M.P.L.A. is itself a merger of various smaller groups and is organized on a non-racial – some of its members are white – as well as non-tribal basis. One of its founders was Agostinho Neto, and the Acting President, Mário de Andrade, is a poet and former student at the University of Paris. In Paris, he was associated with the society for the promotion of African culture organized round the magazine, *Présence Africaine*.

For several years the Movement's headquarters were in Conakry – Andrade has now apparently moved to a Leopoldville office – which for the Portuguese constituted adequate evidence of Communist attachments. Andrade has enjoyed some verbal support from the Soviet bloc, it is true, and has had an article published in *Pravda*, but there are no serious indications that the Movement is more than a militant nationalist party. Certainly its programme published in March 1961 in the *Portuguese and Colonial Bulletin* was moderate enough. It envisaged the equality of various ethnic groups and even the right to autonomy of national minorities with distinctive characteristics, which, if it means what it seems to say, would quickly lead to trouble in an independent Angola. The programme proposed equal rights for women, a voting age of eighteen years, the abolition of foreign military bases, the end of the forced-labour régime, a minimum wage, and an eight-hour working day. Economically, the party required the distribution of estate lands to African farmers, the abolition of the single-crop system, and the transformation of Angola into a modern industrial country.

Allied to the M.P.L.A. is the African Party for the Independence of Guinea. The several Moçambique opposition groups which have been formed in Dar-es-Salaam have also been invited to participate in the united anti-colonial front. Whether the front will hold together and even increase its strength, however, remains to be seen. If the various anti-colonial movements could form a coalition with the several anti-Salazar Portuguese groups, the Salazar régime would face a potentially formidable opposition; but the spectrum of opinion is almost certainly too wide to permit such an alliance.

The war in Angola has provided the focus for most nationalist activities, because what happens in Angola will determine events in the rest of Portuguese Africa. The Portuguese government has been aware also of the political and strategic implications of the struggle. Shortly after the uprising, the régime apparently decided to make an absolute show of strength and terror in Angola, to make political concessions only against the background of military invincibility. To avoid any difficulties at home during so critical a time, Salazar dismissed the Minister of Defence and assumed the portfolio himself. A new Overseas Minister was appointed, and key positions in the Defence and Colonial Offices given to men of resolute loyalty. Several thousand paratroopers were flown to Angola, followed within the next several months by troopships of soldiers. By the middle of the summer there were an estimated 20,000 to 25,000 Portuguese soldiers engaged in the war. Peripheral to the military effort were the armed raids by white vigilantes, who were offered guns by the colonial authorities, during the weeks of March and April. These informal activities were pursued in and beyond the area of conflict and served to intrude additional racial tensions into Angolan life. The number of murders committed by these white patrols is not known, but the crimes and disorders of the vigilantes reached such proportions that the Portuguese government itself tried to curb their fanaticism in May.

On the military front, however, the government showed no such restraint. The conflict was regarded by many Portuguese officials as a war of extermination which must be fought as such. African villages in northern Angola were bombed indiscriminately; other villages captured by Portuguese troops were razed, the male inhabitants executed, and women and children driven into the bush. Certainly the atrocities committed by African guerrillas have been more than matched by those of the 'civilizing' Portuguese columns. The Portuguese have given no quarter. Newspaper accounts quote boastful Portuguese military estimates of how many thousands of 'black animals' have been destroyed. Again it is impossible to calculate the number of African lives lost; estimates range from 10,000 to 30,000. But the number of refugees fleeing across the frontier into the Congo now exceeds 150,000. Many of these survivors arrive mutilated, burnt, and wounded. They have told incredible tales of indiscriminate Portuguese brutality. In October the Defence Ministry announced that all important settlements in northern Angola had been occupied and that the war was virtually over. Subsequent words and actions by the government, however, have made this statement sound somewhat unconvincing. Throughout 1961 the conflict took on more and more the broader outlines of the long struggle in Algeria.

The size of the African guerrilla force is probably not substantial; it seems unlikely that more than 4,000 or 5,000 men have at any time been directly engaged. The guerrillas are organized in small bands who take advantage of the difficult terrain to raid and harass Portuguese farms and communication centres. They are wretchedly armed, and their greatest advantage has undoubtedly been the Congo frontier, which provides them with a base for operations and a haven for escape. In spite of Portuguese accusations, there is little evidence that the rebels are receiving weapons from Communist countries. Their arms have mostly been those captured from the Portuguese themselves during the early days of the rising or a few guns supplied by sympathetic Congolese troops. A small number of UN guns has also fallen into rebel hands. The majority of African weapons remain scythes and home-made knives and spears. The casualties they have inflicted on Portuguese forces have been minimal; the total is probably less than 1,000, of whom about 300 were settlers and their families massacred in the first days of the war. Yet the military situation for the rebels is by no means hopeless. Additional forces are being trained in the Congo and in isolated areas of Angola, and it is almost certain that their strength will grow from month to month. It seems equally certain that, from one source or another, small supplies of guns and ammunition will reach them.

A factor which may ultimately be as important as guns to the Angolan rebels is an increasingly militant world opinion – one which turned, perhaps decisively, against Portugal in 1961. During 1960 and 1961 the subject of the Portuguese colonies stood high on the agenda of pressing world issues, and the chambers of the UN rang with caustic and bitter denunciations of Portugal's policy in Africa. Some of the speeches were often more vehement than factually accurate, but they all revealed a growing exasperation with the contention that the African territories were integral parts of Portugal, that everything happening in them was a domestic affair, and that Portugal was in no way obliged to respond to UN resolutions. Thus, the Ghanaian delegate Quaison-Sackey said in October:

This revolt is a living one, and so Portugal must perforce come to terms with it. Our brothers in Angola are fighting against dictatorship and slavery. The world must realize that the Portuguese territories in Africa are slave states and have always been slave states.

The hostility of African and Asian nations to the Portuguese presence in Africa was to be expected. But in December 1960 the General Assembly passed a resolution, directed, though not so stated, against Portugal, calling upon colonial powers to end their dominance and to take immediate steps to transfer all powers to the people of their territories. The resolution was passed overwhelmingly. The United States abstained from the vote, but then, on 15 March 1961, voted for a resolution which called upon Portugal to comply with the December resolution. (Britain and France dissented.) On 20 April, by a vote of 73 to 2, the General Assembly appointed a sub-committee to investigate the crisis in Angola. Again the United States and a bloc of Latin-American nations voted for the resolution; Britain and France abstained. On 9 June, the United States joined with Russia – Britain and France abstaining – in calling upon Portugal to desist from its repressive measures in Angola. (These votes by the United States brought forth immediate protests from the Portuguese government, which turned loose street mobs against the American Embassy in Lisbon and the Consulate in Luanda.) By the end of 1961 Portugal could count upon the support only of Spain and South Africa at the United Nations.

Portugal refused to cooperate with the sub-committee or to allow it to enter Angola. Its only concession was to invite the Bolivian Chairman, Dr Carlos Salamanca, to come to Lisbon as a private citizen for discussions. The sub-committee's 141-page report, presented on 28 November, was a statement of the repressive conditions and abuses which had led to the revolt. The document was outspokenly critical of Portuguese policy in almost every regard, although it recognized some positive achievements in the past; the committee urged Portugal to make drastic reforms and to prepare Angola for self-government and the exercise of self-determination. In closing, the committee commented:

The Portuguese authorities face a historic choice: whether to continue to rely on the use of force, with the inevitable miseries, economic losses and uncertainties; or to respond to world opinion and take measures to reassure the population, insure the return of the refugees and build a new relationship with the people of Angola.

What is needed is readiness to understand the new forces in the world; courage to accept changes and wisdom to formulate and pursue viable means towards an enduring peaceful solution.

The UN debates and the voting records of several members of the North Atlantic Treaty Organization have made Portugal impatient and even distrustful of her allies, particularly the

United States. At the NATO meeting in May 1961, Portugal threatened to use her NATO troops in Angola and apparently suggested that she might be obliged to leave the Organization. There is an element of bluff in such threats – although in her resentment Portugal might indeed do anything – for essentially Portugal needs NATO more than NATO needs Portugal. NATO arms, directly or indirectly, are being used in the Angolan conflict, and the Salazar régime gains much in prestige and material advantage from the association. For her allies, notably the United States, meanwhile, the alliance with Portugal has constituted a growing moral embarrassment. It is difficult for America to justify her eloquent concern for African independence in the face of a very real association with an obscurantist colonial power. Clearly the Kennedy administration was early in 1961 trying to resolve this paradox; in addition to its public position at the United Nations, the new administration was beginning privately to put pressure on Portugal to make reforms in her colonial policies. This diplomatic manoeuvring was probably brought up short by the Berlin crisis, which made NATO unity an over-riding consideration, and by feeling in the United States after the Belgrade Conference that African opinion was perhaps not as important as it had seemed a few months before.[1]

Britain, on the other hand, has remained resolutely loyal to her 'oldest ally'. It was hardly to be expected that Britain would vote at the United Nations for resolutions which could, without too much imagination, be used against her in certain ticklish African relationships of her own, but in several other directions the Tory government has seemed bent on smoothing Portugal's ruffled feelings. In a Lisbon speech Lord Home, Britain's Foreign Secretary, did mildly suggest that Portugal consider following the British way in Africa; but, judging from the Portuguese reaction, there is little evidence that the Salazar régime took his remarks very seriously. In spite of concerted

1. In the United States, Portugal has hired the public relations firm of Selvage and Lee to influence American opinion in favour of Portugal's policies in Africa.

protests from the Labour and Liberal parties, and even from some Conservatives, the British government has continued to sell war material to Portugal, including two frigates, apparently undismayed that these materials might well be used in Angola. The position of France toward Portugal has been roughly the same.

In the summer of 1961 the Overseas Ministry began to make changes in colonial administrative policies. These half-measures, which were at once rejected by nationalist leaders, might have had some significance ten years earlier – providing that the Portuguese had then succeeded in doing something they had seldom been able to do before in Africa, that is, enforce progressive colonial legislation and decrees – but in 1961 they could scarcely be considered even a sop to nationalist aspirations. The proposals, however, were significant for what they revealed – that Portugal had begun to yield to accumulating pressures; that her colonial policy was not quite the idealistic force it had been touted to be; and that the Portuguese government was still, alone, so insulated from reality, it believed it could solve complex human problems by improbable legislation. For a few observers (including the writer) these decisions also had an additional significance, beyond the apparent. Perhaps they meant more than simply too little, too late. Was it possible that they represented, unconsciously perhaps, the beginning of a psychological break with the past? Had Portugal taken a hesitant half-step down the road that could only lead to the end of the empire in Africa?

Certainly there was little suggestion of this in Overseas Minister Adriano Moreira's address in Oporto on 28 August. In this very important speech Mr Moreira summed up changes in native policy over the past year and spoke of more dramatic changes soon to be decreed, measures which, in the Minister's words, '. . . prove the sureness with which we contemplate the future, the serenity with which we face the difficulties of the present, and our faithfulness to the course of history.' His words had a familiar ring.

First, Mr Moreira referred to labour reforms during the past year: the revocation in June 1960 of all penal sanctions for breach of work contracts and their replacement by the sanctions of civil law; the setting, in the same year, of minimum wages in all Portuguese territories and the granting of contractual freedom to set wages above the minimum; the establishment of labour inspection procedures in all overseas provinces; the ratification by Portugal of international conventions concerning minimum working ages of minors, days of rest, discriminatory procedures in employment, and the abolition of forced labour. The colonial administrators do not, of course, regard contract labour as forced labour, and there has been no change at all in this basic philosophy of the Portuguese labour code. So long as contract labour remains, marginal improvements are virtually meaningless.

In May 1961, the government abolished the compulsory growing of cotton, and the abolition of compulsory rice-growing is under consideration by the Moçambique Legislative Council. If this abolition is seriously enforced, one of the many sources of trouble in Moçambique will be relieved. At the same time, the various agencies for the control of cereals, coffee, and cotton, other sore spots in both the colonial economy and in race relations, were abolished and replaced by what may prove to be more flexible institutions. Native land laws have been strengthened.

Mr Moreira spoke of accelerating a process begun in the 1950s to replace the native administrative apparatus with the *concelho*, or municipal, administration in those areas where the population had reached a certain cultural level. It may be assumed that in a large number of circumscriptions, a token form of decentralization will be introduced. But Mr Moreira added:

Just as in the sphere of private law our respect for traditional ways of life implies preserving the validity of usages and customs, so in the sphere of local administration we find it neither just nor timely to impose the municipal formula in all circumstances.

Native villages will now, it is said, elect their leaders. The voting lists for the Legislative Councils of the territories will be expanded and the meagre authority of these councils is apparently to be increased. Through the general relaxation of the native administration, the abolition of several of its more repressive aspects, and the introduction on a wider scale of local administrative institutions similar to those in Portugal, the government clearly hoped to create a modest participation in colonial government with no real sacrifice of authority. The native administrative apparatus was really to be left intact, and these changes would not endanger either Portugal's central authority over the colonies or the relatively privileged position of the white population.

Finally, the Overseas Secretary announced the abolition of the *regime do indigenato*. Mr Moreira could not quite argue that the mission had been accomplished; the war in Angola and the lack of any visible evidence that native life had been enriched by this discriminatory and authoritative régime would have made any such pronouncement a mockery. Mr Moreira could only call attention to 'the civilizing effort unparalleled elsewhere . . . [which] bears witness, better than words can do, to the right intention of the system and the genuineness of its execution.' What practically the abolition of the indigenous régime means is not yet clear. The decree ordering its abolition was more a paean of praise for the *régime* than anything else. In essence it means the application of the Portuguese constitution to all the inhabitants of Angola, Moçambique, and Guinea. More specifically, it means that Portuguese civil law, still to be handled in many cases by the administrator, will apply to the African population. It will presumably mean that a larger number of Africans will be able to vote for members of the Legislative Council and in the national elections. Whether the electoral rolls in Angola, for example, will ever reach the metropolitan figure of twenty-five per cent of the population is uncertain. It is too early now to say whether this was a totally meaningless gesture. One can be certain, however, that the *regime do indigenato* was abandoned for one reason alone; it had become too great a liability.

In the same speech, Mr Moreira made clear the Salazar government's intention to continue a policy which had already created disrupting tensions in Angola. 'We believe it necessary', he said, 'to increase the settlement of our Africa by European Portuguese, who will make their home there and encounter in Africa a true continuation of their country.' He spoke of the enormous urgency of the task and of the formation of provincial settlement agencies to expedite the flow of Portuguese to Africa. He declared that many of the young men who went as soldiers to Angola would be expected to remain there as farmers and artisans. And what of the future?

As we clearly proclaim the high priority of the problem of settlement by people from continental Portugal, we wish to underline . . . Portugal's decision to continue its policy of multi-racial integration without which there will be neither peace nor civilization in black Africa.

Professor Melville Herskovits has remarked that in Africa racial tensions rise in direct proportion to the increase in the white population. The rise in racialist sentiment in Angola during the last decade would seem to support him. The Salazar government hopes to take care of Portugal's surplus population and to create in the African colonies an integration based on the cultural attachments of the white population. If Portugal pushes ahead with this scheme, she will be creating even more dangerous problems than those she is presently attempting to resolve.

Another sharp change in Portugal's African policy will take place in the economic sphere. Critics have belittled Portugal's claim that the African territories are overseas provinces for two main reasons: the presence of a *regime do indigenato* and the economic discriminations existing between the mother country and the colonies. Starting on 1 January 1962, Portugal is reducing tariffs – long a bone of contention between the white colonists in Africa and the Portuguese government. All tariffs will be abolished at the end of a ten-year period and a single market established. Trade between Portugal and her colonies already exceeds £50,000,000 a year. And Portuguese economists believe that by eliminating trade barriers this figure can be doubled. After thirty years, the government has finally begun to curb the power and privileged position of Portuguese monopolies in the overseas trade.

All of these changes and proposals reveal an apparently sublime faith in the policy of integration for the African territories. There are, of course, too many imponderables for one to predict what will happen in Portuguese Africa. Or what will happen in Portugal itself, where the Angolan war is causing severe strain on the carefully balanced economy, and where the younger officers of the defence forces are becoming increasingly restless. And what happens in Katanga, in the Rhodesias, and in South Africa is also vitally relevant to the fate of Angola and Moçambique. Portugal has survived any number of crises in the past – though none so serious as those of the present, to be sure – and seems confident that she will again prevail. But if she does, she will be more likely to resort to guns, tanks, and bombs, than to the promises of discredited policies.

There can be no easy answer to the problems of Portuguese Africa. Independence may not itself be the answer, but there will be no satisfactory answer without it.

Selective Bibliography

This small bibliography of works in English which are either totally or partly concerned with various aspects of Portuguese Africa is intended only to be a modest guide to the reader who may wish to read further on the subject. It is by no means complete, since I have for the most part included only works published in the last twenty years, together with a few earlier works which should still be available.

The large majority of sources for *Portugal in Africa* are Portuguese. In addition to colonial reports of the nineteenth and twentieth centuries, colonial and metropolitan newspapers and journals of the same period, the texts of colonial legislation, and statistical annuals, I have found the following selected Portuguese works most useful:

Almeida de Eça, Filipe Gastão de, *História das guerras no Zambeze*, 2 vols., Lisbon, 1953–4.

Botelho, J. J. Teixeira, *História militar e política dos portugueses em Moçambique da descoberta à 1833*, Lisbon, 1934.

   História militar e política dos portugueses em Moçambique de 1833 aos nossos dias, Lisbon, 1936.

Brásio, António, *Monumenta missionaria africana, Africa Ocidental*, 10 vols., Lisbon, 1952–

Cadornega, António de Oliveira de, *História geral das guerras angolanas*, 3 vols., Lisbon, 1940–2.

Delgado, Ralph, *História de Angola, 1482–1836*, 4 vols., Benguela and Lobito, 1948–55.

Enes, António, *Moçambique*, Lisbon, 1946.

Felner, Alfredo de Albuquerque, *Angola*, Coimbra, 1933.

Lobato, Alexandre, *A expansão portuguesa em Moçambique de 1498 à 1530*, 3 vols., Lisbon, 1954–60.

Lopes, Edmundo Correia, *A escravatura*, Lisbon, 1944.

Lopes de Lima, J. J., *Ensaios sobre a estatística das possessões portuguesas*, 4 vols., Lison, 1844–6.

Mousinho de Albuquerque, Joaquim, *Moçambique*, 2 vols., Lisbon, 1934.

Oliveira Martins, J. P., *Portugal em Africa*, Lisbon, 1953.
Silva Cunha, J. S. da, *O trabalho indígena*, Lisbon, 1955.
Vilhena, Ernesto de, *O regime dos prazos da Zambézia*, Lisbon, 1916.

And these books in English:

Axelson, Eric. *'Portuguese in South-East Africa, 1600–1700*, Johannesburg, 1960.
    South-East Africa, 1488–1530, London, 1940.
Blake, John W., *Europeans in West Africa*, 2 vols., London, 1941–2.
Boxer, Charles R., 'Background to Angola: Cadornega's Chronicle', *History Today*, vol. XI, pp. 665–72 (October 1961).
    Four Centuries of Portuguese Expansion, 1415–1825: A Succinct Survey, Johannesburg, 1961.
    Salvador de Sá and the Struggle for Brazil and Angola, London, 1952.
    The Tragic History of the Sea, London, 1959.
Boxer, Charles R., and Azevedo, Carlos de, *Fort Jesus and the Portuguese in Mombasa*, London, 1960.
Childs, Gladwyn M., *Umbundu Kinship and Character*, London, 1949.
Coupland, Reginald, *East Africa and Its Invaders*, London, 1938.
    The Exploitation of East Africa, 1856–1890, London, 1939.
Cunnison, Ian, 'Kazembe and the Portuguese', *Journal of African History*, vol. II, pp. 61–76 (October 1961).
Davidson, Basil, *The African Awakening*, London, 1955.
    Angola, 1961, London, 1961.
    Black Mother, London and Boston, 1961.
    Old Africa Rediscovered, London and Boston, 1959.
Diffie, Bailey W., *Prelude to Empire*, Lincoln, Nebraska, 1960.
Duffy, James, 'Portugal in Africa', *Foreign Affairs*, vol. XXIX, pp. 481–93 (April 1961).
    Portuguese Africa, Cambridge, Mass., and London, 1959.
    Shipwreck and Empire, Cambridge, Mass., 1955.
Egerton, F. Clement C., *Angola in Perspective*, London, 1957.
Figueiredo, António de, *Portugal and Its Empire: The Truth*, London, 1961.
Galvão, Henrique, *Santa Maria: My Crusade for Portugal*, New York and London, 1961.
Gray, John, *Early Portuguese Missionaries in East Africa*, London, 1958.
Harris, Marvin, *Portugal's African Wards*, New York, 1958.
Jack, Homer, *Angola: Repression and Revolt in Portuguese Africa*, New York, 1960.

Jackson, Mabel V., *European Powers and South-East Africa*, London, 1942.

Kup, Peter, *A History of Sierra Leone, 1400–1787*, Cambridge, 1961.

Livermore, H. V., *History of Portugal*, Cambridge, 1947.

Livingstone, David, *Missionary Travels and Researches in South Africa*, London, 1857.

Livingstone, David and Charles, *Narrative of an Expedition to the Zambezi and its Sources*, London, 1866.

Lupi, Luis C., *Portugal and Her Overseas Provinces*, Lisbon, 1961.

Mahala, Chikomuami, 'The Horror of Moçambique', *Africa South in Exile*, vol. v, pp. 50–9 (October–December 1960).

A Manual of Portuguese East Africa, London, 1920.

Moreira, Adriano, *A Policy of Integration*, Lisbon, 1961.

Nevinson, Henry W., *A Modern Slavery*, New York, 1906.

Okuma, Thomas, *Angola in Ferment*, Boston, 1962.

Oliver, Roland, *Sir Harry Johnston and the Scramble for Africa*, London, 1957.

Parsons, Clifford J., 'Background to the Angola Crisis', *The World Today*, vol. XVII, pp. 278–88 (July 1961).

    'The Torment of Angola', *Africa South in Exile*, vol. v, pp. 72–80 (July–September 1961).

Portugal, An Informative Review: this bi-monthly publication of the Portuguese Information Office (S.N.I.) has printed over the last several years many articles of varying importance on Portuguese Africa.

Salazar, António de Oliveira, *Portugal and the Anti-Colonialist Campaign*, Lisbon, 1960.

Silva Rego, António da, *Portuguese Colonization in the Sixteenth Century*, Johannesburg, 1957.

Spence, C. F., *The Portuguese Colony of Moçambique*, Cape Town, 1951.

Strandes, Justus, *The Portuguese Period in East Africa*, trans. by Jean F. Wallwork, Nairobi, 1961.

Theal, George M., *Records of South-Eastern Africa*, 9 vols., Cape Town, 1898–1903.

Tucker, John T., *Angola, Land of the Blacksmith Prince*, London, 1933.

United Nations General Assembly (Sixteenth Session), 'Report of the Sub-Committee on The Situation in Angola' (mimeo), November 1961.

Van der Horst, Sheila, *Native Labour in South Africa*, London, 1942.

Index